Sara's Children

The Destruction of Chmielnik
By Suzan Esther Hagstrom

Sara's Children records how five siblings survived slave labor, starvation, beatings, typhus, exposure and fatigue. The starkly written narrative relies heavily on the Garfinkels' own words and interviews with other survivors from their hometown of Chmielnik, Poland. The non-fiction work begins with what they lost: loving parents, an extended family, loyal friends and a simple but vibrant life-style. Nonetheless disturbing signs of anti-Semitism marred their happy childhoods. Violence and hatred escalated as Germany razed Poland and swept Europe. Each chapter explodes with descriptions of the Garfinkels' terrible ordeal. Heartbreaking testimonials from other Holocaust survivors, maps, photographs from the late 1940s, and written records culled from Germany reinforce and verify their account.

Sara's Children is one family's saga of instinct overriding despair and triumph amid destruction. More momentous than any one could ever imagine, Nathan Garfinkel and his sisters, were reduced to living skeletons, victims of anti-Semitism that raged out of control during World War II. Nazi Germany and its sympathizers brutally murdered more than six million Jews across Europe, wiping out entire families and in some cases villages. Through sheer luck and by helping each other, the Garfinkels overcame seemingly insurmountable odds to evade death and remain full of love, joy and hope.

Sara's Children

What people around the world are saying about

Sara's Children

The fate of the Garfinkel family is written as every account on the Holocaust should be written: detailed and concrete.

Thomas Rahe

Historian at the Bergen-Belsen concentration camp memorial in Germany.

It is important to have depictions of the Nazi persecution of the Jews written and published, as this is one of the weapons that can help prevent a repetition.

Simon Wiesenthal

Founder of the Jewish Documentation Center in Vienna, Austria.

This book demonstrates humane and Jewish values: faith in God, love of family, mutual help, and devotion. This work restores faith in mankind.

Felicja Karay

Holocaust survivor and scholar in Rishon Leziyon, Israel.

Sara's Children *relates the fascinating and exceptional story of five siblings who survived against all odds... a moving story of heroism, sacrifice, and determination.*

Robert Berdahl

Chancellor of the University of California at Berkeley.

This vivid rendering of the Garfinkels' personal miracles puts a human face on the enormity of the Holocaust, enabling the reader to better grasp its stark horror.

S.J. Usprich

Professor of Law, The University of Western Ontario, Canada.

Only known photograph
of
Sara Garfinkel
c. late 1930s

Sara's Children

and
the Destruction of Chmielnik

By
Suzan E. Hagstrom

Sergeant Kirkland's Press
Spotsylvania, Virginia

Published & Distributed by

Sergeant Kirkland's Museum and Historical Society, Inc.

8 Yakama Trail, Spotsylvania, VA 22553-2422
Tel.: (540) 582-6296; Fax: (540) 582-8312
E-mail: seagraver@kirklands.org

www.kirklands.org

Manufactured in the USA

The paper in this book meets the guidelines for permanence and du-
rability of the Committee on Production Guidelines for Book Lon-
gevity of the Council on Library Resources, Inc.

Library of Congress Cataloging-in-Publication Data
Hagstrom, Suzan E.
Sara's children and the destruction of Chmielnik /

Suzan E. Hagstrom.

p.   cm.
ISBN 1-887901-28-0 (alk. paper)

1.Garfinkel family 2. Jews--Persecutions--Ukraine--Khmel§'yëì§'yæ. 3.
Holocaust, Jewish (1939-1945)--Ukraine--Khmel§'yëì§'yæ. 4.
Garfinkel, Sara. 5. Khmel§'yëì§'yæ, (Ukraine)--Ethnic relations. I.
Title.
DS135.U43 G374 2001
940.53'18'0922--dc21   00-052212
[B]   CIP

First Edition
2 3 4 5 6 7 8 9 10

Text edited by Pia S. Seagrave, Ph.D.

Table of Contents

INTRODUCTION

When Helen Garfinkel Greenspun telephones and reaches my answering machine instead of me, her recording is straightforward: "I am Helen. Call me." To ears more accustomed to hearing "This is Sam" or "This is Sally calling," the message sounds a little odd. The direct syntax is easily explained by the caller's Polish origins, but greater meaning underlies the short statement. "I am" is Helen's affirmation of life. She is a Holocaust survivor.

I met Helen in 1990 while gathering information for a magazine article about the Holocaust Memorial Resource and Education Center of Central Florida. Hers was a key interview for my story about the non-profit educational organization in Maitland, Florida. Helen's lectures in schools, churches, and other community forums help fulfill the center's goals of combating prejudice and teaching about the Holocaust.

Though only an adolescent during World War II, Helen was marked for murder because she is Jewish. Under Nazi Germany's "Final Solution" policy, all Jews were isolated in ghettos or camps and killed — if not by disease, hunger, or deprivation, then by firing squads, torture, gas chambers, beatings.

Many non-Jews, including Gypsies, homosexuals, Soviet prisoners of war, Jehovah's Witnesses, Seventh-Day Adventists, communists, intellectuals, and dissidents, also died in concentration and forced-labor camps. Anti-fascists of all kinds fell victim to the Holocaust, known as the *Shoah* in Hebrew. Only the Jews were to be killed to the last man, woman, and child. Many historians regard the Holocaust as the first government-sanctioned genocide.

Germany nearly succeeded in its gruesome task, which often

took priority over adequately supplying soldiers on the battle lines. Of an estimated 11 million people murdered in the Shoah, 6 million were Jews.

Helen was among an estimated 300,000 Jewish survivors freed from death camps in 1945. Ill with typhus, she nearly died after liberation. Had the war lasted even a few weeks longer, German Nazis and their collaborators in other nations might have completed this genocide of Jews.

While interviewing Helen, I realized my research would not end with the magazine article about the Holocaust center. The intricacies of Helen's personal history were remarkable. When she said she had three sisters and a brother who also endured three years of suffering in the death camps, I was dumbstruck. Jews trapped in Europe who managed to live through World War II counted themselves fortunate to have one or two close relatives remaining. Exceptions might be families who had hid in barns, underground bunkers, or in the forest.

For five siblings to emerge alive from the death camps defied the odds. I chose to omit that detail about Helen from the magazine article. Otherwise, readers might have mistakenly assumed that was the common outcome for European Jews when, in fact, hundreds of thousands of families were exterminated without a trace. After fruitless searching at the war's end, many Jews found themselves to be the sole living members of their families and, in some cases, of entire communities. As far as Helen knows, the Nazis killed each and every Jew in Busko Zdroj, Poland, including her Aunt Channah and four cousins. As the late Primo Levi wrote in *The Drowned and the Saved*, Shoah survivors such as he were the exception, not the rule.

"Every one of us who survived has an incredible story to tell," says Tess Wise, the founder and executive director of the Holocaust Memorial Resource and Education Center of Central Florida.

"There had to be a special situation, a special stroke of luck, a special moment for each of us because the circumstances were designed for death, not for survival."

The survival of five siblings in one family may not be unique in Holocaust statistics, but it is rare. How Helen, her brother, and three sisters escaped death is compelling. Helping them convey their experiences in context of the Shoah is a privilege. Documenting their story helps commemorate the people they knew who died: friends, family, neighbors, other acquaintances, even strangers. Writing their story is only possible because of the Garfinkels' courage and generosity. They recognize the importance of studying history to battle bigotry and to avoid repeating past atrocities. They are concerned about the mass murder of Moslems in the Balkans, the resurgence of neo-Nazism in Germany, racism in the United States, and tribal warfare and famine in Africa.

Like Helen, Nathan Garfinkel and Sonia Garfinkel Nothman speak publicly about the Shoah. They participate as volunteers in the Holocaust Memorial Center in West Bloomfield, Michigan, near Detroit. Helen's other two sisters, Regina Garfinkel Muskovitz and the late Bela Garfinkel Soloway Hurtig, are more typical of Holocaust survivors in that they did not routinely discuss their ordeal. Regina lives in West Bloomfield. Bela died in late 1997 in Pompano Beach, Florida.

In 1942, when German Nazis uprooted Helen, Nathan, Sonia, Regina, and Bela from their hometown of Chmielnik, Poland, and sent them to labor camps, they ranged in age from 12 to 22. Left behind were their parents, Kalman and Sara Pearl; their younger sister, Rachel; and their younger brother, Fishel. They, along with other Chmielnik Jews deemed unfit for work, were shipped to Treblinka, Poland. There, in October and November of 1942, the Nazis gassed most of Chmielnik's Jews, particularly children, elderly people, mature adults, and young mothers with infants.

After World War II, Helen, Nathan, Sonia, Regina, and Bela immigrated to the United States. They married, raised families, worked hard — in some cases operating small businesses — saved money, bought homes, and sent their children to college. In short, they overcame great personal anguish to realize the American dream and to lead fulfilled lives. Having each other helped them rise above overwhelming suffering and degradation that has permanently silenced some Holocaust survivors and emotionally crippled others. The Garfinkels discuss past horrors to fight discrimination today and to help prevent genocide tomorrow. In so doing, they not only honor the Shoah's dead but they also provide a voice for those living victims unable to speak.

I chose to write the Garfinkels' story in a journalistic style. Consequently, readers will be pulled back and forth in time, from narrative about what happened more than 50 years ago to the eyewitnesses' present-day descriptions of their ordeals. I felt using direct quotes from survivors and preserving their own words are of utmost importance. After all, it is their story.

Acquaintances aware of this book often ask to what do I attribute the Garfinkels' survival. The question is difficult to answer. No single factor accounts for their survival; rather, it is a complex web of people, events, and circumstances. The region of Poland where they lived, their ages, their specific work assignments in the camps — even the occasional decency of individual Nazis — are among many reasons the Garfinkels are alive.

Although they had many strokes of luck and special moments — the common denominators of survival mentioned by Wise — the Garfinkels' close family ties contributed, in large part, to their having evaded death. Their sense of responsibility to each other was so strong they each rejected chances to escape, to hide, or to pass for non-Jew during the war. At different points of their imprisonment, they risked their lives to save each other. Making sacrifices in the adverse conditions of the death camps was extraordinary, even among family members. Such action sustained the Garfinkels with moral strength when they were too weak to walk. Caring for each other at the edge of death gave them the hope to continue and enables them to describe their past today.

Chapter One
WE WERE SEPARATE

Regina opened her eyes. She was awakening, not from sleep, but from the unconsciousness of serious illness. Through dulled senses, Regina realized she was still alive. The stale air nauseated her. The sounds of labored breathing and groaning penetrated her drowsiness. She felt a body, stiff from rigor mortis, next to her on the cot. The corpse's head was near her feet; its feet touched her head. Regina was too sick to feel repulsed. The sight of cadavers and sick women indicated she was in Bergen-Belsen's hospital. Regina couldn't understand why it was called that. There were no medicines, bandages, beds, or the clean linens associated with hospitals. Only a so-called uniform covered Regina — a long shirt so ragged and dirty its prison stripes barely showed. Many of the patients — the dying as well as the dead — were stacked in piles. Clearly, Regina had not been taken here to be nursed to health. No one left Bergen-Belsen's hospital alive. All the prisoners knew that. Regina hoped she would die soon. Many times she had begged her sisters to let her lie in the snow. Then she could embrace the sleep without dreams, forever. Freshly-fallen snow was cold but clean. Regina preferred it to the barrack floor filthy with excrement, lice, urine, and dying prisoners. If she died, the misery would end. "Leave me alone," Regina had screamed to Bela, Helen, and Sonia. She pleaded on her knees, "Let me die. Please, let me die." Her sisters always pulled Regina to her feet. They held her up. They dragged her back to the disgusting barrack. Her sisters wrapped themselves around Regina to keep her warm.

Now it seemed Regina's wish would be granted. How appropriate it was that the hospital was partially submerged in the earth.

Lying in this English basement, this half-dungeon, was like being buried alive. Regina looked at the windows. The sills, about head-level inside, were even with the ground outside. By gazing up, Regina couldn't see the corpses surrounding her. Sometimes she passed out, losing track of time, but, when she came to, she looked at the windows. Outside, a crouched figure tapped on the glass. The high cheekbones and anguished expression were unmistakable. Sonia. Too weak to move, Regina couldn't reach out or wave in recognition. Drained by her illness, Regina didn't feel relief or joy that her older sister had arrived to save her. She felt arms under her, lifting her from the cot. She felt Sonia's hands encircling her wrists. Someone pushed her up. Sonia pulled. Regina was being dragged through the window.

That incident, forming one of Regina Garfinkel Muskovitz' most potent memories, not only summarizes her family's experiences of helping each other during World War II, but it also symbolizes the Holocaust's grisly conclusion. Nazi Germany, with sympathizers in other countries, had killed most of Europe's Jews by the spring of 1945. Allied soldiers who liberated concentration camps in Germany and Poland snatched the surviving Jewish prisoners from the clutches of death — the same way Sonia had pulled Regina from the macabre morgue that passed for a hospital in Bergen-Belsen. Jews still alive hardly appeared human. They were so emaciated they resembled skeletons. It's obvious from countless photographs and numerous documentary films that no Jews would have remained had the war continued. Some prisoners were so far gone they died by the thousands each day after liberation.

Each Holocaust survivor has a story to tell, not only about being pulled from death's clutches, but also about the people they knew, their communities, their way of living. The Garfinkels' story begins not with the war, not in Bergen-Belsen, not with Regina's extraordinary rescue. It starts with their happy childhood, in their hometown of Chmielnik, Poland, with ordinary, everyday concerns. The backdrop, the story of the Holocaust, began before the Garfinkels were born because it culminated centuries of hatred against Jews.

Anti-Semitism, deep-rooted and widespread in Europe, greatly aided Germany in its campaign to kill all Jews. The Garfinkels grew up amid discrimination. In Chmielnik, Jews comprised the majority of the population, but they were second-class citizens. The Garfinkels lived near the post office, which did not employ a single Jew. Jews were not allowed to hold government jobs, to work for the railroad, or to teach in public schools. They were excluded from political office, which was based on appointments rather than elections. The governor of the province chose the mayor, for example. There were a few exceptions. Chmielnik's city council may have had one or two Jewish representatives. One of the Garfinkels' teachers, Mr. Laks, lectured weekly to Jewish children in public schools about Judaic history, culture, and religion. Catholic children, meanwhile, attended a similar course focusing on Christianity. Long before World War II started, some of Chmielnik's Polish shops displayed signs reading: "Don't sell to Jews" and "Don't do business with Jews."

Characteristic of many European towns, Chmielnik's central square served as a hub of activity. Streets, including the road to Kielce, where the Garfinkels lived, fanned out from there. A grocery, bakery, pharmacy, general merchandise store, hardware supplier, milliner, shoemaker, fabric vendor, tailor, stationery shop, and clothiers surrounded the square. Second-floor apartments had views of it. A wealthy Polish family lived in a large home at one corner. Farmers and merchants filled the space on Thursdays with their produce and wares. In the evenings, young couples strolled arm-in-arm, teenagers gathered with friends, and families went for walks. A nearby movie theater featuring Polish films attracted young people daring enough to seek secular entertainment. The square, paved in flagstones, contained a water pump and newsstand. Helen often bought newspapers there for her older brother, Nathan — never dreaming the square would set the stage for her own personal drama.

As far as the Garfinkels can recollect from their childhood, they did not witness overt physical violence against Jews in Chmielnik before the war. That contrasted with neighboring cities where pogroms erupted routinely. Kielce, for example, which had once expelled its Jews in 1847, subjected them to beatings in 1918. History books document persecution, murder, rape, and other crimes against Jews throughout the centuries in Eastern Europe. Nearly 300 years before World War II, a massacre depleted Chmielnik's Jewish population, according to *Encyclopaedia Judaica*. In 1655, the Polish Army, led by Stefan Czarniecki, accused Chmielnik's Jews of conspiring with Swedish invaders. In retaliation, soldiers slaughtered 150 Jews.

Such atrocities throughout Europe set the trap for Germany's genocide of Jews and made anti-Semitism a constant tension in the Garfinkels' daily lives. Sonia remembers one conversation that chillingly conveys the entrenchment of ignorance and intolerance in Poland. As they walked to school, Stasia Musial, a Catholic friend, swore Sonia to secrecy before asking her if what the priest had said in church was true. Stasia asked Sonia whether Jews killed Gentile children so they could use their blood to make matzo. Sonia was about 14 or 15 years old at the time. Helen was 11 or 12.

"I was stunned. The priest in church told them this? I couldn't keep my promise. I told my parents this story. They were very upset. My mother was almost near tears. My father explained to me that the Christians were against Jews because they thought the Jews killed Jesus. My friend was very upset about this, too. I don't think she believed this because nobody, no Gentile children, were missing." The "blood libel" myth, prevalent throughout Europe and described in Bernard Malamud's book, *The Fixer*, was Sonia's most vivid encounter with anti-Semitism before the war.

Tosia Fastag Bottner, a classmate of Sonia now living in

Toronto, Canada, describes other unpleasant altercations. "The Poles said, 'The Jews have the businesses. The Jews have this. The Jews have that.' Maybe we would walk on Sunday, people might throw a little stone or something," Bottner said. "The hostility that you could feel was from the parents, not so much from the children."

Usher Tarek, now in Toronto, speculated that anti-Semitism was less strident in Chmielnik because the Jews outnumbered the Poles. "Let me put it to you this way: if Poles were anti-Semitic, they didn't show." That changed during the war, however, Tarek said. "After the invasion, my parents' Polish friends didn't help us a great deal."

Regina got her first, bitter taste of anti-Semitism on entering Chmielnik's public school. "My Polish wasn't very good. I came home crying because I was teased about it. I remember not wanting to come back to school." Her parents spoke Polish at home to accelerate Regina's fluency, but they refrained from coddling her. They wanted to prepare Regina for the realities of prejudice — knowing a Jew speaking perfect Polish would have fewer problems. "If they made a big fuss, it would make it worse." As much as it pained Kalman and Sara to see their daughter ostracized at such a young age, they nonchalantly communicated: "This is just the way it is." That attitude became Regina's code to live by during World War II. It often was the only explanation she had for events that didn't make sense. Regina learned about stereotypes for the first time in public school, too. The priest insisted the blonde girl attend the religion class for Catholic children. "The priest took me by the hand to go with him. I said I was Jewish. He said, 'No, you're not,' with a smile on his face. I came home crying."

Nathan Garfinkel was more acutely aware of bigotry than his sisters and their friends. The eldest child among seven, Nathan always felt the undercurrents of hatred. "In math, I was good. I was harassed. 'You smart Jew.' Polish history I didn't like. I was harassed. 'You stupid Jew.' I was a target then." Nathan preferred

international history to national history. The history of one country
— be it Israel, the United States, or Poland — is too easily dis-
torted, he said. In Chmielnik, Nathan asked his teacher why the
Polish national anthem contained references to reclaiming Italy.
Unable to answer, the teacher made Nathan sit in the corner.
Poland's public schools provided seven years of instruction, but
Nathan tired of anti-Semitic slurs and dropped out after five years.
At his father's insistence, Nathan attended yeshiva for Hebrew
courses and he took private lessons in Yiddish, the language the
Garfinkels spoke at home. Kalman did not tolerate Polish in the
household unless he was helping the younger children master the
language.

Nathan got in fights on the playground when he was attacked
for being Jewish. A close friend, Juzik Stradowski, a Catholic,
helped defend him. "Once Juzik came to the temple with me, but
he never came back because he couldn't reciprocate. He couldn't
invite me to his church," Nathan said. "We Jews understood one
thing. We were separate." Although curfews are associated with
Nazi Germany's regime, they existed informally before World War
II. Jews avoided being out late at night, Nathan said; otherwise,
they might be threatened, beaten, or killed. He recalled instances
of assault against Jews after Christmas Eve's midnight mass. "Why
would I be abused the day God was born?" Nathan asked. "I wasn't
abused as much during Easter when God died. I could never understand this."

On another occasion before the war, police apprehended and
scolded Nathan and Juzik for riding bicycles without lights after
dark. Juzik, the Catholic, went home with a reprimand. Nathan,
the Jew, spent the night in jail. "This made a big impact on me.
There were two laws, one for Jews and one for non-Jews," Nathan
said. "There was a frisk-and-search policy. We all had identification cards. I am a target because my name is Jewish."

A close childhood friend of Nathan, Jakob Lederman, now in
Forest Hills, New York, remembers stone-throwing, name-calling,

fighting with Poles at soccer matches, and hearing about pogroms in other towns. "It wasn't so pleasant. The Poles didn't like the Jews, period. I didn't have Polish friends. I got a bad experience with them. In Holland, they helped the Jews. In Poland, they make concentration camp; the Polish people helped them. When the Germans invaded our town, the Polish people pointed out the Jews. Poland was like a time bomb."

Jakob Sylman, now in Toronto, said Poles from nearby towns and farms flocked to Chmielnik on Thursday, market day. Some adults planted themselves outside Jewish-owned stores and admonished Chmielnik's Poles by saying, "Don't buy from Jews!" "We weren't afraid because we were the majority," Sylman said. "In school, we talked to Poles but as friends, no. In the street they used to throw stones." Kalman Mapa, now in Toronto, said that, even though Jewish children outnumbered their Polish peers, they felt intimidated. Inside and outside the classroom, Mapa said, some Poles made false accusations against Jews, and other Poles bullied Jews.

Such prejudice, evident in academic and professional circles, reduced opportunities for bright, young Jews like Nathan. Universities, for example, limited the number of Jewish students. Although Jews comprised more than 10 percent of Poland's population, they didn't exceed 3 percent of any college student body. When universities segregated Jews to one side of classrooms, Nathan said, they protested by standing up to take notes. Wealthy Polish Jews typically sent their children to college in other countries, but most families in Chmielnik could not afford higher education. Nathan links an acceleration in anti-Semitism to the death of Jozef Pilsudski, Poland's first marshal, in 1935. During his political career, Pilsudski had forged alliances with Jews, and, together, they fought against Russian Communists in 1919. Most other Poles did not share Pilsudski's liberal tendencies and tolerance. Two senators, General Kotz and Madame Pristow, formed the Organization of Polish Nationalist People, which excluded Jews. Another parliamentarian, Premier Sladkowski, spoke of "hitting the Jews," not necessarily physically, but economically. The government became right-wing, known as *endecja* in Polish.

Israel Steinfeld, of Toronto, said anti-Semitism spawned political awareness among Chmielnik's young Jews, and that, in turn, resulted in a generation gap. While the parents seemed completely absorbed in Orthodox Judaism, shunned the outside world, and accepted the status quo of inequities, Steinfeld said, the children read secular books, embraced modern ideas, and questioned the system. "The parents didn't see what we see. Somehow the children felt the dangers that the parents didn't believe. The parents felt that God would take care of everything." Institutional prejudice disenfranchised young Jews, Steinfeld said. "It was no hope for no future. You're locked in a cage and no way to get out."

After finishing public school, Steinfeld worked for Chmielnik's Jewish financial-services firm, Bank Ludowy. His boss, Efraim Zalcberg, had a special license because he had served in the Polish Army during World War I. "There were special circumstances that enabled Jews to advance," Steinfeld said, but they were rare. Steinfeld noticed that some Polish customers took advantage of the Jews' lower status. "If they borrowed money and didn't pay back, we couldn't make them pay. We couldn't take them to court." Despite his good job, Steinfeld felt trapped. Polish people made fun of Jews and things Jewish, such as the *tallis*, or prayer shawl.

Jakob Lederman visited the Garfinkels' modest home almost everyday. He and Nathan went to the movies and attended meetings of Zionist organizations advocating a homeland for Jews. "His father (Kalman) always studied the *Talmud*," Lederman said, referring to the sacred body of Jewish learning. The Talmud's volumes contain hundreds of years of debate and discussion of laws, morals, and traditions. The complex work was written by rabbis, scholars, and jurists. "We didn't want to sit and read the Talmud. We went out."

Even as a child, Regina sensed Nathan's frustrations and his conflicts with their pious father, who ignored discrimination. "There were so many limitations. Why would anybody want to follow in a father's footsteps? To go to synagogue and pray and barely make a living. The old lifestyle didn't take you anywhere," Regina said. "The youth must have been looking for a way out. Jews couldn't have a higher education. My brother was reading different books. Nathan was very devoted to the family but rebellious at the same time."

Israel "Ira" Kaminsky, now in Bayside, New York, encountered fewer generational conflicts because his modern Orthodox father accepted not only Israel's secular activities but also the visits of his sisters' boyfriends. Israel spent much of his spare time acting in the Apollo theater. The plays, mostly historical dramas, were performed in Polish. Kaminsky counted one non-Jew, Henryk Maciejewski, among his friends. During the war, Maciejewski joined the Polish resistance and supplied Israel with underground newspapers.

Jozef Pilsudski's picture, a fleeting sign of progress, hung in the classrooms of Poland's public schools — a relatively new establishment. Chmielnik had one school for girls and another for boys — in separate buildings on different streets. Next to Pilsudski's picture hung the image of an *orzel bialy*, or white eagle, the symbol of Poland. Next to that was a crucifix, a reminder of the dominant culture and religion. Throughout much of its history, Poland has been a theocracy. "There were prayers in the morning," Helen said. "Everyone stood up. The Polish girls prayed and crossed themselves. The Jewish girls didn't pray, but we had to stand out of respect."

Fay Skrobacka Goldlist, of Toronto, said teachers instructed specific groups of students for several years. Goldlist recalls Mrs. Kuchynska, one of Sonia's teachers, as exceptionally effective. "We learned from A to Z everything: geography, sciences, singing, and spelling." Mr. Laks also stood out. "He wanted the children should know about religion. He always had something to say that we should understand more." Public school began at 8 a.m. and ended at 1 p.m. Most families ate their large meal at midday. In the late afternoon, many Jewish children attended religious schools, or *cheder*. Typically, girls went to Beit Ya'akov, or House of Jacob.

Until 1935, the Garfinkels had been somewhat sheltered from bigotry, having grown up in a Jewish neighborhood in Chmielnik's outskirts. Their father, Kalman, made a living as a miller. He bought barley, corn, oats, rye, wheat, and other grains from farmers to make flour. The family's two-room home adjoined his store. Another merchant, a Pole, opened a similar enterprise across the street. "He told the farmers not to sell to us because we were Jewish," Sonia said. "But the farmers had done business with my father for many years. The farmers knew my parents."

Chapter Two
BEFORE THE STORM

Regina, along with her brother, sisters, and other Holocaust survivors, often marvels that she has led a normal life since World War II. Some memories of the concentration camps are so overpowering they fill dreams and spill into the waking hours. Food might remind survivors of slowly being starved from late 1939 through 1945. Clothing may serve as a flashback to the rags they once wore. Simply going places, doing things as they please, can trigger a rewind mechanism, hurling survivors into the terrible period when German capitalists and Nazis enslaved them. As memories, the *laagers*, or camps, loom large, often overshadowing the pre-war years. The contrast between the Holocaust and European Jews' seemingly ordinary lives beforehand is particularly wrenching because it magnifies what they lost — as revealed by Regina's recollection of Bergen-Belsen's shower room:

"It was a large room with a big sink. We were lined up naked. We had to go over to the tub and wash. We had to wash our hair. We didn't get washed but had to get wet. It was freezing." As she waited, Regina observed the long column of young women. In the dim light, she saw silhouettes of skinny bodies, bent and drooping postures, disheveled hair. Completely spent by hard labor and lack of food, the women blended with the gray, dreary warehouse. One at a time, they stepped into a tub of cold water. First they put in one leg and then the other. Regina shivered. The cement floor chilled her bones through her bare feet. It was her turn. "I put one leg in, but I couldn't move my other leg. My foot got stuck to the floor." To Regina's astonishment, her foot froze to the cement. "I had to pull my foot off the floor."

In Regina's camp experience, that washroom represents a

ground zero of sorts. Regina stood there, stripped. In seizing the women's only possessions — some dirty, tattered clothing — the German soldiers tried to wrest away any remaining shreds of dignity. All decency had vanished. The soldiers treated their Jewish captives like barnyard animals, herding them into groups, whipping them into line, and transporting them in livestock cars. During such moments, which stretched into days, weeks, months, Regina couldn't remember what it was like to be human. If she did, it might have killed her. Even now, decades after the Holocaust, describing what the war destroyed — home, family, health, friends, lifestyle — breaks Regina's heart. This is also true for her sisters, brother, and other survivors.

Everything familiar had been taken by the time Regina nearly drowned in the abyss of Bergen-Belsen. A real bath of warm water and soap — with her mother washing her hair — formed an obscure, nearly-forgotten image of distant yesterdays. It was tomorrow's unattainable wish. Remembrance of life before the war, with its banal, daily routines, serves as a reference for what the Garfinkels lost. It helps explain the tragedy of the Shoah and the perpetual grief of survivors.

Despite occasional outbursts of anti-Semitism, life in Chmielnik before World War II had a tranquil rhythm set by the seasons, Jewish holidays, and the Shabbat, or Sabbath. School and play occupied the children; managing their households and caring for their families consumed the women, while synagogue attendance and business transactions absorbed the men.

Chmielnik was famous for its geese and goose sausage, which were sold throughout Poland and exported to Germany. The feathers and down were sent to the United States to make pillows and bedding. The quills went to France for use as toothpicks. Even the goose droppings were converted into fertilizer. Although Jews were prohibited from owning land, they rented poultry coops, farmland, orchards, and forests. They collected eggs, which they preserved in underground cellars. They picked apples, pears, and plums, which they stored in straw in basements and attics. The fruit and eggs were sold in Warsaw, Lodz, and in other large cities during the winter. Ice, carved from nearby lakes and a stream, was kept in a pit so deep it didn't melt and could be sold during the summer.

Some enterprising Jews operated tanneries, where they made leather and leather products from the hides of dead cows and horses. A nearby limestone quarry yielded compounds for making mortar, paint, preservatives, and other products. The forests provided a source of lumber, and one entrepreneur designed homes that could be assembled from a kit. Several factories made textiles, clothing, stoves, furniture, canes, and olive oil. Chmielnik's diverse economy made it a center of commerce — attracting the surrounding farmers to its stores, tailors, and shoemakers.

Be they Jewish or Polish, few homes had electricity and none had indoor plumbing, so the job of women was especially arduous. Sara Garfinkel cooked, cleaned, baked from scratch, and fetched water from wells — to mention a few of her duties. Washing clothes, for example, was a 24-hour chore involving the use of washboards and huge vats for soaking, boiling, and scrubbing.

The Garfinkels remember their mother, Sara, as the first one awake in the morning and the last one to sleep at night. As soon as she dressed, Sara went to the bakery to fill her basket with bread and rolls. Before the children tumbled out of bed, the table was already set for breakfast, water was boiling for coffee, and milk had been delivered by a horse-drawn wagon carrying big metal cans. Sara had a reputation among friends and acquaintances for being clean, industrious, and resourceful. "Even during the war, she always managed to save a piece of bread for tomorrow," Helen said. Helen overheard the neighbors' comments: "Look, look. There's Sara getting the children ready for school." In the summer, she gave the children sponge baths outside and dressed them in navy blue and white school uniforms. Using a fine-toothed comb, Sara searched for lice before braiding the girls' hair. She set pails of water in the sunshine. "By the time we kids got up, the water was warm," Regina said. "She lined us up one after the other. My mother was very clean. Our house was very clean. My mother was spotless." In the winter, Sara readied the children near the kitchen stove, which resembled a fireplace lined with white ceramic tile.

On cold nights, Sonia sat or stood with her back against the warm tiles. She used the light cast by the coal-burning stove and kerosene lamp to read books she had borrowed from Chmielnik's public library. Sara sat nearby to mend and sew. She also embroidered napkins, handkerchiefs, runners, and linens, some of which were displayed in a cabinet full of the family's fine china, crystal, and silver. "My mother never went to bed before anybody else in the house," Nathan said. On arriving home from literary readings, a game of dominos, or a heated political discussion, Nathan saw his mother knitting or darning socks near the stove. "She never went to bed until I came home," Nathan said. "I remember because I was the last to come home. She asked me, 'Where have you been so long?' Then she went to bed. It wasn't late for me, but for her it was late. I never saw in my lifetime, a mother like that. She was beyond compare."

Thanks to a distant relative who survived the Holocaust, the Garfinkels have one photograph of Sara. It shows her and Nathan's friend, Chaim Mikolowski, seated at his bedside in a Warsaw hospital where he had had his appendix removed. The operation, performed in early 1939, saved Nathan's life. Sara stayed with him a week — sometimes sleeping on the floor of his hospital room. According to his sisters, Nathan was the apple of their mother's eye. She called him by his Yiddish name, Nusan, or nickname, Nusale.

"If my mother were here today, she would look like Jane Seymour," Helen said, referring to the British actress. "She was tall, so simple. She had a look of goodness. Not that she was so beautiful, she was refined. She was quiet, polite. She never raised her voice, my mother. Everybody liked my mother." Mrs. Kaufman, a wealthy neighbor, asked Sara to hold her family's money and jewelry during the tax collector's visits. The Kaufmans owned a lumberyard and paint-making plant. "Mrs. Kaufman trusted my mother, not her sons, not her daughters-in-law, to keep her money for her," Sonia said. "That's the kind of person my mother was." Even Regina, who was much younger, cherishes the memory of Sara's kindness. Each week, a tiny woman brought letters for Sara to read aloud and paper for Sara to write replies. Family members complained of the woman's illiteracy, but Sara admonished them not to criticize someone in need. "I would say she was very gentle and very generous, always willing to help others," Regina said.

Sara and Kalman first met through a matchmaker, who initially failed to persuade them to marry. They each wed others, became widowed, and were reacquainted. Kalman had two children, Isaac and Mandzia, from his first marriage. Sara was childless. The same matchmaker succeeded in her second attempt to join Sara and Kalman. "The matchmaker came back and said, 'It's meant to be,'" Sonia said. "My father was religious, but my mother was more out-going."

Like many Jewish women in Chmielnik, Sara attended synagogue, maintained a kosher kitchen, and always wore kerchiefs or wigs. "I never saw my mother without a wig," Sonia said. "Her wigs were dark blonde." Orthodox Jews regard a woman's hair as sensual just as they consider a man's beard virile. After marriage, Orthodox women cover their heads as a sign of modesty — allowing only their husbands to see their real hair. On Saturdays, Sara wore her finest clothes, long gold chains, rings, and brooches. "In Europe, you didn't have costume jewelry," Sonia said. "It was real jewelry." Kalman attended a synagogue for men only. Sara went to a synagogue that admitted women to a balcony overlooking the men — thus maintaining an Orthodox tradition of segregating the sexes. "Many times I went with my mother because I knew how to pray," Sonia said. "My father was so proud that I went with my mother to synagogue." The Garfinkel children sensed Sara was religiously observant to please their father and that she was more vivacious and open-minded than her acquiescence suggested. Kalman faithfully recited prayers and attended synagogue each morning and evening. Each Saturday after the special Sabbath meal, he read to the family excerpts from the Talmud. In that sacred text, Kalman had written his children's birth dates and names, which originally were Bela, Natan for Nathan, Sheindel for Sonia, Chana for Helen, and Rivka for Regina. The children Americanized their names after World War II.

Religious Jews honored Shabbat as God's designated day of rest; starting at sundown on Friday, they stopped working for 24 hours. When Kalman took naps on Saturday afternoons, Nathan sometimes invited friends over to play cards. "Father didn't know. My mother is religious, too, but she looked the other way. My mother wanted to please the kids, you know," Sonia said. "She was very out-going. Good — how can I tell you? — kind, considerate about others. And she understood." Many times after the Saturday meal, Nathan left the house to see friends because he didn't want to participate in Kalman's Talmud readings. Although Nathan had attended special schools (such as cheder, as a child, and yeshiva, as a teenager) in order to study Hebrew, Judaism, history, and culture, he wasn't interested in religion. "This wasn't for me because I have no answer. I looked for more reality in life," Nathan said. "On Saturdays I would get up early, and we would go to talk about books. This was my synagogue." Nathan and his friends met in the fields on sunny days and discussed the works of Tolstoy and Shakespeare. Nathan especially liked the play *Romeo and Juliet*, which depicted idealistic youths defying the established order of their parents.

Kalman clung to Judaic traditions and ancient rituals. Once, in the morning's wee hours as everyone else slept, Nathan discovered his father lying on the floor near the bedroom's doorway.

Ashes smeared on his forehead, Kalman muttered what Nathan believes to have been *tikkun hazot* or *hatsos,* a prayer of penitence. Those seeking forgiveness of sins and improvement often recite the tikkun hazot late at night, when the heart and soul are thought to be more receptive to self-examination. "I could tell he didn't want me to see him. I saw some disappointment and shyness in him," Nathan said. "I didn't say anything." Nathan kept silent out of respect, although he dismissed such practices as pure superstition.

Sonia considered her father modern for an Orthodox Jew. He kept his beard and sideburns short. He did not wear long coats. Sonia said Kalman resembled the U.S. song leader, Mitch Miller. He showed a progressive streak by stressing secular education. "My father told us over and over: 'You can lose everything, but things you learn you'll never lose,'" Helen said. Sonia echoed Helen: "It was knocked in my head constantly that I cannot be without school, that school was the most important thing." Despite their differences, Nathan admired his father's business acumen. "He smells the raising of prices or lowering of prices from wheat," Nathan said. "If he were here, he would be a rich businessman, he would be a Wall Street person now."

Regina recalls Kalman being surrounded by friends, mostly merchants, who attended the same synagogue. They included Mr. Shore, who owned a tobacco store, and Mr. Zunshein, who owned a stationery shop. "I perceived him as head of the family always, like he fulfilled his role as a father, yet I don't remember him being a strict man," Regina said. "We knew what was expected. We always did what was expected. I remember listening to him. I remember him explaining."

Sonia thought Kalman was very wise. "My father taught us right from wrong," she said. "This I can't ever forget. He gave me ten *zlotys* — to save five *zlotys* in the savings bank and to keep five *zlotys* to spend." The bank teller at Polska Kasa Oszczednosci mistakenly gave Sonia extra cash. "My father said, 'You know it's wrong.' He made me go back to the bank. I was ashamed to go back," Sonia said. "When my father looked at my face, he knew when I lied. It was like he would look inside me and find out."

Nathan viewed Kalman as the disciplinarian and Sara as the diplomat. "My father slapped me one time. I forgot what happened, but he hit me. My mother talked back. She said, 'You never hit our son,'" Nathan said. "My mother was keeping peace between me and my father. My mother tried to calm my father down. She tried to say to the children, 'Is it hard to listen to your father? Listening doesn't mean you agree with him.'"

Inside Kalman's grain store, wooden storage bins lined the walls from floor to ceiling. A huge scale sat in the corner. Activity peaked on Thursday, when farmers delivered corn, wheat, oats, and rye. Kalman hired a neighbor to carry the huge sacks of grain. "For my mother it was a double work day," Nathan said. "She helped in the store because she wants to do it. Then she cooked. She had so many children to take care of, and she did with love."

Behind their business, the Garfinkels lived in two large rooms. "It's not like here where every child has a room or every two children have a room," Helen said. The younger children — Regina, Rachel, and Fishel — slept in their parents' bedroom. Nathan, Bela, Sonia, and Helen slept in the kitchen, which functioned as a living or family room by day and as a second bedroom by night. The furniture, made of blonde wood, was versatile. "You lifted the top off the bench, and there was a bed," Helen said. The dining table's top also lifted to reveal a storage chest for quilts. One armoire held the family's clothes. Another armoire contained sheets and linens. Although the rooms were few, they were large. "If you compared life here in America to life at home in Poland, you would call it (Poland) poverty level, but at home we called it middle class," Nathan said. "People in America who are poor would be considered middle class in Poland."

Shabbat, beginning Fridays at sundown, served as the week's focal point by drawing families together. As Sara lit candles on the kitchen's brass candlesticks and on the bedroom's silver candelabra, she recited a prayer to inaugurate the Sabbath. The ceremony's simplicity and beauty fascinated Sonia. "I used to love Friday nights. It was a festive day. We put the candles on. We had lots of food. We had wine, of course, every Friday night. My father said prayers." Little did Sonia know the flickering flames in her Chmielnik home would assume greater meaning decades later. "I still light the candles on Fridays. I do it for my parents." Special foods prepared in advance for Friday and Saturday might include chicken soup, fish, calf's liver, chicken, geese, lima beans, sweet-and-sour cabbage, cookies, chala, and, in the summer, cakes made with apples or blueberries. On Thursdays and Friday mornings, Regina and Helen carried the raw dough to the bakery for cooking.

Many Friday evenings, as Shabbat began, Kalman brought a poor person home for dinner. Fulfilling the commandment to provide charity was one Judaic practice of which Nathan approved. Sara always gave the guest a package of pastries and a little money. Sometimes the guest was Icekle, a raggedy, homeless man who slept in Chmielnik's synagogue. "He went from house to house. Each house gave him a penny or two pennies," Helen said, referring to *groshen*, the Polish equivalent of pennies. Helen never forgot Icekle because, years later, she identified strongly with him.

Like other Jews worldwide, Chmielnik's Jews observed the Sabbath as a day of rest. "We couldn't do any work on Saturday. That's why we cooked so much on Friday and Thursday," Sonia said. "On Saturday you cannot comb your hair. You cannot polish a shoe. You cannot water a plant. I thought God would strike me." In the winter, the Garfinkels hired a Polish laborer to light a fire in the stove on Saturday mornings and to rekindle it later. "We give this man some money and some cake," Helen said. On holidays requiring Jews to fast, Regina and her friends tested each other to see whether they had eaten. They demanded: "Let me see your tongue. If the tongue is white, that shows you haven't eaten,"

Regina said. "For kids, it was a big deal not to eat." During those special days with her family, Regina never imagined that not eating would mark her existence or that her tongue would turn white for months at a time.

The Garfinkel children showed signs of independence reflecting the changing times. Bela lived with her maternal grandparents in Lodz because she preferred the bustling city to Chmielnik's sleepy ambiance. Nathan disappointed his father by dropping religious studies. Sonia baffled her parents by refusing to get her ears pierced even though it was customary for young women to wear small, gold hoops. Helen elicited her father's disapproval by learning to ride a bicycle from Nathan. Although the children didn't always conform to their parents' wishes, no disputes destroyed the family's feeling of togetherness. "A mother have 10 kids. Each kid is different," Sonia said. "We're four sisters, and each of us is different."

The quiet and sensitive Sonia loved to read, anytime, anywhere. On warm days, she took books and a blanket to the fields and sat under an oak tree. Kalman tried to persuade Sonia to become a religion teacher. "When I was young, I listened. When you eat a meal, you have to say a prayer. When you take a drink, you have to say a prayer. When you wash your hands, you have to say a prayer. When you went to bed, you have to say a prayer. We used to say, 'It's so hard to be a Jew.'" Unlike Nathan, Sonia did not shun Judaism, but she was attracted to the big city, its crowds of people, varied activities, and modern conveniences. Sonia thought of moving to Lodz, where so many of Chmielnik's young people had migrated, including her older sister, Bela, and her best friend, Lola Warszawska, who got a job in a soda fountain. Sonia could live there with her half-sister, Mandzia. "I thought I might get a job doing embroidery by machine. Mandzia was going to help buy me a machine because you could make lots of money by embroidery. Mandzia was like my mother," Sonia said. "The only thing about Lodz, I would miss my parents, I would miss my sisters."

If not for World War II, Nathan might have stayed in Chmielnik to operate and, eventually, to take over his father's grain store, but Sonia feels that is unlikely. "My father predicted that Nate would never be a businessman. My father knew," Sonia said. "If my brother would win today the lottery, he wouldn't keep it. He would give the money away, to the poor, to people who need." Shoah survivors from Chmielnik describe Nathan as energetic. He taught many acquaintances, including Israel "Ira" Kaminsky, to ride a bicycle. His good-natured personality and sense of humor made Nathan popular. If Nathan took an exceptionally long time in the outhouse, Sonia said, the children threw rocks against the walls. Sonia said many girls in Chmielnik were infatuated with Nathan for his intelligence and good looks. Marriage, children, and even a career were far from Nathan's mind. He wanted to read books, study, learn. He wanted to explore and travel. "I was thinking of going to a bigger city, maybe Lodz or Warsaw or out of the country completely. Maybe I would go to France where my aunts were, maybe to Palestine. I didn't think I would stay in Chmielnik. There was nothing in Chmielnik," Nathan said. "It was my dream to be a teacher but not in the yeshiva. I still had the hope to go to university to become a teacher."

Israel Steinfeld admired Nathan for having the courage to be his own person. Nathan openly participated in modern activities taboo to Orthodox Jews such as sports and political debate. "I loved sports. I loved soccer. I went to soccer matches. Hidden I played," Steinfeld said. "Hidden means without permission of the parents. Some people went out from the shadow. Others stayed hidden. That's the nature of youth." Steinfeld's father, known as the honest Joshua, led prayers for about 40 men who were followers of Rabbi Szydlow. Peers saw Nathan as happy-go-lucky, Steinfeld said, while parents saw him as rebellious for stepping out of the shadow.

Helen was too young to contemplate Chmielnik's generation

gap although she was aware of the tension between her father and older brother. Helen believes she would have followed the town's young Jews, including her sisters Bela and Sonia, to Lodz, but, as a child, she didn't think much about the future. After arriving home from school, Helen played with the neighborhood boys and girls — in particular with her younger brother, Fishel, and the Kaufman children. They devised games: hide and seek, jump rope, and hopping on one foot while balancing a rock on the other foot. The children invented their own version of golf by digging holes and using sticks to hit stones into the holes. They counted the number of stones required to fill the holes they had dug. The abundance and variety of toys owned by Helen's grandchildren remind her of how much today's United States differs from the Poland of 60 years ago. The only store-bought toys Helen and her friends owned were yo-yos. "Nate bought me a yo-yo," Helen said. "Oh, that was a big thing."

Kalman Mapa, of Toronto, played with Helen often because his best friend, Chaim Kaufman, lived near the Garfinkels. Like other Shoah survivors from Chmielnik, Mapa describes the Garfinkels as a hard-working and personable family. Although he lived near Chmielnik's center, Mapa ventured to the outskirts to visit friends. "I know Chanka very good," Mapa said, calling Helen by her Polish nickname. "All the sisters were fine girls. Chanka's brother, Nusan (Nathan), he used to teach lots of children to ride bicycles. They were nice people." At that time, Mapa's childhood was untroubled.

Regina's memories of those happy years preceding the German invasion are fleeting. She played outdoors with homemade toys, but she was not a tomboy like Helen. "I don't remember playing with Helen. I remember her being more daring than anybody else. Helen would do certain things others wouldn't do," Regina said, noting that Helen jumped, ran, climbed trees, rode a bicycle, and played in the dirt. To play "store," Regina rubbed broken dishes against rocks to shape the ceramic into coins. Regina owned a rag doll, sewn by Sara, and collected swatches of fabric from the dressmaker to make doll clothes. After mastering Polish, Regina enjoyed school, and history was her favorite subject. Regina cannot speculate on how her life might have unfolded in World War II's absence. "I have no idea because I really had no life before, so I have nothing to compare it to. I always think it would have been different or it should have been different." Regina feels Nazi Germany robbed her of the chance to grow up and finish school. "I lost a childhood. I feel very bad for my lack of education. I am angry because I was deprived of an education," Regina said. "I went from childhood to adulthood. It's not the same as going step by step. You always think, 'what if, what if.'" Regina might have been content to stay in Chmielnik. Not only did the residents know each other, but also their jobs of serving each other gave them a sense of purpose. Visiting old-fashioned communities, such as Mackinaw Island, Michigan, reminds Regina of Chmielnik's pleasant lifestyle. "I love that feeling of a small town."

Chmielnik's teenagers spent their spare time with friends cultivating the art of conversation. "Everyone has their own group of friends," said Mania Poper Cherston of Queens, New York. "We had a place where every evening we would meet. We would talk about politics, about books, what was going on in the world." Teenagers created their own entertainment. "People in Chmielnik were very poor. It was a low standard of life. Each family has seven, eight kids. To put them with clothes, books, and school supplies, that was a big accomplishment." Yet the town sparkled with a rich cultural life, Israel Steinfeld said, noting that Chmielnik had several libraries. Several newspapers — called Hinnt or Heint, Fockshtimeh or Volkshtimeh, Moment, and Nasz' 'Przeglond — circulated. Many residents, especially the teenagers, were well read and self-taught.

Anti-Semitism seemed to make studying the only outlet. "You couldn't develop the economy because no one let you. You couldn't emigrate because no one let you in. This was the situation in the

1930s," Steinfeld said. "You don't know what to do. You could only do one thing — read, read, and read. This was the opium for the youth."

Adults earned a living by catering to each other. Each year, the shoemaker measured the Garfinkel children's feet to make shoes for them. "My father would watch him and insist that we buy the shoes one size bigger," Sonia said. "I wanted to get shoes a size smaller because I wanted a small foot. I was tall for my age." The self-conscious and shy Sonia saved her zlotys to buy the smaller shoes. "My father never knew." But a Polish water carrier in the neighborhood noticed and liked to tease Sonia. "I tried to avoid him, but he would always see me and call out, 'Tight shoe. Tight shoe.' The shoes hurt me. When I walked, it took me longer."

Possessions were few but they were high quality — a sharp contrast to today's mania for consumption in the United States. Like many families, the Garfinkels had their clothing custom-made. "We went to a store and bought materials, and we took to a tailor to make clothes. I remember the store. I used to go with my mother," Sonia said. "How she loved us kids. She put us before her always. Everything for the kids. Everything for the kids, with the food, with the clothes." A special garment Sonia will never forget is a fully-lined coat that Bela's boyfriend, Isaac, made for her. Isaac, who worked in a dressmaker's shop in Lodz, fashioned it from swirling panels of green wool. He designed a similar coat for Bela in royal blue. Sonia's coat, which was sophisticated for a Chmielnik teenager, prompted her to buy a matching hat, shoes, and purse.

Tosia Fastag Bottner said most Jews in Chmielnik focused on their families, synagogue, and simple pleasures, such as reading in the library and taking walks. "You can't compare it to life now," Bottner said. "There was no TV or news commentaries. There was lots of tranquility. People didn't know any better. They didn't need luxuries. Most of the shtetl (town) were Orthodox. I come from a very religious family, a very loving family. We were pro-

tected, sheltered." Growing up in Chmielnik in many ways resembled the calm before the storm, making the catastrophe that
befell the town's Jews that much more devastating.

Chapter Three
BLITZKRIEG

One of history's most demonic eras commenced with Germany's invasion of Poland in September, 1939. World War II maps illustrate better than words what happened to Europe's Jews. Within three years, Germany secretly built, in Poland, at least six highly-specialized factories and equipped them with gas chambers for suffocating people and crematoria for burning bodies. The estimated 6 million Jews forcibly transported to these slaughterhouses thought they were going to resettlement zones. Some maps identify Auschwitz, Belzec, Chelmno, Majdanek, Sobibor, and Treblinka with swastikas or with skulls and crossbones. Those ominous symbols surround the Garfinkels' hometown of Chmielnik.

To kill Jews, German fascists first tried to kill the freethinking and morals of European civilians. They were largely successful in Poland, where they placed almost all of the death camps. Anti-Semitism raged at a higher pitch in Poland than in Germany. In a hideous irony, German industrialists and Nazis compelled Jewish slave laborers to build the extermination sites. Besides collaboration, the goal of genocide required careful planning, ample resources, and several years' time. In the interim, Germany controlled civilians through curfews, censorship, food rationing, work quotas, and other regulations that were nearly impossible to obey. The harshest restrictions applied to Jews, but the unwritten law of fear ruled everyone.

To obliterate an entire group of people, the Reich exploited fear as much as hatred. For example, Germany's army and S.S.

shot and hung families in public to punish the alleged transgressions of just one member. The relatively few Poles who were tolerant, therefore, grew afraid of reprisals — a reason so few individuals helped Jews. The Garfinkels' non-Jewish customers and acquaintances who ignored anti-Semitic jeers and taunts before the German occupation risked beatings, imprisonment, and execution for associating with Jews. While some Poles welcomed the new fascist regime, many dreaded it. Jews — even without the existence of death camps in 1939 — especially feared the Nazis.

As Usher Tarek notes, Chmielnik Jews had read newspaper articles the previous year about Kristallnacht, the infamous "night of broken glass." On that night, November 9, 1938, fascist hoodlums burned synagogues in Germany, vandalized Jewish businesses, and looted homes. The brown shirts also arrested, beat, and killed Jews. Helen heard ugly rumors about the advancing German soldiers, that they mutilated and castrated young Jewish men. Word of such atrocities and murders prompted thousands of Polish Jews to flee east as soon as Germany invaded.

Among those refugees was the Garfinkels' older half-sister, Mandzia, from Kalman's first marriage. Mandzia's husband, Morris "Julek" Singer, tells a dramatic story of fleeing from Lodz, Poland, to the Soviet Union. Shortly after the invasion, Morris was taken with other Jews for forced labor assignments. After enduring several such round-ups, Morris concluded Jews had no future in Poland. "The fascists were so sadistic. I saw how they treated people," Morris said. "They put the heaviest work to old men. We were unloading barrels of ammunition. For an old man, this was impossible. I tried to help this old man beside me, and the German beat the hell out of me."

Morris could not persuade Mandzia to leave Lodz. Despite violence in the streets, she did not want to travel with an infant, their daughter, Renia, to an unknown destination. Mandzia told Morris to prepare a new home and send word. After reaching Bialystok, he sent his brother, Leibl Singer, to fetch her. Leibl assured her Morris had found a place to stay, even though Morris really hadn't. Bialystok, a Polish city that Germany temporarily turned over to the Soviet Union, was teeming with Jewish refugees. "Basically, I tricked her, and I saved her life." Leibl couldn't persuade his own wife to leave — losing her and their two children forever to the flames of the Holocaust.

Morris, Mandzia, and baby Renia's harrowing escape involved finding each other in the forest and traveling thousands of miles to the Ural Mountains, where the parents toiled in factories as slave laborers. "The Soviets treated us the same as their own citizens, which was bad," Morris said. "They gave you a card for bread every day but not always the store have the bread. The soup was like water, but it was hot. If you followed the orders, they didn't beat you. If you didn't follow orders, they send you thousands of miles away, to Siberia." Life was dangerous for Jews in Russia, but Morris was certain it was preferable to staying in Poland. He didn't really know, however, until the war's end. All of Morris' blood relatives left behind in Poland, including his mother, brother, and two sisters, perished.

The Garfinkels' older half-brother, Isaac, who served in the Polish Army, met a different fate than Mandzia although he, too, went to the Soviet Union. The family surmised Isaac's final months from a soldier and from Isaac's letters, some dated as late as June, 1941. The Soviet Union, which had conspired with Germany to divide Poland, captured Isaac with other Polish soldiers. As a prisoner of war, Isaac toiled in the Dombas coal mine. He escaped to Lvov, Nathan Garfinkel said, where, in all likelihood, he was murdered with other Jews. Before joining the army, Isaac had worked as a tailor in Lodz and Kielce.

Before the war, "Isaac tried to get the entire family to move," Nathan said. "My mother wanted to go, but my father didn't want to go, so we stayed." Isaac had a wife and children who later died in Treblinka's gas chambers. Isaac had suggested the Garfinkels move to Lvov in eastern Poland, near the Ukraine. The city's history of passing from one nation to another subjected its Jewish residents to the bigotry of the Ukrainians as well as the Poles.

Several weeks after Germany stormed Poland, the Soviet Union took over Lvov, Poland's third largest city, along with the region of Eastern Galicia. That annexation, accomplished under the Soviet Union's pact with Germany, provided a temporary haven to Jews. During late 1939 and throughout 1940, about 100,000 Jewish refugees from western Poland flocked to Lvov, which already contained about 110,000 Jews. "People used to lay on the border and sleep outside, with no food, without money," Sonia said. "I have friends who lived through the war being in Russia. How could you go with seven kids? It was impossible."

Many Jews debated whether or not to leave Poland. Tarek recalls such discussions within his own family, which operated a butcher's shop in Chmielnik. "My parents were against it," Tarek said. "They didn't believe the Germans would be that barbaric. Germans were the most educated, the most advanced people in the world."

Israel Steinfeld said moving was impractical for most. "You have to understand. Most families had a minimum of five children. The attachment of parents to children was to such a degree some people could have saved themselves, but they wouldn't separate from their families. They kept the families together."

Fleeing to the Soviet Union presented its own special perils. The Communists transferred some of the Jewish refugees from Lvov to sparsely-populated regions farther east, enslaved others in labor camps, and banished yet more to Siberia. Despite such mistreatment, Jews had a slightly better chance of survival in the Soviet Union. For that reason, Nathan said, he would opt for communism if he were forced to choose between communism and fascism.

Many others shared that sentiment. When Germany broke its treaty by attacking the Soviet Union on June 22, 1941, about 10,000 of Lvov's Jews followed the retreating Red Army. The Germans entered the city June 30, 1941, renamed it Lemberg, and established a reign of terror.

Isaac Garfinkel could have died any number of ways in Lvov. He could have been beaten to death in the streets during an immediate series of pogroms, known as the Petliura Days. Isaac might have starved in Lvov's Jewish ghetto, created in November, 1941. He might have been deported with more than 70,000 of Lvov's Jews to the gas chambers and crematoria of Belzec.

Given his young age and physical strength, Isaac was probably shipped to the nearby work camp of Janowska — the destination of Simon Wiesenthal, a talented Jewish architect in Lvov. Wiesenthal survived. Isaac did not, and the Garfinkels can only speculate about their half-brother's death. To avenge the murders of millions like Isaac, Wiesenthal devoted himself to hunting down Nazis who committed crimes against humanity. The Jewish Documentation Center he founded in Vienna, Austria, has helped bring more than 1,100 Nazi war criminals to justice. Wiesenthal has honored the dead victims by writing books and lecturing against anti-Semitism.

Nathan knew young Jews who had evaded the Nazis by going to the Soviet Union. His close friend, Jakob Lederman; Lederman's sister, Bela; and wife, Betty, sought temporary refuge in Lvov, where they met Isaac Garfinkel by chance on the street. The encounter was brief, Lederman said. There was no serious talk about Isaac's prisoner-of-war experience or the troubles facing Jews in Europe. They took a photograph of Isaac which Lederman gave Nathan after the war — a memento Nathan treasures to this day.

Lederman's passage in the Soviet Union was typical. "I went to the Russian side. I left Poland because I was scared about the Germans. They took Jews to work. They took Jews to jail. I run away. Thousands of people ran away, but those thousands didn't survive," Lederman said. "When I left Chmielnik, I thought we would be gone two or three weeks. It was like a storm. You escape the storm for a few days and be back." When Lederman returned, eight years later, Chmielnik was a ghost town. "Who knew they would build concentration camps?" When the Soviet Union was an ally of Germany, it suspected Jews of being "Polish spies," Lederman said. When Germany betrayed the Soviet Union, it considered Jews "German spies." The Soviets rounded up Lederman, his wife, and sister to send to labor camps in Siberia. In Lederman's camp, about 1,500 men and women cut down trees in the forest to make fuel for electrical power plants. "The conditions, you can't describe the conditions. It was terrible," Lederman said. "It was harsh to survive. Hundreds of people died in Siberia. It was so cold, people couldn't take it." After the war, Lederman learned how superior his Spartan living quarters were compared with the concentration camps of Poland and Germany. In Siberia, families were allowed to stay together. Each barrack, accommodating about 100 to 150 people, had a kitchen and wood-burning stove. "When people told me stories about the concentration camps," Lederman said, "I couldn't complain."

Jakob Sylman also eked out a tenuous existence in exile. A few months after Germany seized Chmielnik, his parents instructed Jakob to accompany his sister, Tema, and niece, Ann, to Lvov. There, they would meet Tema's husband, Icek Frydman, who had served in the Polish Army. The two-week journey became a terror-filled obstacle course, Sylman said, challenging them to avoid getting killed by Poles and Germans. As soon as they crossed the border, they were arrested and detained in a Soviet jail for a week. "We had all kinds of incidents. It was scary all the time," Sylman said. "To tell the story, it would take all night." Conditions in Lvov deteriorated so much Sylman and his sister registered to return to Chmielnik despite the horror stories they had heard about the murder of Jews in Poland. "There were rumors of all kinds of things the Germans did," Sylman said. "Nobody believed." After collecting names and addresses, the Soviets used the information to find Jews and send them to Siberia and other regions. Sylman and his relatives ended up in a Moslem city. At one point, he and

Icek were forced to work in gold mines. "It wasn't a work camp, but we were under military control," Sylman said.

Nathan chose to stay in Chmielnik. "If I rescue myself, my family will be alone," Nathan said. "I didn't go because my family wanted to stay together." When German soldiers entered Chmielnik in September, 1939, Nathan was 19, Bela was 18, Sonia was 16, Helen was 12, and Regina was 9.

Israel "Irving" Buchbinder, then a 12-year-old, witnessed Chmielnik's first World War II casualty. "I happened to be out-side when the first Panzer came in," said Buchbinder, who now lives in Toronto. "I was curious." He stood several hundred feet away from the German army tank, which lumbered toward a Jew holding a hunting rifle. The tank spat a volley of fire. "I saw the shots flying. This was not just bullets. This was from a heavy machine gun." The Jew crumpled like a rag doll. "This was in front of my eyes." Buchbinder ran into his grandmother's home, but that first image of war — the tank mowing down a human being — chased Buchbinder the rest of his life.

The Garfinkel family and their neighbors vacated their homes the day the German army arrived. Kalman broke part of the picket fence separating the town from the orchard. The women and chil-dren slipped through first, and the men followed. "My father said everything would be all right, that he was praying to God," Helen said. "I was afraid." The families huddled under the trees. They heard the sounds of war: rifle shots, rumbling military trucks, sol-diers marching, the vibration of tanks, and shouts. Helen believes a Jew was shot in the fruit orchard, but she did not witness the murder. Someone demanded, through a loudspeaker, that every-one raise their hands above their heads and proceed home. Ger-man soldiers threatened to kill people who failed to turn in weap-ons and ammunition. They inspected people's homes, including the Garfinkel residence, but they were not particularly abusive, Helen said.

The German invasion abruptly ended Regina's stable and

happy childhood, transforming it to a faint memory. She spent years trying to regain a feeling of security that had been ripped away in an instant. "I remember spending the time in fear. I remember clinging to my mother a lot. We had to stay indoors most of the time," Regina said. "That puzzled me the most. I wondered why. It wasn't explained to me. It's obvious there was no explanation. The answer was: you're different. It was a question on top of a question. What did I do that was different? Why am I different?" Her mother told Regina, "This is the way things are now," that the war was only temporary. Germany occupied Poland, however, for six agonizing years. "It was an immediate cut-off," Regina said.

People's fear fed and grew on escalating violence. A few days after the invasion, soldiers raided the neighborhood and dragged out four or five families, including the Garfinkels and the Kaufmans, to stage an execution. "The Nazis lined us up, 20 or 30 people. The officer put machine guns in front of us like they were going to shoot," Nathan said. "Three machine guns were aimed at us. My father was standing in front of me with my mother. My mother was very calm. My father was praying. He said a prayer, the last rites," Nathan said, referring to the *viddui*, a confession recited annually on Yom Kippur and also just before death. "I didn't pray. I think, 'This was the end of it.' I tried to be calm."

Nathan, his parents, and youngest siblings — Helen, Rachel, Regina, and Fishel — faced the firing squad's loaded weapons for about 30 minutes. "We were afraid they were going to shoot any second." Inexplicably, their would-be executioners changed plans. Brandishing sticks, the soldiers chased the group home. "They wanted to scare us. My father said, 'Thank God we were not killed.' I thought, 'This was not the end of it.'"

When war first spread to Poland, Bela and Sonia were visiting their maternal grandmother, aunts, uncles, and cousins in Lodz. "You couldn't help but be scared with the guns, with the shots," Sonia said. "We hid in the attic." The Germans seized Lodz on

September 8, 1939, annexed it with the region of Warthegau on
November 9, 1939, and renamed it Litzmannstadt on April 11,
1940. The significant presence of *Volksdeutsche*, or ethnic Germans, protected Poland's second-largest city from bombs and other
immediate destruction. However, about one-third of Lodz' population, more than 200,000 Jews who enriched the city's artistic
and industrial life, was doomed.

"My aunt said if it's going to be bad, she would come to
Chmielnik with her husband, her child," Sonia said. "People didn't
believe that Germans would come to little cities and towns. We
didn't believe they would take us to camp, they would kill."

Chapter Four
UNDER CURFEW

In Chmielnik, the Germans swiftly and ruthlessly imposed new laws governing Jews. Children were not allowed to attend school. Most merchants, including Kalman, were prohibited from conducting business, so they could not earn a living. The Germans began taxing Jews, typically by trying to seize bank accounts, said Israel Steinfeld, who worked in the Jewish institution, Bank Ludowy. "We felt, 'Who are we to ask people to bring in so much money?'" Steinfeld's boss, Efraim Zalcberg, decided to close the bank rather than be coerced into cooperating with the enemy. "The day the Germans walked in, everything disintegrated in Chmielnik," Steinfeld said.

Strict curfews, from about five o'clock in the afternoon until eight o'clock in the morning, confined people to their homes. The Germans required Jews to wear the Star of David as identification. In Lodz, Bela and Sonia sewed yellow stars on the front and back of their clothing. In Chmielnik, Nathan wore a white armband bearing the blue outline of a star. The Germans searched homes to confiscate weapons, silver, gold, artwork, and anything else of value. Sara turned in some possessions, such as silver candleholders and golden chains.

"As soon as Germany invaded the town, people had to give up their radios," Helen said. "The Germans didn't want people to be informed." Very few Chmielnik residents, however, owned such modern devices. Some neighbors who lived near the orchard, the family of Kopl Kaminski, turned in their radio. Helen believes the wealthy Polish family near her neighborhood managed to keep theirs. Disobedience resulted in reprisals. Mr. Laks, Helen's Judaic history and religion instructor, was later shot for giving private lessons. A Jewish baker by the first name of Menashe was shot for secretly making bread in his home. Helen overheard her parents talk about a child in Chmielnik who was executed for failing to wear the star.

"My father always prayed to God. He made excuses for God every time," Sonia said. "First, they started taking everything from us. Then, little by little, they took us." Indeed, the Germans' steady diatribe of regulations encumbered every aspect of Jewish lives. "It was a drastic change," Regina said. "We didn't even have any writing paper. It was very scarce. Pencils or pens you had to be so careful with so it shouldn't get lost." The Germans barred Jews from Chmielnik's public libraries and forbade all the town's residents from using lights at night. Extinguishing the human spirit, not to mention the survival instinct, was not so easy. Sonia, determined to feed her passion for literature, still managed to borrow books and read by the light of her family's kerosene lamp. "The Germans said if they catch anybody with lights on they would kill people." Sonia felt secure with the windows' wooden shutters outside and curtains inside. "My father would come out and say, 'Shut the light. We could get killed.' I would say, 'Just two or three pages more, and then I'll shut the light,'" but Sonia continued reading until the wee hours of the morning.

Saul Jurysta, a Shoah survivor in Vineland, New Jersey, noticed the despair in his hometown when he returned from Warsaw in late 1939. Before the Germans overran Poland, Jurysta's maternal grandfather, Jakob Knobel, became one of Chmielnik's wealthiest residents by operating a thriving wholesale leather business. The Germans forced Knobel to sell his inventory to Poles for a pittance and seized the family's valuables. "They sold the leather, but the money, the zlotys, was worthless. We have to accept the money," Jurysta said. "It was an excuse to show that the Germans weren't stealing. My grandfather became a poor, poor man. They did this to everybody."

Poles who had seemed friendly before — or at least neutral

— showed their true feelings, Usher Tarek said. "There were stool pigeons and double crosses. All of a sudden, they took advantages because they knew the Jews are hated by the Germans. They were trying to rob after the invasion," Tarek said. "There were no safe places. The Polacks didn't help much. The cooperation was almost zero."

Nathan, Israel "Ira" Kaminsky, and other Chmielnik survivors mention a dreadful crime occurring within a few days of Germany's blitzkrieg. They heard that the Nazis had locked a dozen prominent Jews in the synagogue and set the building on fire. The Jews inside escaped, but some of them were shot. Jakob Sylman knows exactly what happened. His father, Leibl Sylman, was there. According to Jakob, the Germans employed a Polish collaborator to identify about 25 of Chmielnik's Jewish leaders. The group of rabbis, merchants, and other notables included Leibl Sylman, who owned a beer tavern, or *piwiarnia*, as it is known in Polish. The Nazis literally dragged Leibl from his home. Terrified, Jakob, his two brothers, four sisters, and mother, Rachel, hid in the basement, where they spent an anxious day and night. They could not see the enemy, but they heard gunfire and smelled smoke.

Leibl was taken a short distance up Siekiewicza Street to the *beit midrash*, or house of learning, next to the synagogue. The Nazis threatened to kill their captives if any shots were fired against Germans. Inevitably, shots rang out — probably Germans firing into the air, Jakob mused. "There were shots, but Jews weren't shooting. They didn't have weapons," Jakob said. Leibl and the others were led outside, one by one. Each man expected to be executed by a bullet to the head. Instead, the German officer pointed his gun toward the sky, fired, and said, "Run away!" Then the Nazis set the beit midrash ablaze. Leibl and most of the Jews reached their homes, but German soldiers apprehended about eight of the men and shot them in the streets, Jakob said. Among those dead was Berl Trembecki, caretaker of the beit midrash.

From the window of their home, Kalman Mapa and his family saw red flames lap and cover the beit midrash. His parents and siblings cried. "They didn't say anything." Mapa watched in stunned disbelief. "You didn't know what to do. It was a bad experience." Jakob Lederman also lived close enough to see the beit midrash burn. "It scared a lot of people. Then they run to Russia." Lederman joined that exodus about a month later. "The Germans went into Jewish stores and empty everything and sell it. They robbed everything from the Jews."

Rachel Wygodna Herszlikowicz, now of Melbourne, Australia, lived with her widowed mother near Chmielnik's beit midrash. Their flat was upstairs from a staples store her mother owned and operated. "My older sisters came to our house and hide. The whole night was shooting. Our house had hundreds and hundreds of holes from the bullets," Herszlikowicz said, referring to executions, which began the night the beit midrash burned and which continued throughout the German occupation. "They took a lot of Jews to the cemetery and shoot them, too."

Despite death and destruction, Jewish teenagers wandered the streets the next day, Jakob Sylman said, and mingled in the marketplace with German soldiers, who gave them chocolate and trinkets. In retrospect, that scene, with the beit midrash still smoldering in the background, was surreal, Sylman said. "As a kid, you're not afraid. You don't think about things like that. I was 15 at that time. It was hard for me to realize that deeply what this meant." Much later, after the war, Sylman learned the Germans had routinely burned synagogues as they swept east through Poland and the Soviet Union. According to numerous accounts, they deliberately locked Jews inside before igniting the buildings.

"The Nazis showed their real intentions of how they will behave," Kaminsky said. "The Nazis were very dangerous. Everyone was hiding." The Germans converted Chmielnik's large synagogue to a warehouse. After the war, Holocaust survivors formed an organization to buy the historic structure, dating back to 1638. Today, the building remains gutted. Plywood covers the windows and doors. The stone walls bear swastikas and other hateful graffiti.

The 1939 arson of Chmielnik's beit midrash, calculated to intimidate, was mild compared with what Simon Wiesenthal described in his reference book, *Every Day Remembrance Day: A Chronicle of Jewish Martyrdom*. He recorded, for September 5, 1939: "In Chmielnik, district of Stopnica, Poland, 14 Jews are burned alive at the stake." Although the Garfinkels did not know about that specific atrocity, news of other incidents instilled a constant sense of danger. Any misstep could spell disaster, yet they tried to live normally. Nathan, in particular, came and went as he pleased. He was not one to heed warnings or to follow rules, and, for that insubordination, he was nearly killed twice in Chmielnik.

Nathan first confronted death one evening in late 1939, as he rode his bicycle home. He had just delivered dead chickens and geese to his uncle, Wolf Garfinkel's, poultry store in Kielce. He returned with lamp oil. In Chmielnik's outskirts he saw some German officials approaching. Realizing it was too late to turn around or to change direction without drawing attention to himself, Nathan dismounted and pretended to fix his bicycle. He removed his armband to avoid being immediately discovered as a Jew breaking curfew.

The Germans stopped and demanded identification. Learning he was Jewish, they became enraged and hauled Nathan to a special office. They strapped him into what is called a "guillotine chair" and beat him senseless. "Nobody ever got out of this office alive. I don't know how I got out of there alive — maybe because I was young," Nathan said. "I understood then I was a victim, but there was also a war. Physically, that beating was the worst." The Nazis resumed beating Nathan the next day, broke his bicycle, and sent him home. He was so swollen and bloody his mother failed to recognize him. At his parents' insistence, Nathan tried to be more careful. However, with his blonde hair and blue eyes — non-Jewish traits in the eyes of Nazis — Nathan often traveled without identification.

Not wearing his armband may have saved his life, Nathan believes, when he was caught taking a shortcut through a farm near Celiny. Germans had appropriated the ranch and dairy from its Jewish owners, the family of Ojzer Sztrauch. He was one of the few Jews who owned land because he had distinguished himself as a soldier during World War I and even had lost a leg in battle. Sztrauch's privileged status among Poles did not matter to the Germans; they murdered him. To escape a similar fate, Nathan had prepared a story. If questioned about his ethnicity, he would say his armband had slipped. He never had a chance. The Nazi officer, Warner Munde, marched Nathan to the blacksmith shop, forced him to bend over an anvil, and flogged him with a horse whip. "After four or five lashes on my back, I can't feel anymore. Warner Munde probably would have killed me if he had known I was Jewish."

Whipping wasn't enough punishment. Munde said, "I take you home now." Munde tied a rope to Nathan's right hand and dragged him while riding a horse through a field. "If it were cement, I would have been dead." After a mile or two, Munde let go of the rope. Left for dead, Nathan groaned in pain. He was swollen, bleeding, unable to move. A farmer passing by in a wagon initially mistook Nathan for a corpse. The farmer, who happened to know the Garfinkels, carried Nathan home — an act of decency that was all too rare during the German occupation.

Anti-Semitism, bolstered by the new fascist regime, grew more ugly and violent, a change evident even in Chmielnik's signs. Slogans that formerly read, "Don't buy from Jews," now read, "Don't buy from the dirty Jews." Helen remembers that some thugs beat an elderly Jewish couple who operated a grocery store in Chmielnik. "After the invasion, my parents didn't want us to go out much." Unbeknownst to the Garfinkel children, Chmielnik's daily curfews were just the start of six years of bondage.

Chapter Five
SARA'S SISTERS

Bela's recollection of the years preceding the Shoah provides a different perspective of the Garfinkels' family history and of the Jewish experience. In 1933, when she was 12, Bela persuaded her parents to let her live with her maternal grandparents, the Tarkeltaubs, in Lodz. The eldest of the Garfinkel sisters, Bela relished the excitement of Lodz, one of Europe's leading textile producers. The city, located about 100 miles northwest of Chmielnik, sparkled as a cultural and commercial center. Poland's second-largest community of Jews after Warsaw, Lodz offered a greater variety of activities, a higher quality of education, and more young people than Chmielnik.

Bela basked in the extra attention at her grandparents' home, a brick apartment in the Jewish quarter. Her aunts, the younger sisters of Sara, doted on her, made her dresses, braided her hair, gave her presents, bought her ice cream, and included her in their outings. "I went to synagogue with my grandparents. They were so good to me. They treated me like a daughter," Bela said. "My aunts were young and single. Their boyfriends had motorcycles with seats on the side. I got to ride with them." That was a stark contrast to Chmielnik, where horse-drawn buggies were the main mode of transportation and only one or two families owned automobiles. "My mother came to pick me up. I didn't want to go home. I was hiding," Bela said. "I said, 'Next time I am going home,' but in reality I didn't want to go home. Who knows how many days my mother schlepped to see me? Once I went home. I just didn't like it. Lodz was more forward."

Mandzia, Bela's older half-sister, also lived in Lodz, and Bela admired her as a role model. "Mandzia was more modern. She lived with friends. She worked in a very big company. She made nice money. She was always well-dressed," Bela said. "I didn't even know she was my half-sister. She was no different. We were very close." Mandzia worked for a large textile factory that made sheets, pillowcases, and quilts. Her future husband, Morris "Julek" Singer, was impressed by Mandzia, too, because he knew the struggles underlying her accomplishments. Mandzia was like many young Jews who had left small towns and villages to find their fortunes in the big city. Getting a job was difficult because many employers did not hire Jews and unions excluded them from membership. "She didn't look Jewish. She was blonde, so they let her in," said Morris, who became a designer of women's sweaters. "There were small factories or companies where Jews could find jobs."

Because of his political activism, Morris was more aware than Bela of the dynamics of anti-Semitism. He joined the Socialist Front Organization to change the status quo. "I felt the system at that time is not the way we wanted it to be for the people," Morris said. "I wanted to eliminate discrimination against minorities — not just Jews, but you had Russians, Ukrainians. I wanted to eliminate discrimination against working people." Both Morris and one of his brothers were imprisoned for attending Socialist meetings. Police used the fear of communism as a pretext for arresting young people — especially Jews — who gathered in groups. "This was a way of harassing people," Morris said. "They accused me of being a member of the Communist Party. This was usually the charge if they arrested somebody. They even accused my mother of being Communist because she have a son like me." To protect themselves, Socialists adopted code names to address each other. That way, government spies infiltrating the organization would not know the Socialists' true identities. Among his comrades, Morris was known as "Julek." Although she had no political affiliations, Mandzia was arrested, along with Morris' cousin, at an afternoon tea. "That's why I met her," Morris said. "Mandzia attracted me as being a good-looking, good-thinking girl. Her personality was out-going, and she likes people." After dating for a few years, they married, and the Garfinkels attended the wedding. Sara still could not persuade Bela to go home to Chmielnik.

Bela considered Lodz' public education to be an advantage. As in Chmielnik, the schools required students to wear navy blue and white uniforms. There were separate religion classes and prayer sessions for Jewish and Catholic children. When Poland's marshal, Jozef Pilsudski, died in 1935, the high school chose Bela to hold the Polish flag at a ceremony commemorating him. "It was an honor. My grandfather couldn't believe they let me carry the flag," Bela said. Her grandfather, a cabinetmaker, had been accustomed to discrimination, but Bela's blonde hair and blue eyes defied the Jewish stereotype depicted by fascists. "I was tall and pretty and the best student," Bela said. She graduated with honors and spoke German and Polish fluently. "In Poland, you treat teachers with respect. If you don't do your homework, you get double work. The teacher was something special."

Popular as a teenager, Bela attracted many potential boyfriends. Only one stood out. Isaac lived on Bela's street, called Piotrkowska. They met secretly to take walks, to go dancing, to watch movies, and to drink ginger ale. "We liked each other, but no one knows about it. People were very strict. Parents were very strict. If my parents know I danced with a boy — oh, God!" Bela said. "We don't talk to each other about it, but we have so much feeling for each other." Isaac worked as an apprentice in a dressmaking shop catering to wealthy women. Bela was certain Isaac would become a clothing designer. She asked him to sew her a coat, and he fashioned one of royal blue wool with a fur collar. "I always ask him, 'Please, let me pay for the material.' Isaac wouldn't let me," Bela said. "Sonia was crazy about this coat. It was so elegant. You don't see coats like that. People looked back at me. I treasure that coat. If not for the war, I am sure I would marry him."

In subtle and dramatic ways, anti-Semitism shattered Bela's hopes and dreams. She pictured herself as a bank teller handling money, but Poland prohibited Jews from working in financial institutions unless Jews owned them. Discrimination did not emerge at school although it erupted elsewhere, Bela said. Like Nathan, she remembers that ugly incidents proliferated in the 1930s, especially after Pilsudski's death. Poles vandalized Jewish homes and businesses and beat Jews in the streets of Lodz. Pogroms intensified after Germany seized the city on September 8, 1939. "German soldiers and local German inhabitants entered Jewish shops and houses and walked off with whatever took their fancy, with no one to restrain them," according to *Encyclopedia of the Holocaust*. "Jews could no longer engage in the textile business, and Jewish enterprises were put in the hands of commissars, meaning, in effect, that they were confiscated and taken over by Germans."

Henik "Henry" Moszenberg Kaufman, a Shoah survivor in West Palm Beach, Florida, was among those Lodz Jews whose property was looted after the blitzkrieg. The Germans ousted his parents from their beauty salon and barbershop on Drewnowska Street and sent the entire family to the Carpathian Mountains near Czechoslovakia. They disguised themselves as Polish peasants to travel to Chmielnik, the town where Henik and his parents were born. Despite the hospitality of many relatives in Chmielnik, Henik's mother, Chana Skoczylas Moszenberg, was determined to reopen the beauty shop in Lodz, so she could earn a living.

Relying on bribes and persuasive storytelling, Chana Skoczylas Moszenberg managed to reclaim the family's apartment in Lodz and to resume business. She even sent for Henik to join her — just before the ghetto's creation. Life was difficult, Henik said, but his mother's services as a hairdresser were in great demand. "My mother needed no money. She needed food," Henik said. "She did a lot of work for the big shots. She cut their hair, making permanents. That way she got enough food. We got the white bread and cut it into pieces and we kept it. We made like Melba toast and stored it for a year."

Bela's uncle, Yosel Tarkeltaub, a milliner in Lodz, also suffered under the German regime. He made hats, barrettes, and other accessories in a second-floor workshop and sold his creations downstairs. A gang of hoods threw rocks through the windows, and one of the stones struck Yosel in the head. Discouraged, he later became ill and closed the shop. As far as Bela knows, Yosel died in Lodz' Jewish ghetto, referred to by Germans as the Litzmannstadt ghetto.

Ghettos, the neighborhoods used by Nazis to isolate Jews from other city residents, functioned as death traps. In *Every Day Remembrance Day*, Simon Wiesenthal describes March 1, 1940: "This day is known as Bloody Thursday in the history of Lodz in central Poland. The German army organizes a pogrom against the Jewish population of Lodz for not moving into the ghetto quickly enough. Several Jews are slain and the others are driven into the ghetto without being able to bring any belongings."

Hate crimes before and during the war spawned a wave of emigration from Poland that engulfed Bela's beloved aunts. With the exception of Golda, they left one by one. Aunt Dora departed first, accompanied by her husband and two children. After settling in Paris and establishing a couture, she sent money to the family. Then Aunt Lonia and her husband relocated to Paris. By the time Aunt Sheindel and her boyfriend decided to flee, emigration was barred, so the couple was smuggled to Paris via Belgium. Sheindel's clandestine journey, combined with her elopement, deeply wounded Bela's grandfather. Bela believes he died of a broken heart. "He cried and cried day and night," Bela said. Had Mr. Tarkeltaub lived to witness the destruction of Lodz' Jews, he surely would have shed more tears, but he might have understood the absolute necessity of Sheindel's secret departure.

The aunts sent letters indicating they would secure emigration papers for Golda. Even if the documents had arrived, chances are Golda would have stayed. Pregnant, she was awaiting word from her husband who had escaped to the Soviet Union, and she felt an obligation to care for Bela's grandmother. Before the war's outbreak, Bela daydreamed about joining her aunts in Paris. She even imagined Isaac becoming a fashion designer there. Instead, the night before Germany invaded, Isaac begged Bela to accompany him to Lublin in eastern Poland. "He said the Germans are coming in, and they're going to kill everybody." Bela was more conservative than her Aunt Sheindel. "I can't go. In those days, you don't go off with a boy, not married, and travel. No. That's not possible." Besides, Bela was committed to staying with her grandmother and Aunt Golda. "I said, 'I'm not going to leave my family.' I cry a lot after he went away. Nobody knows that I love him. Only he knows."

As Isaac had predicted, the German occupation was brutal. Although Jews represented one-third of Lodz' residents and contributed greatly to the city's world-renowned textile industry, they were mercilessly terrorized. Poles of German descent, or Volksdeutsche, accounting for about 10 percent of the population, zealously participated in such atrocities as the public hangings of Jews and the burning of synagogues. As mentioned in a previous chapter, Germany annexed Lodz on November 9, 1939, and renamed it Litzmannstadt on April 11, 1940.

Morris "Julek" Singer's experience of being forced to work in chain gangs motivated him to flee Poland with Mandzia and their baby, Renia. On several occasions before the escape, an anti-Semitic neighbor helped Morris hide — an odd gesture revealing the perverse nature of bigotry. A close friendship between Mandzia and the neighbor's wife influenced the seemingly-good deeds. "Whenever Germans came into a building looking for Jews, he would tell me to go into the attic," Morris said, recalling the times he climbed on the roof's water tower and watched his neighbor remove the ladder. "I was his dog. I was his pet Jew. He said, 'No one is going to kill my Jew. I'll kill him (Morris) if I have to, but no one else can,'" Morris said. "This is the psychology of anti-Semitic people.

If they know a Jew, they see a good side."

Like her family in Chmielnik, Bela was subject to many regulations. The Nazis compelled Lodz's Jews to wear yellow stars and prohibited them from attending synagogue or school, observing Jewish holidays, using public transportation, accessing their own bank accounts, and walking the streets between 5 p.m. and 8 a.m.

Helen Rozenek Jurysta, a Holocaust survivor now living in Vineland, New Jersey, remembers yet other ways the Nazis tried to degrade Jews in Lodz. "It was after two or three weeks when the Germans came in: they made a law that the Jews couldn't walk on the sidewalk, that we have to walk down in the street. That way, they would know who the Jews are," Jurysta said. "Life all of a sudden turned around. There was no food. We stand in line for a small loaf of bread. We stand all night. The lines were miles long. After all night in line, we come home with nothing. Right away the Germans start taking away first the men to work to do all kinds of undignified things... hard labor, dig ditches, and to do things unnecessary. The Germans went into stores. They emptied them out. They broke furniture. They started beating people. Life was unbearable in Lodz after a few months."

On December 1, 1939, the Nazis began creating one of Poland's first large-scale ghettos by confining Jews to certain neighborhoods.

"You took chances going out. They would kill you in a minute," Bela said. "We all think, 'It's going to be bad.' We all predict, 'It's going to be worse.' I didn't think about it, that we're going to go to camp."

Despite mounting persecution and the random beatings of Jews during the late 1930s, the Garfinkels traveled between Chmielnik and Lodz to see each other. An avid cyclist, Nathan rode his bicycle, while Sara and Sonia took the train from Kielce to Lodz. Bela went to Chmielnik occasionally, but she was always anxious to return to the Tarkeltaub household in the big city.

On one such trip, to circumvent rules banning Jews from trains, Bela removed the yellow stars from her clothes. Like her brother and sisters, she trusted that her fair features would deter questions, but she felt her nervousness would betray her. "If you are scared, this didn't help you. What I did was not legal." Bela arrived easily enough to Chmielnik, but she could not return to Lodz. Her parents learned the Nazis had sealed the Jewish neighborhood containing the Tarkeltaubs' home with fences, barbed wire, and guard towers. Restrictions, starting with curfews and confinement to the old city and Baluty quarter, had finally led to the setting of permanent boundaries. The Nazis made the Jewish ghetto official by physically blocking off neighborhoods on April 30, 1940, and by ordering all of the city's Jews to move there on May 1, 1940. Her parents concluded Bela would be safer in Chmielnik, but she couldn't stop thinking about her grandmother and Aunt Golda.

The notorious Lodz ghetto contained 48,100 rooms to accommodate a total of 204,800 Jewish men, women, and children. More than three-quarters of the ghetto's population were forced to resettle there from other neighborhoods, nearby towns, and other countries. The enclosed area, measuring less than two square miles, did not have sufficient running water and sewers to handle the influx of people.

For Henik "Henry" Moszenberg Kaufman and his mother, conditions were somewhat tolerable for a few years despite the desperate circumstances surrounding them and the separation from his father, sister, and brother. They lived in their own apartment but were forced to share it with another family. Even after Lodz' Jewish elders obligated Chana Skoczylas Moszenberg to close the salon and to work in a textile factory in 1942, she got food by going to her clients' homes to fix their hair. What she procured was barely adequate. In another part of the ghetto, Henik's grandmother died of hunger. As the ghetto shrank in 1944, mother and son were evicted from their apartment.

Bela's inability to return to Lodz was as traumatic as any physical hardship she later endured in the death camps. Bela acknowledged she had difficulty recalling the war years in detail, partly because she was so distraught about being detained in Chmielnik. "I cried day and night. I said, 'Why did I leave the ghetto? Why did I leave the ghetto?' We couldn't even write letters," Bela said. "I was very sad because I left my Grandma, I left my beautiful Goldie. My Grandma and Goldie depended on me. I would go out to get bread for them. If I knew I couldn't go back to Lodz, I wouldn't have gone to Chmielnik."

The aunts in Paris who survived the Shoah also felt profound loss and guilt that Golda was left behind. Overcrowding caused the Lodz ghetto — similar to those in other European cities — to develop unsanitary conditions. Jews died of hunger, disease, cold, and exhaustion. In 1942, an estimated 55,000 were deported to Chelmno to be exterminated in gas vans. Chaim Mordecai Rumkowsky, appointed by the Nazis to serve as Lodz' Jewish leader, or *Judenaeltester*, tried to buy time and save lives by promoting the ghetto as a labor source. That controversial strategy temporarily spared some young adults while sacrificing children and the elderly to gas chambers. Rumkowsky's plan backfired in the summer and fall of 1944, when more than 76,000 Jews were shipped to their deaths in Auschwitz.

Henik and his mother, Chana, tried to avoid those transports by hiding in the basements of empty houses. With only a change of clothes and some dried bread in their knapsacks, they lived as fugitives for several weeks. One day, they were startled by the cry, "Hands up!" in German. They had been discovered. "We have no place to go no more," Henik said. "They brought us to the Lodz station. There were hundreds, maybe thousands, of people there." Mother and son were separated upon their arrival at Auschwitz. Henik was shipped to a work camp. Chana, ever resourceful, lied about her age and ingratiated herself to the German commandants with her hairstyling skills.

Few residents of Lodz were so lucky. The Garfinkels believe their grandmother, Aunt Golda, and her baby starved in the Lodz ghetto. "My aunts feel so badly about Goldie, they'll never forgive themselves. Maybe they could have done more," Bela said. "But Goldie didn't want to leave my grandmother. It's not like today where people don't give a damn about you."

Chapter Six

A BOTTLE OF VODKA

The Garfinkels welcomed Bela's return as a light-hearted distraction from the grim yoke of German occupation. She was the sophisticated older sister with a fashionable wardrobe from the big city. "Bela was good-looking. Boys came to visit Bela. She got a lot of attention," Sonia said. "My father used to adore her, Bela. He ordered her boots. My parents wanted to make up for all those years Bela wasn't home. They tried to show her love. We were assured of this love. She wasn't. Whenever Nathan went out, he took Bela and his friends."

Helen describes Bela as striking. She wore makeup and stylish clothes — like the royal blue coat made by Isaac. Bela used *rumianek*, or chamomile, to make her blonde hair even lighter. She picked the little flowers and boiled them into potions. Bela reminded Helen of the time when Jews traveled freely in Poland, when Helen accompanied her mother to her grandmother's house. Bela also reminded Helen of past visits from the Tarkeltaubs, including her Aunt Sheindel, who brought a little dog on a leash. Another maternal aunt, Channa, from Busko Zdroj, used to stop in Chmielnik whenever she traveled from Lodz, Regina said, recalling the black beads of mourning Channa wore around her neck. Now Jews were running for their lives.

Despondent over leaving Lodz, Bela hardly noticed the fanfare her arrival caused in Chmielnik. "I kept thinking I would go back to Lodz. I thought I would wait another week. I felt guilty because my grandmother and Goldie didn't know I was not going to come back. Some of my friends expected me back." For Bela, the only advantage to being in Chmielnik was getting to know her parents better. "My mother was always neat, always nice. When you go in my mother's house, you could eat from the floor," Bela said. "She was not elegant beautiful. She was average beautiful. She was nice beautiful. She was dedicated beautiful."

Bela's impression of her father paralleled that of her brother and sisters. She viewed him as progressive about secular education but ultra conservative in religion. She questioned his good deed of inviting a homeless person to dinner on Fridays. "I say, 'Why my father have to bring home a poor man? We are not rich.'" Kalman's insistence that his daughters attend a special school to learn Yiddish and Hebrew reflected his advanced thinking, Bela said, noting such lessons were considered unusual for girls. Acquaintances called Kalman the *chuchem*, or smart one, Bela said, and they often sought his advice to solve problems and to mediate disputes. "In those days, he was like a lawyer, but he wasn't a lawyer."

Many Jews relocated to join their immediate families, a source of comfort in troubled times. Whether they returned to small towns or migrated to large cities, no place in Poland was safe. In Chmielnik, Jews lived with the daily threat of beatings, shootings, and executions. They also faced the prospect of slowly starving with the advent of work restrictions and food rationing in late 1939. The Germans virtually abolished free commerce, forcing Jews to restructure their businesses and to create an underground economy. The Thursday markets diminished. Regina noticed that the town square attracted fewer farmers and peddlers; they offered less variety at higher prices. "I was given money to buy certain things. Naturally, it had to be the basics, bread, potatoes, carrots," Regina said. "I remember coming home and saying, 'I didn't have enough money.'" Germany's siphoning of Poland's agricultural production and other resources reached a point where, "Even if Jews had money, they had no access to food," Regina said. "Nine out of ten farmers said they didn't have enough food for themselves, let alone share it with anyone else."

The absence of food stood out during Sabbath meals. "We

did all the same things," Regina said. "We said the prayers. We lit the candles. We had foods, but it was in a mock form." Bland wheat boiled in water replaced the savory feasts of chicken, fish, vegetables, bread, and cakes. "Fishel asked about the different foods," Regina said. "We had a neighbor who was cooking for Shabbat. All she had on the stove was empty pots of water. Can you imagine? It was that pride." Deprivation forced some Jews to see greater meaning in Shabbat. For Regina, a mere child, the food no longer mattered. She drew nourishment from the tradition. Being with her parents and siblings as they recited prayers and lit candles recaptured the sense of security — if only for a few moments — that Regina had felt before the German invasion.

"Everybody struggled to survive, to keep alive," Fay Skrobacka Goldlist said, recalling German mandates that prevented Jews from earning a living. "That was their aim so that people should get weaker and weaker to give in to their demands." Goldlist's parents, Michael and Malka Skrobacka, operated Chmielnik's kosher dairy with the help of their eight children. The Skrobackas, along with other Jewish merchants, tried to adapt. Jews could not travel more than one mile outside Chmielnik, Goldlist said, so collecting milk from farms was impossible. Even Regina noted that milk deliveries ceased shortly after the blitzkrieg. "I don't remember, during the war, having milk at all," Regina said.

The Skrobackas became produce vendors, relying on Polish farmers to bring them potatoes and vegetables, which they resold to Chmielnik's Jews. When those activities seemed too dangerous, Fay and her sister, Cesia, set up a sewing workshop in their home. "This was our breadwinner," Goldlist said. "Cesia was the dressmaker. I was the sales girl. We sold the material, and my sister was paid for the sewing. Many times myself I can't understand how we survived. People in these times really didn't have what to eat."

Sonia watched her mother, Sara, scrape the empty bins in Kalman's store and boil bits of grain in water to make soup. The cellar, where the family stored food, was empty. "Many times, my mother would say she had already eaten, so there would be more for the rest of us. My mother would cook some potatoes for a soup. My mother would say, 'I ate,' but I know she didn't eat." Helen echoes Sonia: "We were really, really hungry. There were times my mother wouldn't eat so we would have more." Nathan tells similar vignettes about Sara. Sometimes the farmers allowed Jews to gather unwanted food, such as potatoes that had been exposed to rain and sunlight. The discarded vegetables were rubbery, but Sara boiled them in water to make soup. "She said, 'I ate while the potatoes were cooking,'" Nathan said. "We found out she only drank the water from the potatoes." Regina noticed her mother's worries mounting with the hardships. "I always remember my mother feeling bad for Nathan during the war," Regina said. "She knew Nathan was very different, that he wanted education. She used to say, 'There's barely enough food to keep him alive.'"

Hunger precipitated life-threatening problems for Jews: poor health, disease, light-headedness, and not being able to think straight. In turn, getting proper care for illness and injuries posed a major challenge. Medicines were in short supply, traveling was restricted, and the German government interfered with the medical profession by forbidding Polish doctors to treat Jews and Jewish doctors to treat Poles.

The Garfinkels grappled with an emergency shortly after the German invasion, when Bela and Sonia remained in Lodz and Nathan was not home. It was a cold winter night, Helen remembers. Her father slept, and her mother sewed. While playing, Fishel knocked over the kerosene lamp and caught on fire. Sara responded by smothering the flames with a blanket and rolling Fishel in another blanket. Fishel screamed in fear and pain. Without access to a doctor or drugs, Sara improvised. To soothe the burns, she coated Fishel's face, neck, and arms with egg yolks. Helen carried the eggs from the cellar and helped her mother break them into a bowl. In an eerie way, the accident foreshadowed Fishel's fate. "I distinctly remember what he said," Helen said. "He said, 'I want to live. I want to live.'"

Another crisis erupted a few months later, when Sara fell sick. Gripped by a high fever and swollen throat, she couldn't move for days. The image of her father praying stays with Helen. Kalman wore his *tallis katan*, a shirt adorned with fringes — similar to a prayer shawl. He recited the viddui. Nathan decided to take more action. "Then, strep throat was serious. My mother almost died." One night, Nathan went to fetch Dr. Skwara, Chmielnik's Polish physician, who lived closest to the Garfinkels. The Jewish physician, Dr. Balanowski, who had diagnosed Nathan's appendicitis, lived near the center of town. Driven by his mother's past vigilance of him, Nathan sneaked through back yards, crossed alleys, and jumped over fences. He couldn't forget that Sara had slept on the floor of his Warsaw hospital room after his appendectomy. Dr. Skwara agreed to visit Sara. Gunshots sounded as they climbed into the doctor's car. Then Nazis emerged from the darkness. Dr. Skwara assured them Nathan was his assistant.

The next day, Nathan risked his life again by cycling to Busko Zdroj, the resort town where Aunt Channa lived. He found an orange — a feat Helen calls a miracle. "An orange during the war was unheard of," Helen said. Nathan's orange, Kalman's prayers, and Dr. Skwara's medicine — which all resulted from her family's concern and care — helped Sara recover. Her death would have devastated Kalman and the children. Without exception, all of the Garfinkels refer to their mother as an angel. In relating their own physical and emotional torments, they are relatively unmoved, yet the memory of Sara brings tears to their eyes. Regina conveys some of the reverence she and her siblings held for their mother: "When my mother went to get the water, we wouldn't let her carry the pail. Someone always ran to get it."

Nathan said Christian acquaintances, including Mrs. Musial, thought highly of Sara, but anti-Semitism so imbued Poland that prejudice laced their compliments. "The neighbors called my mother 'the Jewish Christian lady,'" Nathan said. Although that remark puzzled him at the time, Nathan considered it praise acknowledging everyone admired Sara's good nature and kindness. To him, it meant his mother embodied the best of all religions. Determined to eliminate the barriers of race, religion, politics, culture, and even gender that separate human beings, Nathan philosophized about the words, Jewish Christian lady. "I think maybe that's what it means to be a human being — you have to be a Jew and you have to be a Christian to be a human being." Many years later, Nathan grew to regard Mrs. Musial's comment as an insult. Even if she sincerely intended it as a compliment, it still offended, implying only Christians could possess such virtues as charity and honesty. Furthermore, the remark impugned Sara's dedication to Judaism and her heritage. The best that can be said of "Jewish Christian lady" is it was a back-handed compliment, resulting from ignorance and insensitivity. The Garfinkel sisters are furious their brother ever looked favorably on "Jewish Christian lady." Chmielnik, they say, was too polarized between Christians and Jews. Sonia doubts whether the neighbors uttered those words. "I never heard this before in my life," Sonia said. "Who said this? Jewish Christian lady? He's nuts. Take this out."

Despite this dispute, the Garfinkels agree all their neighbors, Jews and non-Jews, recognized their mother's devotion to her family. Sara and Kalman worried about caring for seven children as food supplies dwindled by the day. "I think my father was always most concerned about providing for us," Regina said. "That was the utmost in his mind — providing for us." Like many parents, Kalman and Sara explored the possibility of asking non-Jews to keep their children for the war's duration. The children would be useful — working in exchange for being fed and sheltered somewhat from direct persecution. Some Poles risked their lives to hide Jews for no other reason than "it was the right thing to do." Israel has honored such individuals — few and far between — as "righteous Gentiles."

Other Poles sympathized, but their willingness to help hinged on financial incentives. They not only accepted payment to harbor children but they also expected more money after the war. Good intentions were short-lived, however, when the Germans decreed that hiding Jews was a capital offense. Most Poles stopped sheltering children, even those who looked stereotypically Germanic. Such were the farmers who kept some of the Garfinkel children.

Although Regina was young — 10 years old — she could not adjust easily to living with strangers. She felt uncomfortable assuming a new identity despite her parents' assurances that pretending to be non-Jewish would be temporary. Crossing herself as though she were a Catholic felt unnatural. The idea of attending church bothered Regina. She refused to go. A tinge of guilt set in as she ate meals combining meat and dairy products — a violation of kosher rules. Working outdoors, in and of itself, was unsettling. "I was out in the field all day. I had trouble getting the cows and the geese into the barn. The geese went in all different directions. I was in tears," Regina said.

Most of all, Regina missed her family. She couldn't resist returning home on Fridays to reconnect to that feeling of togetherness Shabbat always exuded. In the candlelight's soft glow, "I felt secure, I felt comfortable, I felt at home, and that's where I wanted to be."

Sara explained that, if Regina stayed with the Poles, there would be more food at home for the rest of the family. "While I walked back to that farm, I felt so guilty. I felt guilty for eating," Regina said and cried. "I sat down, and I was sick, and I threw up all the way to the farm." Regina continued returning on Fridays. "My parents said, 'If you don't like this farm, we can send you to another.'" The farm wasn't the problem. If anything, Regina appreciated the farmer's kindness. The times she wrapped bread in a napkin to take to Chmielnik, he told Regina not to sneak food from the table, that he would give her food for her family. "At dinner I always saved my bread, and I wanted to take it home. The man said, 'It's okay. You don't have to hide the bread.'

"I told my mother, 'I don't mind being hungry. I'm not hungry.'" Regina gave away food to prove to Sara she wasn't hungry. "I remember another time I came home, and my mother gave me a carrot, and I ran out and gave the carrot to Nathan." Time and again Sara sent back Regina. "My mother said, 'It's only temporary.' She said it was dangerous to return home." Pretending she was a non-Jew made no sense, Regina reasoned. She asked herself, "Why am I doing it now?" She thought masquerading as a Christian was more dangerous. "I said I was Jewish anyway. I felt I would have given myself away probably by the way I acted. I felt the whole village would know. I felt the farmers would know," Regina said. "You can't change who you are." Yet her parents kept instructing Regina not to tell anyone she was Jewish.

Sonia worried about Regina's ability to cope alone, away from the family. Her younger sister was so withdrawn. When Sonia stopped to visit, Regina begged to go home. "She said, 'Sonia, I won't eat anything. Let me come home.' I brought her home on Friday. We both cried on the way home. I felt so sorry," Sonia said. "Regina at her age wanted to be with us. My father wondered why, but deep down he wanted her to stay." By disobeying her parents, Regina fulfilled their hearts' desire. She refused to return. "I decided I just don't want it. I just couldn't do it. I was not willing to. I don't think I could. I didn't give myself a chance."

Some history texts contain heart-breaking accounts of Jews turning over their children to Polish families. Many parents didn't live to retrieve their children. Those who did or other surviving relatives sometimes found the children not only had assimilated to another culture but also had bonded with their Gentile families. Mendel, the younger brother of Israel "Ira" Kaminsky, lived temporarily on a farm, but Kaminsky couldn't find him after the war. Kaminsky figures that Mendel, too, became homesick and returned to his parents and younger siblings — ultimately to accompany them to Treblinka's gas chambers. Mendel's eagerness to help his family and bring home food is one of the few memories that makes Kaminsky weep.

Some adults with a deep sense of foreboding tried to pass for non-Jew during the German occupation. This was a slim possibility for individuals with financial resources, political connections, and a supposedly Aryan appearance. To save Sonia in such a way, Kalman and Sara asked Mr. Opalka, a Pole in Chmielnik's city hall, to make a false identification card for her. Sonia describes Mr. Opalka as a kind man who offered to draft papers for all the sisters and other Jews. The Germans later gunned him down in the street.

Another individual, Kurczmarczyk, a Volksdeutscher, also tried to get bogus credentials for Sonia. He was one of the few farmers who risked his life to sell grain to Kalman. His motive, however, was to earn extra money, not necessarily to help Jews. Nathan believes Kurczmarczyk wanted to marry Sonia — an idea Sonia labels preposterous. "Never, never, never," she said. "No German would marry a Jew and take on those problems. I would rather go to camp than marry a German." Sonia is certain her parents would have rejected a marriage proposal from a non-Jew. They did, however, try to persuade her to live in a Catholic convent. "I heard he (Kurczmarczyk) make papers for me. Maybe he felt sorry for us...

"My mother took me aside and said, 'None of us will survive the war. You go there (the convent), and somebody will survive. If anybody from family is to survive, you survive,'" Sonia said. Sonia ran outside to the lumberyard to be alone. "I cried. I said, 'I want to be with my brothers and sisters. Whatever happens to my brothers and sisters, I want to be with them. What if I'm the only one after the war? I couldn't live with myself.' I cried. I couldn't eat. I didn't want to leave."

A neighbor who was roughly Sonia's age, Rosa Kaufman, spent the Shoah in hiding. Zigmund Kolagosky, a Pole who was in love with Rosa, rescued her from Chmielnik's ghetto. They married and had twin sons. Although Rosa avoided the misery of the death camps, she silently bore another kind of suffering. Kolagosky was an alcoholic, and he mistreated her. After Germany's defeat, her uncle, Yosel Kaufman, returned to Chmielnik to arrange the escape of Rosa and her sons to Israel. "I don't think Rosa Kaufman was in love with Zigmund Kolagosky. Maybe she didn't want to go to camp. Lots of people married because of this," Sonia said. "It's possible that Zigmund loved her. He saved her."

Germany's bloody conquest of Europe compelled Jews to seek ways to break free from the trap of anti-Semitism. "There was a great turmoil," Goldlist said. "We'll never forget the fear and commotion. People didn't know which way to turn. People start migrating from the west to the east. They run away from the Germans. People were walking. People came from towns to us, families." Goldlist's relatives from Jedrzejow appeared at her family's doorstep. "They stayed with us quite a few days, and they went back. There was nowhere to go." Goldlist's brother, Lejbus Skrobacka, who ended up in Lvov with other Polish soldiers, returned to Chmielnik to get married. "I wish he stayed in Russia so I have a brother," Goldlist said.

Zosia Kalmowiez Kiman, a survivor in Flushing, New York, fled Kielce's Jewish ghetto to join her grandfather in Chmielnik. She, along with her father, stepmother, and five siblings, paid a Volksdeutscher to smuggle them from the ghetto and a Polish farmer to guide them through the forest. Like the Skrobackas, they improvised to earn a living in Chmielnik. On at least one occasion, Zosia returned to Kielce's ghetto to get chemicals so her father could resume tanning leather. He created a workshop in Pierzchnica, near Chmielnik, for that purpose. They operated the business in secrecy. "My sister and I smuggled the leather under our clothes," Zosia said. "Polish people needed shoes for the kids in the wintertime. For a piece of leather, they give you some food."

Adding to the chaos, Germany evicted many Jews from their

homes throughout Poland. Influxes of displaced families arriving from Plonsk and Radom, Goldlist said, exacerbated the hardships of Chmielnik Jews who could not adequately support themselves. Despite her dark hair — a decidedly Jewish trait in the eyes of Nazis — Goldlist traveled outside Chmielnik to buy food for her family. "I tied a big kerchief — like a shawl I wore — to hide the armband," Goldlist said. "It was very risky. If you went out of town, you could get killed. I was always going out with one sister, Mindela. If you couldn't go out to the country to buy food, you starve."

Kalman and Sara desperately wanted to save their children. Undeterred by Regina's resistance to living away from home, they arranged for Helen and Fishel to stay on a farm in nearby Celiny. The two siblings worked as shepherds by day. At night, they slept on haystacks inside the barn. As the farmer coached them on how to pray and cross themselves, Helen visualized the crucifix hanging in Chmielnik's public school. "It was the same thing the children said in school," Helen said. Growing homesick as Regina had, Helen and Fishel also returned to Chmielnik to visit their family and to bring food.

One day, fear, rather than loneliness, prompted Helen to take Fishel home. "I saw a sign," Helen said. "It offered a bottle of vodka and 100 zlotys for farmers to tell the Germans where the Jewish children are. My brother couldn't read. He was only seven. I got scared. The next day we walked home."

Helen and Fishel left either very late at night or in the wee hours of the morning. Arriving in the dark, Helen tapped the window with a stick to awaken her parents. Fearful, Kalman did not open the door until he was sure no one was watching. After hearing Helen's story about the sign, Kalman said, "Don't worry. The farmers know me. I paid them. Nothing will happen to you."

So Helen and Fishel trudged back, but not for long.

One day, as the children herded cows toward the barn, the farmer greeted them frantically, saying two Germans on motorcycles were approaching. He hid Fishel and gave Helen a scarf and apron to wear. He instructed Helen to milk a cow and not to talk, even if she were asked questions.

"The German asked me, 'Where are the Jewish children?' I shook my head. I kept milking the cow," Helen said. "All I could think of was the Germans are going to find my brother, and my brother will tell." Circumcision made Jewish males easily identifiable. Men and boys bore the humiliation of being ordered to drop their pants in public. "All I could think of was my family would be shot in the middle of the marketplace like the Jewish teacher," Helen said, referring to the fate of Mr. Laks. After the Germans left, the farmer served lunch to Helen and Fishel. He explained he could no longer keep them. He had a family, and he was afraid.

Nathan empathized with his parents' conflicting emotions: the sorrow of parting with their children and the joy of being reunited. "As parents they had done the best they could without realizing that tomorrow it's going to be worse," Nathan said. Many parents were torn in choosing the best course of action. "My mother was afraid of being separated from my father and from the children. How to keep life together. That was tragic."

Helen knew other Jewish children in Chmielnik who worked on farms until liberation. In her heart, though, Helen felt the same as Regina, Sonia, Bela, and Nathan. She preferred going hungry and staying with her family over being well-fed and homesick. "I wanted to come home by then. I was scared," Helen said. "When you're afraid, you want to be with your mother and father. They can protect you."

Chapter Seven
INSIDE THE LODZ GHETTO

I ts scarcity throughout World War II made food the obsession of European civilians. Rations to Jews, even before the Shoah's death camp phase, were woefully inadequate. The act of gathering provisions for self-preservation became known as "food organizing" among Jews. German Nazis, however, regarded the practice of buying on the black market or outside the rationing system as stealing — a crime punishable by death.

"We didn't depend on the rationing system because we had some money," said Usher Tarek, echoing other survivors. He often went to farms on behalf of his parents and siblings. "You had to risk your life to go out in the country to buy some food. We had armbands, but I didn't wear the band. First of all, I looked almost like every Polack in Poland. I spoke the language as well as a Polack. Still, I was lucky I wasn't caught."

The Reich's diabolical plan to starve and kill Jews disrupted the natural order. Children found themselves in the peculiar position of providing for their parents and grandparents. As Saul Zernie, now of Toronto, notes: "A young boy could get away with food organizing easier than an older Jew." Zernie often went to farms to get potatoes, flour, and other staples, as did his father, who was still a young man in his late 30s.

Kalman Mapa, who was only 12 or 13 years old, stepped into the role of family breadwinner. While his parents and older brother feared the dire consequences of breaking the rules, Mapa possessed a bolder temperament and greater willingness to assume risk. Even though he did not feel he could pass for non-Jew, Mapa often ventured outside Chmielnik to buy food from farmers.

In the Garfinkel household, the responsibilities of buying food and operating Kalman's business in secret fell to the children. "It was pitiful to look in their eyes," Sonia said. "My parents couldn't help us. They couldn't support us. My father had so much pride. It was humiliating for my father. He couldn't take it. Men couldn't go out. Jews couldn't go out. They were beaten. They were killed."

Shielded by their Aryan looks, the Garfinkel sisters often went to purchase bread, eggs, cheese, grains, vegetables, potatoes, whatever was available. Kalman gave his daughters money, cloth, and other items to be bartered. Later, when the money ran out, the children exchanged the lovely linens embroidered by their mother, Sara. Kalman instructed Helen that, if she were stopped and asked, she should say she had begged at different farms. "My father said, 'If Germans catch you with food, never say you paid,' because farmers weren't supposed to sell to Jews."

Helen often pedaled a bicycle to different villages and farms. Once, two Germans on motorcycles detained her. Learning she was from the predominantly Jewish Chmielnik, they demanded identification, concealed by the sweater draped over her shoulders. After debating among themselves in German, the Nazis released Helen. "Helen was more aggressive. She was like a tomboy, a real tomboy," Sonia said. "She would run. She was the first girl in Chmielnik to ride a bike. She wasn't afraid. She was more of a go-getter. Active. Very active." One image of Helen's dedication to the family etched itself forever in Sonia's memories. "I remember once seeing Helen coming back from a farm with a sack of potatoes on her back. My heart was bleeding for it."

Sonia went to distribution centers reserved for non-Jews. "I stood in the lines with Polish people to get bread," she said. "If they saw a girl with dark hair and dark eyes, they would take her out of the line and beat her. Many times I thought this would be the last time. Whenever a German looked at me, I thought, 'This would be the last time.'" Sonia felt her mother could read her mind and sense her fears. "My mother knew me well. She said, 'Maybe you don't have to go next time,' but I had to go because if I didn't go, we would not have anything to eat. I would do anything so my father wouldn't have to go out." An older man who appeared Jewish was an easier target, she knew, than a blonde teenager. "My mother begged me, 'Maybe you shouldn't take off the star.'"

Sonia and Nathan often traveled without the required badges, but Sara insisted that her young children never leave the house without their blue-and-white armbands bearing the Star of David. They wore the bands above the right elbow. Sara instructed the children to throw a sweater or jacket around their shoulders to cover their upper arms. That way, they would not be identified from afar.

In a departure from Helen, Regina seldom wore her armband. Regina's light blonde hair was almost white, enabling her to contribute to food organizing. Nazis apprehended Regina on several occasions but never suspected her ethnic background. "If I did risk my life, I wasn't aware of it," Regina said. "As a child, I never gave it any thought."

The oppressiveness of German occupation altered the perspectives of even the most conservative individuals on the smallest matters. Kalman, who formerly frowned on Helen's bicycle riding, now valued it as a family resource. Transportation in and near Chmielnik was still rudimentary; many people, especially in the country, relied on horse-drawn wagons. One family in town owned a car, Helen said, and there was a *taksowka*, or taxi, for shuttling people to the train station. Chmielnik offered minimal rail service linking it to a few neighboring towns, but people bound for Lodz, Warsaw, and other large cities departed from Kielce's train station. The Reich's new rules confined Jews to ghettos and prohibited them from using public transportation. Although Nathan was often mistaken for a non-Jew, he never risked taking the train. On at least three occasions, he rode his bicycle to Lodz.

Although the Garfinkels often downplay the danger, the *Encyclopaedia Judaica's* entry for Chmielnik documents the perils of food organizing: "The establishment of the ghetto in April 1941 drastically worsened the plight of the Jewish population which was greatly reduced by hunger and epidemics. From December 12, 1941, when a death decree was issued against anyone caught leaving the ghetto, many Jews were shot for smuggling food into it." In *Every Day Remembrance Day*, Simon Wiesenthal's entry for December 12, 1941, states: "The municipal police arrest and execute several hundred Jews who try to bring food to the starving inmates of the ghetto of Chmielnik."

As time ticked away, supplies dwindled, people grew more hungry, and tension within the family increased. "Bela and my mother were worried about me," Regina said. "I remember going to town to the marketplace and looking for food. Bela told my mother I was walking around like a crazy person. Bela told my mother that. My mother slapped me for it." That Sara would strike any of her children — an uncharacteristic lapse — indicates the emotional toll of hunger, fear, and uncertainty.

Being older, Sonia knew the consequences of food organizing and conducted herself with more caution. Leaving her Star of David at home, Sonia traveled to other towns as a non-Jew to help relatives, friends, and acquaintances. "It got around that I looked Aryan, and I went into cities." Once Sonia delivered a letter from a Chmielnik Jew to a Polish man in Krakow, who, in turn, gave her a package to carry back. Sonia never opened the parcels or read the correspondence. The journey gave Sonia a disturbing glimpse of the future: Jews confined in a ghetto. "I saw a fence. There was no place to go out. There was no place to go in. I felt so sorry for those people." As she sat in Krakow's public streetcar, which passed the ghetto's boundaries, Sonia's heart pounded and her spirits sank.

"My father didn't want me to go to cities anymore," Sonia said. "He thought it was too risky, that I would be killed. If they found out you were Jewish and you weren't wearing a star, they would kill you or beat you to death." News of such punishment injected great anxiety in the Garfinkel household whenever Sonia or Nathan went out, Helen said. "I remember my mother used to say, 'Thank God, she's home. Thank God, she's home.'" Sonia heard Sara utter those same words. "Many times my mother saw me coming back. She thanked God, and she kissed me," Sonia recalled. "She would say, 'Thank God, you're home.'"

As leaving home became more treacherous and the number of executions escalated, even Nathan reached a point when he stopped going out. Circumcision would betray his heritage. Like his parents, Nathan relied on his sisters to make contact with farmers. "It's a close family. If she cannot do it, I do it for her. If I cannot do it, she does it for me. It's normal family relations. My parents were worried because we risked our freedom, our health, our lives. When Sonia left, my mother didn't sleep for days. My mother worried a lot about Sonia and everybody else."

In the book, *Holocaust,* British historian Martin Gilbert writes about Polish Jewesses who risked their lives by delivering such contraband as food, medicine, guns, underground publications, and money. Such women relied on their Germanic features to avoid questions and on their wits to respond when questions arose.

Sonia most often went to Lodz to visit the Tarkeltaub clan — her maternal grandmother, aunts, uncles, and cousins. She carried poultry and bread for her relatives in a knapsack. She returned to Chmielnik with cloth, shawls, linens, and other items to sell for cash or to exchange for food. "I used to go at night," Sonia said, "so nobody should recognize me. I put on a scarf. I would always take a Polish book and read so I don't have to talk to anybody. If I wasn't reading, they could ask me questions. If I am reading, I'm occupied." Although she was fond of Tolstoy and Dostoevski, Sonia packed the works of Polish authors. "I was afraid to take a Russian writer because the Germans hated the Russians." She almost always carried *Wrzos,* a romance novel written by Maria Rodziewiczowna. "I knew the book already. If they ask me, I know what it is." Sonia used the taxi to reach Kielce, where she caught the train to Lodz. The 100-mile trip took several hours.

Unlike some provincial Jews, Sonia, along with her siblings, spoke Polish perfectly. Therefore, she did not reveal her identity when interrogated. She was careful not to show she understood German, which is similar to Yiddish, the language spoken in most Jewish households.

Reaching Lodz required travelers to pass two checkpoints, or borders. The city lay within the Warthegau region annexed by Germany on November 9, 1939. Sonia's last trip to Lodz was significant because she managed to see her relatives after April 30, 1940, when the Nazis erected a permanent barrier around the Jewish ghetto. The Litzmannstadt ghetto was one of the Reich's most heavily-guarded and restricted urban neighborhoods for Jews. *Schutzpolizei*, a special unit of police, surrounded the area.

Outside the barricade of wooden fences and barbed wire, Sonia felt lost, but she walked down the street purposefully, so as not to attract attention to herself. A teenage girl approached. Sonia sensed she was Jewish and might know how to slip into the ghetto. Before Sonia could ask, a German policeman appeared. The two girls silently passed each other. Sonia entered a courtyard and hid by wedging herself between the entry gate and wall. Just as Sonia intuitively knew the other girl was Jewish, she suspected that the policeman arrested her. As she reminisces about such chance encounters with strangers, Sonia still wonders what the outcome was.

After remaining behind the gate for what seemed like hours, Sonia proceeded to another apartment complex where she knew some residents. She spoke with the building's caretaker who operated a thriving business smuggling people and contraband into the sealed ghetto. To protect herself, Sonia always devised plausible stories, a practice that came in handy on many occasions. "I said I was Polish, that we used to have a store, it used to be in the ghetto, that we no longer had a way to make a living," Sonia said. "I said I would sell my food and come back."

The caretaker helped Sonia and some merchants sneak in that night. They waited in the foyer of a building until dawn. "I closed my eyes." When she opened her eyes, she was alone. The merchants had vanished, leaving their goods behind. "I saw three Germans. I thought I was dreaming. They were speaking German to me. I didn't answer. I spoke Polish." Terrified, Sonia repeated her story. "I thought I was dead. I thought this was the end. I thought for sure they would take me to the station and kill me."

The three Germans discussed what they should do with Sonia. They inspected her knapsack but didn't take anything. Instead, they confiscated the live chickens and eggs abandoned by the merchants. "The Germans didn't take any dead food from people. They thought it was poisoned." After they left, Sonia went to her grandmother's house, where the pregnant Aunt Golda lived. They were astonished that Sonia had penetrated the ghetto's barriers and tight security. To say that the contents of Sonia's knapsack were welcome is an understatement, given the extreme shortages.

"People were dying in the streets. I didn't know whether to go home or to stay," Sonia said. "My aunt said, 'Please go home. Maybe you have a better chance than me.'" Sonia's cousin, Isaac Tarkeltaub, worked in the Jewish fire brigade inside Lodz' ghetto. He arranged for her to leave in a wagon. "I never went back. Deep down I knew I would never see them again. I knew."

Chapter Eight
BIALA PODLASKA

In Chmielnik and other Polish towns, German Nazis appointed Jews to committees or councils to help impose regulations, to issue orders, and to manipulate the population. The evil intent lurking behind such a convenient arrangement was to make Jews accomplices in the Nazis' crimes. By serving in these administrations, many Jews thought they might be able to reason with their oppressors or to exert some kind of influence — if only to reduce the number of killings. In some isolated instances, Jews participated to curry favor, to gain special privileges, or to save their own lives.

The Germans exploited Chmielnik's *Judenrat*, or Jewish Council, to round up slave laborers, usually men in their teens and early 20s. Once or twice a week, Nathan worked sweeping streets, shoveling snow, feeding livestock, or digging ditches and graves. He even cleaned the office where he was had been nearly bludgeoned to death. "The Nazis were abusive, mostly verbally. They beat us. They didn't kill us," Nathan said. "They didn't kill us at that point, because that would create an uprising. If they kill someone, then Jews wouldn't go to work."

Usher Tarek often toiled in road maintenance with hundreds of Chmielnik Jews. During the winter, they cleared the streets and highways of snow. In the summer, they resurfaced roads. Some workers went to marshes to cut squares of turf for fuel. With each season, the German supervisors became more brutal, Tarek said. They executed his good friend, Mordechai Pasternak, on discovering that Mordechai's 13-year-old brother, Philip, was working in his place. "The inspector came. He reported it to the police. They picked Mordechai up on Wednesday, and Thursday morning they shot him."

At age 12, Israel "Irving" Buchbinder was too young to report for work assignments, but he earned money by replacing Jews on the chain gang. "I worked for those people who could afford to pay." Buchbinder's father served in the Polish Army and was likely dead or trapped indefinitely in the Soviet Union. As the de facto head of household, Buchbinder did anything he could to help support his mother, sister, and three brothers. His maternal grandmother, Frimetel Mendrowski, formerly known for her wealth, generosity, and charitable deeds, also depended on Buchbinder. "I worked almost every day. In the summer I had to break big stones to smaller stones. In the winter we had to keep the roads open every day. The snow was so high, 20, 30 feet high."

Work brigades dotted Poland. Jewish leaders in larger cities, such as Warsaw and Krakow, preferred an organized system of filling German quotas for Jewish slaves over having young men abducted at random, as Martin Gilbert writes in *Holocaust*. By late 1939, Poland's Kielce region alone contained 21 forced labor camps, according to Gilbert.

Nathan objects to the word *slave*. He feels it imprecisely describes the Jews' forced labor experiences in the Shoah. Most slave owners preserved their investment, he argues, by feeding, clothing, and otherwise caring for their chattel. "Even slaves had value, but the Jews had no value. I call myself worse than a slave. A slave had to be kept alive for profiteering. I wasn't kept for profit. I was kept only until I was out of breath. Then they kill me."

Saul Jurysta has often compared Nazi Germany's cruel treatment of Jews with the immoral system of slavery in the United States. "There's no comparison," he said. "The slave owners paid for the black man. They wouldn't take the black man and kill him. They make him strong. They want the black man to have children so they can have more slaves."

Although the word *slave* connotes value to many individuals, including historians specializing in economics, the dictionary's definitions are more broad: "a person held in servitude as the chattel of another... one that is completely subservient to a dominating influence." The origin of the word is Slavic, according to *Webster's Collegiate Dictionary*, stemming from "...the reduction to slavery of many Slavic peoples of central Europe."

History repeated itself during World War II, when Germany set a goal of enslaving anti-fascist enemies and the Slavs to the east. Government propaganda depicted the Poles as sub-human. The simultaneous enslavement of Europe's Jews, deemed non-human, was a temporary measure. The Jews' experience as forced laborers destined for genocide defies description; it was so utterly horrific. Hence, survivors like Nathan, other eyewitnesses, and Holocaust scholars in their wake struggle to select words that convey what happened. Even the words *Holocaust* and *Shoah* have been subject to debate because their religious nuances imply that the S.S. and their collaborators presided as officiating priests. "I like to make a distinction between genocide and Holocaust," Nathan said. "Holocaust is indiscriminate destruction. With genocide, it's discriminate killing. But both mean destruction of humanity." Non-Jewish victims of the Holocaust could, possibly, save themselves by embracing fascism, he speculates, while Jews were denied such options.

Israel "Ira" Kaminsky was among those Chmielnik Jews dispatched to the Wisniuwka labor camp and quarry in early 1941. "They just picked from a list." It was such a terrible episode in Kaminsky's life, he can barely talk about it. Prisoners broke rocks into gravel while guards watched and taunted them. "It was very, very bad. People were severely, severely punished." For example, guards forced some prisoners to stand in barrels of water. Kaminsky is convinced he would have perished in Wisniuwka if he had not escaped with two acquaintances. Upon returning to Chmielnik, Kaminsky hid to avoid being sent back or killed.

Kuba Zaifman hauled stones, crushed rocks, dug ditches, and leveled earth on the road linking his hometown of Kurowenki to

Chmielnik. A German engineer overseeing the project learned of Zaifman's sewing talents and ordered him to make a pastel-colored, linen suit. The engineer traveled to Chmielnik, where German officers admired his new garments. Their inquiries led to Zaifman's reassignment and transfer. He found himself in a Chmielnik warehouse containing a sewing machine and bolts of fabric. Zaifman, who had been a tailor-apprentice under his father's tutelage, sewed night and day. The S.S. were so pleased with his work, they supplied him with measurements and materials to make clothes for their wives, children, and other relatives. They shipped his creations to Germany. In a quirk of fate, Zaifman's skills saved his life by sparing him from hard labor, yet his father and two older brothers, who were also master tailors, died along with his mother and three sisters. Only three of his relatives — cousins who hid with the partisans — survived. Zaifman, who now lives in Toronto, said that, as far as he knows, only one other Jew from his hometown of Kurowenki survived the Holocaust. Everyone else was gassed in Treblinka.

In January of 1940, Chmielnik's Judenrat chose Nathan, Joseph Kiman, and about 900 other young men for a special assignment. They didn't know where they were going or what they would do. When Nathan returned more than one year later, he was emaciated, bruised, and scarred from beatings. He was filthy, and his hair was full of lice. "It was a shock to see his condition," Sonia said. Helen watched her mother wash Nathan — his first bath in months — cut his hair, and put baking soda on his wounds. "My mother was crying," Helen said. "He looked terrible. He was really hungry. I was happy when he came home, but I was afraid."

During Nathan's long absence, Helen and Sonia did not know his whereabouts, and they wondered whether or not he was alive. "We had packed things for him. We gave him postcards and a pencil, but he wasn't allowed to write," Helen said. "For a while, we thought my brother was dead. We didn't know."

Concern for Nathan increased the family's feelings of loss and helplessness. "Nathan's friend came every day, He said, 'Why didn't you pay money?'" Sonia recalled, noting that savvy Jews tried to buy their way out of dangerous situations. Transferring to a work camp was preferable to awaiting deportation to Auschwitz. "Then, there were ways to bribe."

Many months after Nathan's departure, a Jewish man came to inform Kalman and Sara that their son was alive. The man had twin sons who had been taken to the same place. He would not specify the camp — which, as it turned out, was near Biala Podlaska. "He said, 'Don't ask questions,'" Helen said. "That's all he knew."

Kalman and Sara tried to shield the children, especially Helen, Regina, Rachel, and Fishel, from their worries, fears, and from the news of Chmielnik's latest atrocities. Regina sensed her parents' anxieties, nonetheless. "There was a lot of denial. We were hearing rumors about the different camps," Regina said. "A lot of things weren't done or said in my presence. It didn't make any sense. I thought it was something that was just going to pass. I guessed that it was something that happens between adults and between countries and that it was just going to pass."

Although Nathan's appearance on returning from Biala Podlaska appalled the family, he tends to minimize the camp's brutality because it was less onerous than subsequent camps. The Germans shipped Chmielnik's young Jewish men by truck to Kielce, then by train to Biala Podlaska, a city overlooking the River Bug near the Soviet border. The journey was nearly 200 miles.

Some of the camp's first inmates, who had arrived a few weeks before Nathan, were Jewish prisoners of war who had served in the Polish army, according to *Encyclopaedia Judaica*. The S.S. compelled those POWs to walk many miles from Czarne and Lublin through the bitter cold, shooting and torturing individuals en route. Gilbert's description in *Holocaust* is especially gruesome. The POWs' trek to Biala Podlaska is considered one of the first "death marches" of World War II. Such columns of prisoners on foot are more typically associated with the war's end.

Within the first week of having entered Biala Podlaska's camp, Nathan heard that the Germans had locked some of the Jewish POWs in a barn and set the structure on fire. "We were afraid of what was going to happen to us." The S.S. executed their captives at random but not with the frequency Nathan later observed in other camps. In his book, *Every Day Remembrance Day*, Simon Wiesenthal notes for May 15, 1941: "The Nazis murder 12 Jewish prisoners of war in Biala Podlaska, Poland."

Surprisingly, having enough to eat was not a problem, Nathan said. Representatives of the city's Jewish community sometimes visited the inmates and brought food. "What was bad was the dirt and lice," Nathan said. "There was no way to bathe or take a shower." The camp's filth and infestation of lice made the prisoners susceptible to illness, especially typhus. Nathan estimated that about 20 percent of the camp's population died. The mortality rate of subsequent camps was much higher.

The prisoners deepened a channel in the River Bug and dug ditches from the river through the fields to create an irrigation system. They also loaded and unloaded train cars at the border where the wider Soviet railroad tracks met their Polish counterparts. Prisoners moved Soviet fruit, wheat, and oil to trains bound for Germany. Sometimes German coal was shipped eastward, but the trains to Russia usually departed empty. "We believe that the Russians were paid by the Germans in gold. I don't really know," Nathan said.

"It was easy to escape. This is why the Nazis didn't mistreat us as much. I never considered escaping because I was worried about my family at home." Nathan believes a Jewish acquaintance from Chmielnik, Joseph Maly, escaped from Biala Podlaska to the Soviet Union. Maly survived the Shoah and settled in Israel. Joseph Kiman, of Flushing, New York, also fled Biala Podlaska, but he returned to Chmielnik. Like many survivors, he is unable to talk about his concentration camp experience for fear of breaking down emotionally.

The S.S. designated Nathan to be a nurse in the camp's so-
called medical clinic, which had no drugs, bandages, or supplies.
All he could do was heat water for patients. It was not a job Nathan
wanted. The S.S. had executed the previous nurse, accusing him
of having cared for patients who were not ill. "The Germans yelled
at me. Everybody was afraid of catching typhus," Nathan stated.
"I was afraid of being killed like the nurse before me."

The camp's foreman was a German Jew who spoke several
languages, including Polish, Yiddish, French, and Russian. He had
accompanied his elderly parents to their hometown of Biala
Podlaska after 1935, when Germany stripped its Jewish citizens of
basic rights. The government used the Nuremberg laws to expel
thousands of longtime Jewish residents to the countries of their
birth. Unlike other prisoners confined in the Biala Podlaska camp,
the foreman lived in his parents' home in the city's Jewish ghetto.
Nathan cannot recall the foreman's name, but he exemplified many
assimilated Jews who associated themselves more closely with their
country than with their bloodlines and ethnic heritage. Some of
those Jews had distinguished themselves in the German military
during World War I.

A Czech Nazi known for his cruelty once knocked the Jewish
foreman to the ground. The foreman got up and declared, "I am
a German patriot before I am a Jew." He showed the Czech Nazi
the World War I medals he had earned as a German soldier. "The
Czech Nazi saluted his medals and said, 'Heil Hitler,'" Nathan said.
The foreman disappeared shortly thereafter, and Nathan assumes
he was killed. The foreman's parents most likely were gassed to
death in the killing centers of Sobibor or Treblinka, to which Biala
Podlaska's 8,400 Jews had been transported during 1942.

Ironically, the Biala Podlaska camp prolonged the agony of
Poland's Jews. Nathan later figured the irrigation ditches he and
other prisoners had dug were fortifications for the German army.
After Nathan had been shipped back to Chmielnik, Germany invaded the Soviet Union on June 22, 1941.

Germany's betrayal of its ally coincided with an accelerated campaign to annihilate Jews. During Nathan's enslavement in Biala Podlaska, the Nazis restricted Chmielnik's entire Jewish population to the town. The boundaries were officially set on April 1, 1941, according to Simon Wiesenthal's book, *Every Day Remembrance Day.* Chmielnik's ghetto, unlike its larger counterpart in Lodz, had not been sealed with barriers. It was an "open ghetto." Jews could easily sneak in and out, but execution was certain punishment if they were caught. When the Nazis disbanded Biala Podlaska's labor camp during the summer, Nathan returned to a prison of another sort, the Jewish ghetto of his own hometown.

Chapter Nine
KALMAN'S BEARD

Despite all the suffering and degradation they endured at the hands of Germans during World War II, the Garfinkels reserve their tears for the indignities and torments inflicted on others, especially their parents. To this day, Helen gets goose pimples and weeps as she recalls her father's screams. She still feels guilty that, as a 13-year-old, she could not prevent the attack on her father.

Once as Kalman walked home from synagogue, two Nazis lunged at him with knives. Helen was playing outside with two friends. Hearing shouts and a scuffle, she looked up to witness the Nazis knock her father to the ground. They kicked Kalman. They punched him. To cut off his beard, they slashed his face with knives. Their German shepherds jumped on Kalman. Lying on the street was the velvet sack containing Kalman's *siddur*, or book of daily prayers; his *tallis*, or prayer shawl; and *tefillin*, which are small cases containing scriptures.

"I covered my eyes. I covered my ears. I went forward. I went back," Helen said. "If I am a father or a mother, I would go to help if my children were being beaten. But I was a child. I was scared." That she didn't intervene still bothers Helen. Often it's the actions not taken, the words not spoken, or the comments uttered in haste that haunt survivors of the Shoah.

Sonia, for example, can never forget her unfulfilled promise to her little brother, Fishel. In a game requiring children to wager bets with walnuts, Fishel extended his participation by using buttons from his clothing as nuts. Unable to win back his buttons, the distraught Fishel confided in Sonia. "I said, 'Fishel, don't worry. I'll find buttons.' The following day, they took us away. I never saw him," Sonia sobbed. "I often wonder what Fishel thought, that I was going to find the buttons, and I never came back."

In another instance of unfinished personal business, Sonia regrets once losing her temper with her father. She accompanied Fishel to private Hebrew lessons despite the harsh penalties for that — beatings, imprisonment, even death. "I told my father, 'What's the use to go to school? We see killing and robbing,'" Sonia said, crying at the recollection. Kalman answered, "They can take everything from you — silver and gold — but they can't take away education. Education is knowledge."

Helen remains remorseful that she hadn't rushed to her father's side a few seconds sooner. Kalman, cradling his face in his hands, couldn't stand, so Helen and her two friends dragged him. By the time they got home, his knees were scraped raw.

Before Kalman arrived, neighbors had brought news to Sara that Germans were beating her husband. "I wanted to run out, and I wanted to take a knife and kill them," Sonia said, expressing an uncharacteristic rage. Her reaction is unusual for Sonia, whom Helen later regarded as too kind-hearted to survive the death camps. "I would run out. I would fight with them. I would hit them. I would kick them." But someone, Nathan or Sara, restrained Sonia. "For myself, I didn't care, but my father. I wanted to help my father," Sonia said. That incident, occurring a few months after Germany's blitzkrieg of Poland, marked a turning point.

Kalman did not leave the house again, not even to attend synagogue. Ashamed, he covered his face with a white handkerchief to hide his shorn beard. For Orthodox Jews, cutting or shaving represents a desecration of one's body. For men, losing one's beard equates to a loss of everything — from the physical (strength) to the abstract (wisdom) and to the ethereal (holiness). Every day Kalman chanted the viddui, the Jewish equivalent of a deathbed confession. He gave up his profession and contact with the outside world, leaving the operation of his miller's shop to the children. In defiance of Nazi prohibitions, Nathan and Sonia transacted business with farmers willing to sell grain.

Once three Germans, accompanied by a Jewish informant, burst into Kalman's store. Just as they exploited the Judenrat, the Nazis employed Jewish collaborators and Jewish police to maintain order and to carry out unpleasant tasks. Although sometimes disdained and criticized by other Jews, such individuals tried to prevent beatings and killings. "He tried to help. He didn't do any harm to Jews," Nathan said of Chmielnik's Jewish informant. "They destroyed him. They killed him after there were no more Jews." Bela flirted with the informant but was terrified of him at the same time. "If he's good, he's good. If he's bad, he can say bad things about you. He acted rough and tough. He did this to survive. Everyone was afraid of him," Bela said. "He was good to us. I'll never forget. He says, 'Close the store now. The Germans are here.'"

Esther Pasternak Tarek of Toronto saw the Jewish collaborator riding his motorcycle every day through her neighborhood to visit his Polish girlfriend. Tarek felt no resentment, she said, because he did nothing to hurt her or her family. He was simply trying to stay alive like everyone else. "He was nice to the Germans, but they killed him anyway," Tarek said. "He helped the Germans, and afterwards he was shot."

Unlike Tarek and the Garfinkels, Bela Nozyce Strauch did not have a favorable or sympathetic impression of Chmielnik's Jewish informant, who raided her home with the Germans. While they ransacked the house, their dogs ripped out her father's beard. Bela, who now lives in Toronto, begged that the informant's identity be withheld even though her family suffered at his direction. The informant's nieces, nephews, and other descendants don't know they had such a relative, and Bela wants to spare them the shame.

The instant the informant entered Kalman's shop with the Nazis, Sonia figured she would be killed. "The Germans had guns. I was afraid," Sonia said. "They saw the sacks of wheat, but he said, 'Come on. Let's go.'" The Germans left, but they easily could have executed Nathan, Sonia, and the entire Garfinkel family. "He helped us," Sonia said. "In the end, they killed him. They shot him."

Sonia often wonders why her father wasn't killed in late 1939, rather than merely roughed up. Ugly episodes of beard-cutting had happened elsewhere, including in nearby Kielce, according to Martin Gilbert.

Helen Rozenek Jurysta remembers one such incident in Lodz. She left the house to search for her grandfather. "We didn't know what happened to him," Jurysta said during an oral history taped in 1995 in New Jersey. "The Germans probably took him to work. Maybe my grandfather was working in the street." As she walked the streets, Jurysta spotted a group of men lying on the ground. They seemed to be in pain. "I thought, 'Let me see if I could help these men.'"

She didn't know why, but she found herself drawn to one of them. "There was a man. He called out to me, 'Channa! Channa, you don't recognize me? I am your grandfather!'" Jurysta was in shock. All Jewish men who were religious had beards, and now they were shorn like sheep. "I didn't know this man was my grandfather." Then she noticed blood on the faces of the men who had been beaten to the ground. "They shaved off his beard. They took out some of the pieces of skin from his face. I didn't know my own grandfather," Jurysta said, in tears. "It's the first time I am talking about it. It's all hidden in my mind."

The arbitrary and unpredictable nature of violence spawned constant terror. Many Jews in Chmielnik were bludgeoned to death or shot dead in the streets. Some were even buried alive.

Regina remembers the commotion of Helen and her friends dragging her father home. "They only hushed it up, because they didn't want the children to hear what was going on," Regina said. "That was the worst part, not really knowing. My parents would try to protect me, but I still heard about incidents."

That Nathan and his father did not see eye-to-eye about reli-

gion or politics still troubles Nathan because their divergent view-
points created a silence between them. Kalman used prayers, the
Talmud, and simple faith in God as his guides in life. He desired
Nathan to pursue Judaic studies and become a rabbi or religion
teacher. However, Nathan had doubts. "I asked the rabbis questions. They couldn't answer me," Nathan said. "I couldn't de-
nounce God, but I didn't know whether I believed in God, either."

Nathan participated in movements advocating Zionism, the
creation of a separate homeland for Jews in Palestine. First, he
attended meetings of Bethar, an organization that he later perceived as militantly anti-Arab. "I got fascinated with it," Nathan
said. "My neighbor was a member. I was involved with it for the
dancing, singing, but I didn't understand the philosophy of it."

Finding Bethar too conservative, Nathan explored the other
extreme, the Hashomer Hazair, or Young Watchmen, a group so
liberal it was accused of harboring Communists. "It was more
progressive. The purpose was to build a Jewish state with a labor
movement," Nathan said. "I believed in the idea of a Jewish state.
I eventually wanted to move to Palestine, but access was restricted.
It would take 100 years."

In 1935, Germany's enactment of the Nuremberg laws de-
priving Jews of basic rights alarmed Jews across Europe, especially
in virulently anti-Semitic nations like Poland. Government-sanctioned prejudice crystallized Nathan's previous experience of discrimination and his impression that Jews would never be treated
equally in Europe. Hence, Nathan was among thousands of Polish Jews who felt an affinity for Zionism. Open to ideas, Nathan
studied other ideologies. One of his teachers in Chmielnik, Mijer
Gorlicky, was a Communist, and some of his non-Jewish friends
were members of the Polish Socialist Party. If Nathan could not
break away from Kalman's grain store, he coaxed Helen or Regina
into fetching newspapers and books from Gorlicky. "Nate bribed
me. He give me a nickel or a dime," Helen said, referring to Polish
groshen. Regina looked up to Nathan as an adult wielding the

same authority as her parents. "There was a lot of exchange of newspapers, magazines, and books," Regina observed.

Sonia and some of her friends, including Tosia Fastag Bottner and Lola Warszawska, joined the more conventional Bethar. Helen, who was too young, became jealous; she wanted to wear uniforms and to attend meetings with her older sister. A close friend of Sonia, Rachel Wygodna Herszlikowicz, joined Mizrachi, which Herszlikowicz described as "a very Orthodox organization just for girls." "We had a very nice crowd," Herszlikowicz said. "We danced, and we sang. We learned about Israel."

More interested in culture and fellowship than in politics, Sonia was furious with Nathan for associating with Mijer Gorlicky. "Mijer was a very knowledgeable mind. Mijer tried to convert Nate to communism. He tried to convert me, too." Sonia viewed Mijer as a hypocrite; he made money by smuggling gold from the Soviet Union. "I despise this Gorlicky until this day. He said to Nate that there is no God. My brother listened to Mijer Gorlicky more than to my father. My mother cried over this. She said (to Mijer), 'Please, leave my Nusale alone.' My mother loved Nate so much."

Nathan contends his mother was not necessarily opposed to Gorlicky's leftist ideas but merely worried that Nathan might be arrested. Poland had outlawed communism long before World War II, and Alter Goldstein, of Chmielnik, was imprisoned for being a Communist. Nathan admired Gorlicky's intellect and ability to speak French, German, Flemish, and several other languages. Educated in Belgium, Gorlicky worked in Chmielnik's public library. "When I met Mijer Gorlicky, I told my father I didn't want to be a rabbi or religion teacher. My father was very angry about this," Nathan said. "He didn't protest against my interests because he knew the more he protests against communism and other studies, the more my desire would be. Forbidden fruit tastes good."

So Kalman disapproved silently of his son's quest for secular knowledge. "Only God will help," Kalman said. "God will give us

Israel." Nathan could not relate to his father's fundamentalism. "With people like this you cannot talk," Nathan said. Many friends and acquaintances empathized. Saul Jurysta, for example, could not communicate with his maternal grandfather, Jakob Knobel, who was the family patriarch. "I couldn't adjust to my grandfather," Jurysta said. "He was very religious. I became a Zionist." Consequently, Jurysta left Chmielnik for Warsaw in 1932, when he was only 17. Upon returning to visit his hometown during the war, he argued with his grandfather, who was shocked that Jurysta spoke of fighting and resisting the Germans.

Jakob Lederman, describing the generation gap in Chmielnik, said, "You know something? They were so fanatic, the parents. They were religious people. The teenagers went to the organizations, Zionist organizations. We went. The parents didn't like it. The teenagers, they read papers. They know what happens in the world. The fathers, the parents, didn't know nothing about this. Nathan was modern already. Nathan was like a rebel in the eyes of his father."

Nathan's brother-in-law, Morris "Julek" Singer, noted that the children couldn't win over their parents to political activism. "My mother agreed with the Socialist ideas except Socialism didn't have religion. When the police accused my mother of being a Communist, she said, 'I would be a Communist if they believed in religion.'" Morris said he often clashed with his mother. "The religious movement, Jewish or non-Jewish, they always cooperate with the system." Morris perceived Nathan as being more fanatical than he. "Nathan wouldn't hear of any criticism of Socialism. The movement is God," Morris said. "Nathan is more an idealist. He felt this political movement was his entire life."

Acutely aware of disagreements between her father and brother, Regina intuitively understood the conflict. "I think Nathan could have persuaded my mother more to his ideas than my father. She would have been more understanding. Nathan was the apple of her eye. Of course, my father wanted Nathan to be the image of him."

Helen overheard arguments involving mundane matters, such as Nathan's habit of breaking curfew to play dominos with friends or to visit a non-Jewish girlfriend, Marisia Marcishevska, across the street. "My father screamed at Nathan that he should not go out at night. Nathan didn't listen," Helen said. "This girl used to help Nathan, but her family was afraid. They didn't want to help him later on." Nathan also visited Mijer Gorlicky's sister-in-law, which upset Kalman and Sara, Helen said, because she was older than Nathan. What's more, she was a leftist.

Nathan was always at odds with his father. "I was closer to my mother. My father tried to persuade me to go to his side. At age 15, my father gave up on me. By age 15, I found out what's going on. I have no place in Poland," Nathan said. Even at age 13, Nathan thought of his bar mitzvah as a ceremony commemorated by a sponge cake and a bottle of whiskey. It was not the profound spiritual awakening of taking moral responsibility for his actions. "We had no conflicts openly. I didn't feel tension with my father, but I'm afraid that he felt tension because I didn't do what he wanted for me. I could understand his point of view, but he couldn't understand my point of view."

Nathan understood that Kalman cherished his beard as a symbol of religious faith and manhood, but he found his father's passiveness and immobility exasperating. Kalman remained humiliated after his cuts healed and his beard grew back. If he had been violated once — for Orthodox Jews considered beard-cutting on par with emasculation — he could be violated again. Kalman felt defeated.

"After that, my father said the prayer of last rites," Nathan said. Kalman recited the viddui's opening pleas: "O my God and God of my fathers! Let my prayer come before Thee, and disregard not my supplication. O forgive all the sins I have committed..." Those words, the entire prayer, and his father's behavior enraged Nathan. "After his beard was cut, my father was ready to die. I asked him, 'Why are you saying the last rites? You're not dying. If you want to die, why don't you kill yourself?' He said that was against God's law. 'Nusan (Nathan), if I kill myself, I am a murderer. I kill God's property.'"

That conversation makes Nathan weep. "Later on, I felt sorry I said it." Nathan was angry with his father, but Kalman, always calm and composed, was not angry with Nathan. "I hope he forgives me for asking that," Nathan said. "I hope he forgives me."

Chapter Ten
THE FORCED FAREWELL

The mere persecution, plundering, and massacre of Jews failed to satiate German Nazis and their Polish collaborators. The Shoah exceeded any reasonable person's comprehension of evil in the oppressors' insidious and blatant efforts to dehumanize Jews before enslaving and murdering them. In one attempt to dispirit Chmielnik's Jews, German officials scheduled a transport of young people to labor camps during Sukkot, an eight-day holiday that follows Rosh Hashanah, the Jewish New Year, and Yom Kippur, the Day of Atonement. Sukkot, a "harvest festival" also observed by the non-religious, is a time of thanksgiving. Jews celebrate by building temporary shelters to honor their nomadic ancestors. Because Sukkot coincides with the new year's first days, Jews add honey, sugar, and fruit to foods in tribute to life's sweetness.

Although the Garfinkels believe they were deported in September, 1942, the departure date cited in history texts is October 1, 1942. In that particular year, October 1 corresponds to the 21st day of Tishri on the Jewish calendar. Sukkot starts on the 15th day of Tishri, a month roughly interchangeable with September. The Garfinkels and other survivors describe the weather in Chmielnik as unseasonably warm for fall — like an Indian summer — the day the Nazis abducted teenagers and young adults. An order — emblazoned in German on posters — demanded that Jews from age 16 to 40 report to the central square for work assignments.

In the Garfinkel family, the order governed only Nathan, 22; Bela, 21; and Sonia, 19. The children — Helen, Regina, Rachel, and Fishel — were too young. Bela did not respond because she

had sores on her hands and arms. Sonia reassured Bela that staying home would be best. Two workers would be enough sacrifice
for one household, Sonia said. Despite the sunny weather, she
wore the green coat Bela's boyfriend had made.

Nathan and Sonia proceeded to the square together, having
said their good-byes. They had no idea where they were going,
what kind of work would be foisted on them, or how long they
would be gone. "My mother was crying," Helen observed. "She
felt very bad for my brother Nate because he had been to a labor
camp before."

Mass confusion, weeping, and heart-wrenching farewells overwhelmed Chmielnik's square. Parents begged the Germans not to
take their children. Thousands of Poles crowded the center of
town to watch the spectacle. Sonia felt trapped. "All of a sudden,
I saw the Germans. Then a little farther, I saw open trucks. There
was no way you could run away. People tried to run away. They
let the dogs on them. I was scared of German shepherds."

Nathan saw the Germans divide Chmielnik's Jews into two
groups. He, Sonia, and other young people destined for work were
steered to the right. "Everyone else went to the left," Nathan said,
referring to children, grandparents, mothers with babies, the physically disabled. Those rejected workers later died in Treblinka's gas
chambers. "But it was chaotic. There was nothing orderly about
it. Thousands of us were there." So disorderly was the scene, Sonia
did not notice the division between left and right.

The German officials did not rely entirely on age to choose
workers. Some eyewitnesses, including Cesia Zaifman, of Toronto,
were pulled aside for work while relatives of the same age were
deliberately left behind. "We had no birth certificates," Nathan
said. "It depended on how you looked." The selection process was
random. Zaifman, who was age 20 at the time, walked to the square
with her sister, Hinda, who was a year older. "We were like twins
we looked so much alike," Zaifman said. "My sister was not taken.
She was sent home. I thought she was the lucky one. She was

going home. It was terrible. She was thinking the same thing. She was thinking maybe I was going someplace good. Later, in the labor camp, I was upset. I thought maybe we both could survive. I am the only survivor from all of my whole family. I am the only one."

Fay Skrobacka Goldlist spoke with her sister, also named Cesia, for the last time in Chmielnik's square. The two young women had supported their parents and siblings with their dressmaking business and by working on a Nazi-operated farm near Chmielnik. The farm's Volksdeutsche supervisor, waving a list of names, tried to claim her Jewish laborers. The Nazis compromised by allowing the supervisor to take half of her work force. "The Germans told her, 'You can take one sister. You can't take both.' So she took Cesia, and I was left in the square. I wanted to go with Cesia," Goldlist said. "We hugged and kissed, and she went home. We didn't know the Jews would be taken to Treblinka. With the Germans, you didn't know where they take you. It's incredible and unforgettable. Believe me, whatever we tell, it's not enough. Everybody has more to tell."

Zosia Kalmowiez Kiman and her sister, Chana, were torn away from the rest of their family in an instant. Her brothers were too young, and her father had a crippled arm. On the way to Chmielnik's central square, Zosia decided to safeguard her precious keepsake: a heart-shaped locket containing a photograph of her deceased mother. She unclasped the necklace and handed it to one of her brothers. "I was afraid the Germans would take it away," Zosia said. "I gave this to my little brother. I told him, 'Don't lose this.' I never saw this again. I never saw my brother again. I never saw my family again."

As the Germans swept through Israel "Ira" Kaminsky's neighborhood, they pounded on doors and yelled, "Everybody out!" In his haste to obey, Israel walked to the street in his slippers. "We had to go out right away. They were shooting people." His younger brother, Simcha, brought him shoes, leather ones that laced and covered his ankles. "If I would come to camp with my slippers," Israel said, "I would have been a lost person." The entire Kaminsky family reported to the square, but the Nazis chose only Israel; his brother, Harry; and sister, Rachel. They stood by helplessly as their father, four sisters, and two younger brothers trudged home. Kaminsky's family was split forever. "They were looking for strong people who were capable, whoever presented good health. I was one of about 1,200 young men and women picked. Out of 1,200, it's my estimation about 100 survived."

Several reference books specify October 1, 1942, as the date for Chmielnik's Selektionen — the selection of Jewish laborers from those deemed unfit for work. On that day, the Nazis shipped 1,000 young Jews from Chmielnik to Skarzysko-Kamienna's labor camps, 40 miles away. On the same day, according to Simon Wiesenthal's *Every Day Remembrance Day*, another 500 Jews went to the work camp at Czestochowa. "They pushed us like cows on the trucks," Zaifman said. "They did one truck at a time. They were always with the dogs. These German soldiers, I was afraid to look at them."

The German soldiers and Polish police mercilessly beat Jews who tried to flee, including Saul Jurysta and his late brother, Elia. Jurysta felt the terror. "Volksdeutsche saw us running away. They beat us up. Blood was running from my brother's head. The dog bit me. I was forced to sit with my brother on the stones. The Volksdeutscher said, 'If you try to run again, I shoot you.' They chased us on the truck, me with my brother. We had no choice."

Saul Zernie, then 17, walked to the square with his father, still a young man at age 38. The urge to escape was so overpowering, Zernie bolted. A Jewish policeman pursued and caught him, just as he entered a building. Zernie was forced back to the square. He felt like a hunted animal. "We were surrounded by German and Jewish police," Zernie said. "They started lining up the people, picking the healthy ones and the younger ones."

Kalman Mapa watched in horror through the window of

Chmielnik's Red Cross clinic, where he had volunteered as a nurse's aide. The clinic had about 15 patients, including Kalman's older brother, Chil. "I play a game to help him (Chil)," Mapa said. "I took him in the back. We pretend he was sick." Kalman was 16; Chil was 18. "They put all the young people on the trucks. It took hours. Some trucks make trips. There was screaming, running away." Although Kalman and Chil evaded the roundup that day, their younger brother, Arthur, was cornered. "They took him away to Skarzysko and killed him. My cousin, too. They were young boys. He was 11 years old."

Israel "Irving" Buchbinder looked older, taller, and huskier than his 15 years. The Nazis picked him but dismissed his sister and three brothers, all of whom were younger. As Buchbinder climbed into a truck at gunpoint, his mother, tears streaming down her face, pushed her way through the crowd. "I was in one of the first trucks to leave. My mother come to see me taken away. She gave me a piece of bread. They chased her away. That's it. That's the last time I seen her." As far as Buchbinder knows, his mother, sister, and brothers were gassed in Treblinka. "My mother is from a very large family. She had 16 brothers and sisters." Buchbinder had more than 100 cousins, but only four survived the Shoah. "The truth is sometimes you don't believe yourself what you went through. The majority of towns in the area had the same fate."

Etka Raitapfel Baumstick, of Toronto, said the melee enabled some people to sneak away, unnoticed, down side streets. A cousin, Miriam Raitapfel, who was the same age as Etka, joined those escapees. Miriam, 15, did not survive the Shoah. Neither did Etka's parents or younger brothers, ages 9 and 12. "I am the only survivor of my entire family. We thought we were going to register for work and then we would go back home," Etka said. "We didn't know we were going to be taken from our homes... to camp. We saw all the wagons that were prepared to us. Everybody was quiet. Everybody was frightened. Nobody said a word. There were Germans with dogs."

Mania Poper Cherston found herself encircled by Germans, Poles, and Ukrainians armed with rifles and dogs. The Nazis accepted young married men as workers, she said, but spurned women with children. Cherston, age 20 and single, was the youngest of seven children. Across the square she spotted her brother, Efroim Poper, 23. He had left his wife and little boy at home. The Nazis segregated men from women, she said. "I could see him. He could see me. We had an order that everybody should sit on the floor," Cherston said. "A Jewish policeman came over to me. He said to me, 'Your brother told me to give you this money.'" It was 60 Polish zlotys. "We were told to present our working papers. This was a lie," Cherston said. "First, they took the women. We didn't know where we were going."

The fate of Jews left behind unfolded within a week. On October 3, 1,270 Jews from Szydlow and Drugnia were relocated to Chmielnik. On October 6, 8,000 Jews from Chmielnik, presumably including those from Szydlow and Drugnia, were transported to the Treblinka killing center. A special task force of German police and Ukrainian auxiliaries organized the killing, according to Simon Wiesenthal.

Although Selektionen determined who would live and die, both groups were condemned. The S.S. routed the weak and sick, the children and elderly to immediate extermination. In some Eastern European communities, these Jews were shot and buried alive in mass graves. The S.S. temporarily spared some teenagers and young adults who looked healthy and strong only to work them to death over a period of months or years.

Henik "Henry" Moszenberg Kaufman and his mother were trapped in the Lodz ghetto — separated from his father and sister who took shelter with relatives in Chmielnik. Henik learned of their fate from other Shoah survivors and from Polish neighbors after the war. His father, Israel Moszenberg, walked with a cane — making him a vulnerable target during Chmielnik's liquidation. A German arbitrarily shot Israel in the marketplace. Henik's little sister, Helcha, rushed to her father's side. The same German shot Helcha, too, to silence her screams. "Why they shot my father because he cannot walk so fast?" Henik asked in anguish. "My sister went after him and start to cry, and they shot her on top of him. What kind of barbarism is this?"

On October 1, a few hours after Nathan and Sonia left, Sara sent Helen after them. She had wrapped a sandwich, socks, and other items for Nathan in paper and string. Helen carried the package to the square. "There were trucks, male and female separate," Helen said. "These children were packed like animals. The Germans always with their guns toward us. I looked and looked to see where my brother was." Nathan was already on a truck.

As Nathan grasped the bundle from her hands — before she could say goodbye — Helen felt gun barrels jabbing her back and sides. She heard shouting in German. Helen shouted back, yelling that she was too young to go to the work camps. Using rifles, the soldiers pushed and prodded her toward a truck full of women, forcing her in. Sonia was on that vehicle, and the two sisters were to be inseparable during the next three years.

Glossing over her own misfortunes, Helen often speaks of the heartache her mother, Sara, must have felt, not knowing the welfare of her children. "Now that I am a mother and a grandmother, I think about my mother. I wonder how she could stand the pain. My mother expected me to come home, and I never came home," Helen said. "Now I know my mother must have been made of steel. Her children were taken from her."

Unbeknownst to her parents, Regina had left the house to see the deportation. From the square's edge, she spotted Nathan and Sonia. Some Germans soldiers chased Regina and released their dogs. Regina was terrified the German shepherds would bite, but they only knocked her down and straddled her. The soldiers began flogging Regina with a whip, tearing her clothes, and commanding her to get out, to go home. They probably didn't suspect she was Jewish, Nathan said; otherwise, they would have killed her or forced her into the trucks.

"I didn't tell my parents that anything had happened." That night, they looked at her bruised and swollen back when they thought Regina was asleep, but she was just pretending. The next day, Regina's parents confronted her. "I remember them asking me why I went to the square. I told them I just wanted to go and see Sonia and Nathan."

Sonia had seen Regina from a distance. "I saw Germans beat her. They pushed her away. I wanted to talk with her," Sonia said. "You couldn't move a step without the Germans noticing you. There were thousands of people there. We were in the middle. They (the Nazis) pushed people back. They pushed people in who weren't supposed to go. Some parents came and tried to take back their children. The parents were pleading and crying. The Germans pushed them back and beat them. It was terrible, terrible, how can I tell you? We thought we would be gone for a week or a month, that we would come back. We were so naive. I thought we would be hurt but not to this extent."

The forced farewells linger in the memories of Shoah survivors. Helen often wonders about the pregnant woman who approached the trucks with her five-year-old daughter. The woman begged the Germans not to take her husband. They responded by striking her and unleashing their dogs to attack her. Helen's final image of Chmielnik's square includes that woman doubled over near the cast iron water pump.

Sonia held Helen's hand. The two sisters traveled with the other women by truck to the work camps of Skarzysko-Kamienna. Nathan said that he and the men went by truck as far as Kielce, where they transferred to trains bound for Skarzysko-Kamienna.

Nathan's group waited many hours in a park near the Kielce train station. Male prisoners who had to urinate or defecate were taken to a patch of prickly bushes, forced to drop their pants, squat over the bushes, and relieve themselves in public. Some were forced to remain crouched in that position, Nathan said, while curious

Poles gathered. The prickly bushes irritated the skin, causing some prisoners to scratch. "The Nazis belittled us in front of Polish people. They wanted to show the Polish people that those Jews were animals," Nathan said. "You know what they called us? Apes. Malpa. This is the first dehumanization of Jews from my home-town."

Whether Jews were taken by train or truck, they were treated like livestock — really worse than livestock — given the overcrowd-ing and lack of water, food, and any semblance of decency. As Nathan and other men were pushed into a boxcar meant for cattle, German shepherds attacked them and shred their clothes. In the scramble to board the train, some men did not have time to pull up their pants. The dogs tugged at their pants. A dog ripped Nathan's brown jacket.

As the trucks full of women departed Chmielnik for Skarzysko-Kamienna, Sonia caught a glimpse of her home. "This I remember like now it happened. We passed by my house. We passed by. I saw the window. This was the window from our kitchen. I saw my mother. I saw my mother's hands like this." Sonia lifted her hands to her head, palms to temples. "My mother saw me in the truck. She saw me, Helen, and some of my friends." Sonia and Helen didn't know it then, of course, but they would never see their parents again. Nor would they see Rachel and Fishel.

Chapter Eleven
ENCLOSED IN BARBED WIRE

Skarzysko-Kamienna, a Polish town about 40 miles northeast of Chmielnik, contained several slave labor camps dedicated to the production of bullets, explosives, and other ammunition. It is one of the great ironies of the Shoah that Jews were forced to join their oppressors in waging war. The sweat and blood of Jewish prisoners fueled German industry, including the task of weapons making. The illegal confiscation of bank accounts and personal belongings — down to the gold dental fillings of dead Jews — helped finance Germany's fascist regime.

Wooden buildings and iron fences form Helen's initial impression of Skarzysko-Kamienna. "It was a holiday," Helen said. Sukkot was supposed to be a festive occasion when Jews gathered with their families, ate special foods, and thanked God. "I wanted to go home so badly. I was lonely. I wanted my mother. It was the first time I was in a prison. I couldn't go anywhere. From behind the barbed wires, I saw a dog barking. I wished I could be that dog. I saw butterflies flying. I thought, 'If I could be a butterfly! If only I could fly!'"

The abduction from her family and from Chmielnik left Helen in a state of shock. She and several thousand other Jews trapped in Skarzysko-Kamienna's work camps didn't know how long they would be there, what they would do, or how harsh their lives would become. Her first few weeks of incarceration remain a blur to Helen. She vaguely remembers that women did not work in the beginning. Instead, they cried for several days. "Ask Sonia. She remembers better."

Unlike most Holocaust survivors who lost entire families, the Garfinkels fill in each other's blanks, so to speak, and bolster each other's memories. Interviews with other survivors from Chmielnik confirm the Garfinkels' testimony and provide more details. Each account is heart-rending.

The truck transporting Mania Poper Cherston stopped about one kilometer outside Chmielnik. German and Ukrainian guards stationed at each corner of the truck announced that, for the price of 100 zlotys, anyone could jump out. Cherston pleaded with a guard to accept her 60 zlotys, which her brother, Efroim, had given her in the town square. She promised the guard he could collect 40 zlotys from her and her parents the next day. "He pushed me away with the rifle," she said. "We were on the truck, 200 women. Twelve or 15 had things to give the guards. They went back home." Cherston stayed on the truck.

After unloading in Skarzysko-Kamienna, the trucks returned to Chmielnik. "The trucks go back and forth. I know my brother is supposed to come," Cherston said. "It was night. I said, 'Where is my brother, Efroim?'" Eventually, some acquaintances informed Cherston that her brother never left Chmielnik. In the town square, a Nazi read a list of names including hers and her brother's; he released those individuals. Cursing her bad luck, Cherston assumed her parents or sister-in-law had bribed the Germans. Unbeknownst to Cherston then, her destiny veered away from death and toward the possibility of life. "I never saw my parents, I never saw my brother anymore. That's it," Cherston said. "A week or a few days later, they deport all these people to Treblinka. So you see, we couldn't figure out what was good."

Besides the endless weeping, Sonia remembers that the women were taken to a large, empty building. A Ukrainian guard clutching chalk drew a large circle on the floor. The S.S. ordered the women to disrobe and to throw their money, jewelry, watches, and other valuables inside the ring. The guards inspected each garment by searching pockets and feeling for items sewn inside linings. The women, mostly teenagers, were embarrassed to be naked in front of others. "It was terrible. The girls were crying,"

Sonia said. "A girl was standing next to me. She was shaking from fear. She took off one earring, but she forgot to take off the other earring. They ripped off her earring with a piece of her ear and threw it in. She was bleeding. I don't remember her name. She was from my hometown." In that instant, Sonia felt an odd mixture of horror and relief. She had one less thing to worry about because, contrary to her parents' wishes, she had never pierced her ears.

Cesia Zaifman has similar memories: "They send us in a room like a warehouse. They made us take everything off. They knew people hid money, gold, and things. They took everything away. Everybody cried. We didn't know what they were going to do with us. It was unexpected."

Etka Raitapfel Baumstick wore a short-sleeved, flower-print dress. "It was a nice, sunny day although it was October," she said of the day she rode the truck from Chmielnik to Skarzysko-Kamienna. "Everyone who left was not dressed up warm. We went to camp with whatever we were wearing. The following day it was freezing." Etka had no jacket or sweater. Mania Poper Cherston also describes the day of deportation as a "nice fall day." She wore a skirt, a blouse, a summer coat, and shoes without stockings. She had hidden the 60 zlotys inside her clothes. "After the showers, we were thinking they were going to finish us there," Cherston said. "We were afraid of everything. Women were crying, screaming. Everyone was humiliated."

When Helen lectures in schools, children often ask whether the Nazis raped Jewish women. Such crimes took place, but not so commonly that the Garfinkels personally knew victims. German laws prohibiting sexual relations with Jews provided some discouragement, but, as Helen succinctly notes, the women's condition typically repelled advances. After a few weeks or months, they were dirty and malnourished, their clothes resembled rags, and lice crawled in their hair. However, reaching the conclusion that there were relatively few instances of sexual abuse based on a small sample of eyewitnesses is misleading. Felicja Karay, a former Skarzysko-Kamienna prisoner now living in Rishon Leziyon, Israel, describes various situations in which women were compromised, not only by the Germans but also by Poles and Jews. Karay's book, *Death Comes in Yellow*, is a scholarly depiction of the history, hierarchy, and life in Hasag's slave labor complex. *Encyclopedia of the Holocaust* confirms the crime of rape, often involving new arrivals in Skarzysko-Kamienna. In introducing some of the camp's top officials, the *Encyclopedia* states, "Kurt Krause and his deputies — Fritz Bartenschläger, Otto Eisenschmidt, and Paul Kuehnemann — were notorious for the acts of robbery, murder, and rape for which they were responsible." Sonia recalls the names of several German S.S.: Krause, Georg Hering, Wilhelm Leidig, and Meshner; "They were murderers, killers. I can't understand how they could beat and torture the whole day and then go home to their families," Sonia said. "When Leidig was dead, I said, 'Oh, good. Now it's time for Hering,' but no one killed him. They killed Leidig in a minute, and he tortured people for years."

Nathan witnessed the aftermath of sexual assault in his section of Skarzysko-Kamienna, Werk A, during the first few weeks of his incarceration. Emerging from his barrack one morning, Nathan saw two dead women on the ground; their nude bodies had been burned between the legs. A Jewish doctor in Nathan's barracks speculated that the Nazis had mutilated the corpses to destroy evidence of sexual molestation. As they discussed the crime, Nathan realized he had seen the two women the day before with a transfer of Jewish residents from Skarzysko-Kamienna's ghetto. He had noticed the women were attractive and well-dressed. "I asked, 'God, where are you? Where are you, God?' I asked that all the time," Nathan said, stressing he did not pray, but merely asked questions in Hebrew. "I told Him, 'I don't want to be the chosen people. I don't want to be the chosen one. I want to be You. I want to be them.'"

In Werk B, Helen's and Sonia's camp section, the women wore

their own clothes. After Chmielnik's Jewesses dressed, the Nazis marched them to their so-called living quarters. The wooden buildings, or barracks, each accommodated about 250 women. Bunks for sleeping lined both sides of the long and narrow structure. Each bunk, separated from the others by tiny aisles, held six women on three levels of shelves made of raw, untreated wood. There were no tables, chairs, furnishings, blankets, pillows, bedding — not even sacks of straw. In Sonia's words, "There was nothing." The building was truly bleak. The walls and roof served as barriers to the wind, rain, and snow, but they offered little protection from freezing temperatures. There was no heating system. The only light came from a bare bulb overhead and a small window on the wall opposite the door. Although the women initially found the barrack repugnant, they later called it "home." Helen and Sonia chose a bunk on top. "I didn't want anybody to throw things on top of me," Sonia said. "It was very crowded." They slept on bare wood, huddling under Sonia's green wool coat. Entirely unprepared for the journey, Helen did not have even a jacket. Sonia's stylish coat served many purposes — bed pad, blanket, and wrap. "We covered ourselves with the coat," Sonia said. "It got dirty. It tore. It fell apart... but that coat lasted a long time."

The next day, the S.S. led the women outside to dole out work assignments. A Nazi called Jan Laskowski chose Helen, Sonia, Cesia Zaifman, Etka Raitapfel Baumstick, and about a dozen other women, mostly from Chmielnik. The Garfinkel sisters were unaware of that moment's importance. Looking back, they realize it was a stroke of luck, one of many, that enabled them to survive.

Laskowski's appearance — older, smaller, and less attractive than the other Nazis — disappointed Etka. Compared with the other bosses, who were young, tall, and handsome, Laskowski looked wizened. "When I went to the barracks, I was crying that this guy picked me. I was crying," Etka said. "There were other girls from the town Skarzysko who had been there a few weeks. They said, 'You should be happy because you'll have much better work than the other girls.' People were dying in ammunition."

Laskowski managed Skarzysko-Kamienna's potato mill, a two-story building outside the barbed-wire enclosure. Upstairs, hundreds of pounds of potatoes boiled in huge kettles. Machines removed the skins and sliced the cooked potatoes. Downstairs, the potato slices passed through rollers injected with hot steam to dehydrate them into flakes. Sacks positioned under wooden chutes caught the flakes. With wooden sticks, workers stuffed the flakes into bags, weighing 30 to 50 pounds each. The mill was so much cleaner than the barrack, Sonia looked forward to the drudgery of the assembly line. The potato mill workers were regarded as an elite group. "Everybody envied us," Sonia said. Helen, Sonia, and their co-workers snitched potatoes and potato flakes when the Polish foremen weren't looking. The potatoes served as a precious source of nutrition, helping Sonia and Helen stave off hunger. Their daily food rations consisted of one slice of bread, one ladle of watery soup, and, perhaps, a cup of coffee. Helen and Sonia also exchanged potatoes for items they needed within the prisoners' elaborate and illegal bartering network. Polish supervisors and foremen, who worked in the factories but lived outside the camp in town, smuggled in soap, clothes, and food to sell to those Jews who had money.

The Garfinkel sisters' first possessions were small pots, essential for collecting soup rations. "We never ate from a plate or with a spoon," Helen said. The pots resembled little blue pitchers, and the sisters looped their belts through the handles. "If you lost your little pot," Helen said, "you couldn't have this soup." Sonia later lost her container. It was probably stolen from the stone oven near the barracks, where she sometimes boiled potatoes. Their access to more food made the Garfinkel sisters rich among prisoners, however, so Sonia could "afford" a replacement. She traded raw potatoes for fabric, socks, or old shoes, but she didn't like haggling. She asked an acquaintance to barter for her. "Gutka. She was very handy," Sonia remembered. "She exchanged things for me." Gutka, a Jewess from Chmielnik, survived the war.

Some Jews entered Skarzysko-Kamienna with money, something the Garfinkels had not anticipated before leaving Chmielnik. "A lot of people came with money sewn in the lining of their clothes," Helen said. "They gave money to the Poles for extra food, for clothes, so they had a little more." Mandzia Wajchendler Mapa, now in Toronto, was among the "wealthier" inmates although she had no money on entering the camp at age 14. She attributes her survival to her father's ingenuity. Isaac Wajchendler, a successful painting contractor, architect, and real estate owner in Skarzysko-Kamienna, traded away household possessions to keep his family together, to buy favors, and to get extra food. Before the Germans sent most of Skarzysko-Kamienna's Jews to Treblinka's gas chambers, Isaac arranged for Mandzia and her older sister, Rose, to enter the labor camp. It was a gamble, Mandzia said. "I went willingly because we didn't know what was better. I went at the right time. After that was the Endlösung. They took away most of the people." Her father followed Mandzia and Rose into the camp. Then he persuaded the Germans to transfer her mother, Cyrla, and brother, Abraham, from another city.

"We had valuable things we brought from home, a ring, a leather purse. This Polish girl working in camp helped us out with food, but we paid her. Very seldom did you find somebody with sympathy," Mandzia said. "I remember once my father wanted to help me. He had a leather jacket. He sold this jacket. He got money so he got food. I always said he was left without jacket so he could provide me and my sister with food."

Mania Poper Cherston spent her brother's 60 zlotys to buy bread from Polish workers in her factory. Each week for three weeks, she paid 20 zlotys for one loaf. "I could eat the whole loaf by myself at once," Cherston said, recalling how she was already ravenous in the beginning. "When I had this bread, I share with other people in the barracks. I gave a slice there, a slice there. Before you know it, it was gone." Cherston, who toiled in the Werk

A and B ammunition plants, envied the potato mill workers. "They weren't in ammunition. That was heaven. Why? Because they had food." At the same time, Cherston felt grateful because some potato mill workers shared their extra food with the ammunition workers.

The S.S. considered the taking and eating of potatoes as thefts, crimes warranting the death sentence. Helen and Sonia say Laskowski knew they routinely took potatoes and potato flakes, but he looked the other way. When he occasionally burst into the mill to lecture sternly about stealing, the prisoners understood he was subtly warning them that some brutal guards might be watching or frisking people that day. Laskowski was a Volksdeutscher, an ethnic German who lived in Poland. A small man with a mustache, he was fond of smoking cigars and spitting. Because Laskowski was older, in his sixties, Helen and Sonia speculate he was not so easily indoctrinated into believing fascist dogma and its tenets of anti-Semitism.

The camp's hierarchy started with uniformed German S.S. officers at the top. They employed businessmen and civilian Nazis clad in plain clothes, such as Laskowski, to manage the factories. Differentiating between the S.S. and mere Nazi party members was difficult. Nathan identified Laskowski as S.S., but Sonia said he was only a Nazi. "Most of the Germans operating Skarzysko were S.S.," Sonia said. "All S.S. are Nazis. Not all Nazis are S.S., but they're almost one and the same." To help maintain discipline, the S.S. employed *Werkschutz*, or guards, clad in dark green uniforms. Typically, the guards were crude and ignorant louts from the Ukraine, Poland, and other non-German countries. The S.S. revealed their diabolical streak by establishing a Jewish police force, led by Commandant Lejzer Teperman and his assistant, Josef Krzepicki, to keep fellow prisoners in tow. It was a way to turn Jew against Jew. Women did not serve as police, but they worked as supervisors and foremen. There were few, if any, German soldiers, called *Wehrmacht*, in labor camps. However, the *Wehrmacht*, noticeable in their khaki green uniforms, transported Jews to camps.

"Laskowski wasn't so bad. He never beat me. I never saw him beat anyone," Zaifman said. "Other Meisters were beaters. People in other divisions were beaten a lot." Laskowski looked intimidating, however, despite his slight stature. "He never smiled," Zaifman said. "He came to inspections a lot of times. He never looked at a person straight in the face. He looked at you sideways." Etka Raitapfel Baumstick added, "He didn't do anything for anybody personally as far as I know, but I didn't see him hit anybody. If he was around, I would thank him now."

In October, 1942, Laskowski did not immediately dispatch his "employees" to the assembly line because there were no potatoes to process. To protect the women from the blows of the guards, Laskowski placed them in a barracks. He instructed them to look busy and to start sweeping and cleaning if any guards or Nazi officials came by. Laskowski, a widower, picked a husky Jewess, Bela Jakubowicz of Chmielnik, to clean his living quarters and to cook. Although other prisoners envied Bela Jakubowicz, Helen said, she helped many individuals.

When he found the women weeping the first few days, "Laskowski came in and explained to us that we shouldn't cry, that we should work. He said that he didn't have it so good. He said his wife died, he had two sons on the front," Sonia said, referring to Nazi Germany's easternmost battle line in the Soviet Union. "He gave us a little hope. He said maybe the war would end and we would be free. That it didn't help us, crying."

Later, Laskowski saved Nathan's life, not just once, but twice. "There are two reasons we are alive," Helen said. "That Laskowski was our boss. That we worked in the potato factory. If we did not survive, Nate would not survive."

Chapter Twelve
NUMBER 4048

Skarzysko-Kamienna's complex of work camps, specializing in armaments production, represents the participation of big business in Germany's genocide against Jews. Hasag, which operated the Skarzysko-Kamienna camp, Hermann Goring Werk, and I.G. Farben were among German corporations that exploited Jews as slave laborers during World War II. Upon acquiring several Polish factories in 1940, Hasag began paying the S.S. four to five zlotys a day for each Jewish worker. "Maintenance" costs, which were minimal based on survivors' descriptions of deficient food, clothing, and shelter, were subtracted from the labor bill. The Jews received no compensation for their work — rather, they paid Hasag with their health and their lives.

Hasag's management of camps throughout Germany and Poland underscores the Nazis' reliance on anti-Semitism to involve all elements of society in their crimes. The Fascist government corrupted the legal system to strip Jews of rights, won the silence of most Christian clergymen, perverted the scientific community to make guinea pigs of Jews, and terrorized civilians into apathy. Also subverted was private enterprise, including railroads that transported Jews to their deaths, engineering firms that designed the crematoria, and chemical plants that supplied the lethal gas.

The Garfinkels' "employer," Hasag, started benignly enough in 1863 as a lamp manufacturer in Leipzig, Germany. The government classified it a *Wehrmachtsbetrieb*, a company working for the military, in 1934 and elevated it to a *Rustungsbetrieb*, or armaments company, in 1940. In Germany, Hasag enslaved thousands of Jews at such camps as Buchenwald and Flossenburg. In Poland, the company distinguished itself as the largest Wehrmachtsbetrieb. In 1944, Hitler praised Hasag by dubbing it an "exemplary National Socialist enterprise."

Despite the company's close ties to the Reich, none of its top officials was charged with war crimes. Prisoners remember Hugo Schneider as one of Hasag's leaders. Paul Budin, the business executive designated in 1940 to oversee Hasag, died at the war's end. Some historians theorize that Budin and his wife committed suicide in April, 1945, by setting off an explosion at Hasag's Leipzig headquarters. Another famous German industrialist, by the name of Krupp, was found guilty of war crimes in 1946 during the Allies' famous Nuremberg trials. Krupp spent several years in jail — luxurious quarters compared with his company's wartime work camps that imprisoned Jews and other "undesirable" civilians.

As a Hasag slave, Nathan started on one of Werk A's seven assembly lines, producing anti-tank ammunition. The bullets measured six inches in length and three to four inches in diameter. After several weeks, a German S.S. officer, nicknamed "Brilush" by the prisoners for his oversized glasses, assigned Nathan to make casings for anti-aircraft bullets. They measured 13 inches in length and one to two inches in diameter. Nathan worked with three other Jews in an area containing four machines.

"We got unified," Nathan said. "We agreed to keep our production very close to each other so there wouldn't be a big difference between each individual. We didn't want competition." Women checked the finished product in the big metal drum for defective casings. An error rate of 10 percent or more could result in a charge of sabotage, carrying the penalty of execution. Errors were likely, Nathan said, because the volume required of each worker was so high. "It was a 'Catch 22' because the more I produce, the more I speed up, the more junk I can produce."

Brilush's offer of more soup for more bullets intensified the pressure to speed up. "It was a dilemma. I wanted the soup, but if I produce more, I make more mistakes. I produce junk, Schmelz."

The four workers made enough casings, about 100 each per day, to get two extra soup rations. If they each tried to make 110 casings a day for three extra soups, Nathan said, they increased their error rate beyond 10 percent. Mandzia Wajchendler Mapa, an ammunition laborer in Werk A and B, felt similar anxieties. "You know, it was hard," she said. "It was scary. If you didn't make something right, it was sabotage. They punished. We were afraid every minute for your life. It was such a time. It was very bad times."

Mania Poper Cherston made blanks for target practice under the supervision of Meshner in Werk B. She later transferred to Werk A to make real bullets for pistols and shotguns. Her boss there was the evil Kurt Krause. "I was exhausted all the time," Cherston said. "It was very crowded. It was terrible. We were hungry. We were tired. The conditions, the food, everything. We were always scared. We live day by day."

Manufacturing quotas were less stringent in the potato mill, but most Jews in Werk B toiled in ammunition factories. Werk C stood out as Skarzysko-Kamienna's worst section with the highest death rate. Prisoners there assembled underwater mines and filled them with picric acid. Such potent chemicals turned the skin yellow, poisoned the body, and weakened the immune system. Many of the jaundiced prisoners collapsed from illness and fatigue after only a few months. If they could not continue working, guards marched them outside the camp into the forest, and shot them.

Israel "Ira" Kaminsky remembers how other prisoners stared in astonishment at him and his fellow Werk C inmates on Sundays, as the ragtag group trudged to the Werk A showers. "I was one of the yellow people. We were all yellow. As a matter of fact, when I meet other survivors today, they are surprised I am alive," Kaminsky said. "We were like as if we had leprosy. People were afraid to stay near us. They could smell the picrine and the troilite." Those chemicals saturated his clothes. Kaminsky tried to counteract contact with the poison by washing daily — stripping

to his waist and rolling up his pant legs — even though Werk C
had no showers. "I never had the guts to take off my shorts," he
said, explaining that Werk C's primitive washroom served men
and women. Werk C was considered a punishment. "If somebody did something wrong in Camp A or B, they sent them to
Camp C to finish them off." That happened to Kaminsky's brother-
in-law, Isaac Kwasniewski, who was shot in Werk C sometime after his transfer from Werk B. Kaminsky's experience amazes Sonia
who noted, "I didn't know people lived through Werk C." Israel
"Irving" Buchbinder, who made detonators for bullets and casings for cannons in Werk A, also noticed the Werk C prisoners on
Sundays. "We used to call them *kanareks,*" he said, referring to the
Polish word for canaries.

Kaminsky credits his brother, Harry, with helping him survive. Harry's job of moving big crates of ammunition enabled
him to circulate within Werk C, to barter with Poles, and to bring
food to Israel. "If somebody didn't have any help, they couldn't
survive," Kaminsky said. "I was very lucky that I was healthy. I
never got sick in that camp. If somebody was sick for a day only
sometimes, they took them to the firing place in Camp C. They
were shot." By early 1944, when the Nazis realized they would receive no more Jewish slaves, the executions stopped, Kaminsky
said. At that point, he and his brother, Harry, bribed a German to
transfer their sister, Rachel, from Werk A's ammunition plants to
the dreaded Werk C. They didn't care that Werk C was worse,
Israel concluded. "We wanted to be together."

Although Nathan had the relative advantage of being in Werk
A, he faced an intense struggle for survival. The men's barrack
resembled that of Helen and Sonia, but the building was much
larger — holding between 1,500 and 2,000 people. "It looked like
a big horse barn," Nathan said. And it was, according to Felicja
Karay. Some of Werk A's housing consisted of stables called
Pferdebaracken, or horse barracks, the former prisoner wrote in
Death Comes in Yellow, her scholarly account of Hasag's slave la-

bor camps in Skarzysko-Kamienna. Like his sisters, Nathan chose a top bunk. First, he reasoned, he had the strength to climb, and second, he wanted to avoid the filth of the lower bunks, which collected the urine, diarrhea, and vomit of sick inmates overhead.

In the beginning, when Nathan's brown jacket and slacks still looked smart, the guards taunted him: "You Anglo-American Jew capitalist." After his clothes became grimy and torn, they called out: "You Jew Communist." Hasag did not bother with the expense of uniforms, Nathan said, but the company gave him a label for his jacket, number 4048. Sonia and Helen did not receive numbers or the tattoos associated with Auschwitz, the German government's largest death camp and work complex. Nor were the women addressed by their names. "We had no names," Nathan said. "Our names didn't exist." Sonia speculates that numbers were not given in Werk B because it was too much trouble. Germans had so little regard for their Jewish slaves, Sonia said, they did not bother to establish an identification system. Jewish lives held no value. However, the sisters did receive numbers at some point during their imprisonment — something they did not learn of until more than 50 years after the war.

Skarzysko-Kamienna lacked the gas chambers to kill Jews by the thousands each day and crematoria to dispose of their bodies, but it was a killing center, nonetheless. In the broadest definition, all labor camps were death camps in that they were places where Jews were, literally, worked and starved to death. Each day in Skarzysko-Kamienna, Jews died of illness, malnutrition, and beatings. They were also executed in the forest and killed arbitrarily by guards.

The *Encyclopedia of the Holocaust* estimates that an average of 26 Jews died each day in Skarzysko-Kamienna between October 1, 1942, when the Garfinkels were incarcerated, and January 31, 1943, for a total of 3,241 victims. The inmate population usually totaled about 6,000. That number is verified by Kaminsky's calculations of 1,000 to 1,500 prisoners in Werk C and 3,000 to

4,000 in Werk A. Throughout the war, between 25,000 and 30,000 Jews entered Skarzysko-Kamienna, according to the *Encyclopedia*. Of those, an estimated 18,000 to 23,000 died or were killed there.

In 1942, Nathan could not have imagined that summary of death and destruction, yet he had an inkling of it. An atrocity he witnessed shortly after arriving in Skarzysko-Kamienna clarified his understanding of his own situation. Until that moment, Nathan couldn't believe what was happening to Poland's Jews — despite his first-hand experiences of beatings and torture in Chmielnik and of enslavement in Biala Podlaska. Like many other Jews, he kept thinking the worst had passed.

What he saw not only shattered any lingering hopes but also hinted at the impending genocide of the Jews. An S.S. officer began harassing a young woman who was breast-feeding an infant she had hidden under her shawl. Obviously angry that the woman had defied orders by smuggling her baby into a work camp, the officer's face reddened. His shouting grew shrill. "The German tore off the shawl from her," Nathan reported. "He said, 'Give me the baby.' She said, 'After the baby is fed.' The German pulled out his bayonet. I saw something shiny. He, — he cut off the woman's breast — while she was feeding the baby." The image of blood spurting and the woman collapsing in screams signaled Nathan's turning point from denial to the recognition that he was branded for death. "This changed my life. My whole structure of life, my whole morality changed, too. Then I started to believe what the Nazis can actually do. This was the beginning of the end." Prisoners standing closer to the woman protested by yelling, "Stop, stop! Don't kill! What are you doing?" but the officer shot the woman. Then Nazis armed with machine guns encircled the crowd. "I don't know who this woman was or where she came from."

Being singled out for harassment, beatings, and executions was unpredictable, and that added great stress to a tenuous existence. Nathan nearly lost his life several times in Skarzysko-Kamienna's inhumane environment.

Early in his imprisonment, Nathan volunteered to carry soup two kilometers from the munitions factory to his barrack. The chore entitled him to an extra ration of soup and the right to scrape the pot. One evening, as Nathan and other volunteers lugged the big kettles, a guard played a sick joke. He separated Nathan from his partner and paired them with two shorter prisoners. That way, they would be more likely to spill the precious rations, giving the guard reason to punish them. Nathan compensated by stooping a little. Furious, the guard kicked Nathan in the back. Nathan stumbled, and some soup slopped over the kettle's side.

The guard shouted, "Why did the soup spill?" Intent on survival, Nathan swallowed his rage and carefully thought through his answer. If he were to reply, "Because you kicked me," that would cast blame on the guard. Such a blasphemous statement would be tantamount to uttering his own death sentence. Nathan responded, "Because I am taller." The guard then ordered the shorter prisoner to strike Nathan for spilling the soup. The man reluctantly hit Nathan. The guard bellowed, "I'll show you how to hit him," and knocked Nathan to the ground. Walking by at that instant was Brilush, who stopped the beating and took the guard to the office. "We never saw that guard again."

Nathan does not remember Brilush's real name but recalls the S.S. official as being somewhat neutral, neither cruel nor kind. "He never physically abused us or verbally abused us. He was only interested in production," Nathan said. "I wish the bad Nazis were like him."

Punishment was common, with or without cause. Israel "Irving" Buchbinder was beaten with a serving ladle after trying to get an extra helping of soup. "I was very down. I never tried to do it again. After that I went to the corner and ate my soup. I didn't fight." On another occasion, four Ukrainian guards dragged Buchbinder into a room, pulled down his pants, and held him to the floor so a German called Alfred Wagner could flog his bare bottom with a whip. Buchbinder lost consciousness on the fourth lash. Because Buchbinder defecated before the beating ended, Wagner added more lashes. "To this day I don't know why he beat me. I couldn't lay for six months on my behind. It was the color of liver." A Jewish woman, who had connections inside the camp, helped Buchbinder by giving him cold compresses. "It was a struggle to get through a day intact. I didn't want to get hurt," Buchbinder said. "I didn't have too many people I knew at the time. To survive, I had to mind my own business."

Like Buchbinder, Nathan decided that making himself inconspicuous would increase his odds for survival. After spilling the soup, Nathan did not volunteer for special tasks. He figured the avoidance of beatings and psychological torment was more important than procuring extra food. After his work shift, he conserved energy by resting in his bunk. There, Nathan also learned the danger of staying in the barrack instead of working. Prisoners who were sick or accused of feigning illness were removed from the camp and shot in a nearby forest. The guards did not always check the barracks though, so one day Nathan risked staying inside to recuperate from exhaustion.

That one day, however, the guards discovered Nathan and a dozen other prisoners resting. With a torrent of shouts and blows, the guards drove the group before Fritz Bartenschläger, an S.S. officer known for his sadistic executions. The guards lined up the prisoners by height. Bartenschläger carried a piece of bread in one hand to taunt his victims and a revolver in the other hand to shoot them. Starting with the shortest man, he instructed each prisoner to open his mouth for the bread. Instead of feeding his captives, Bartenschläger fired the gun in their open mouths. Nathan was eighth in line. The seventh person had just had his brains blown out. Death was inevitable, but all Nathan could think of was life. If he could not save himself, at least he could salvage his humanity. "There was no fear. I wanted to die with dignity."

When Bartenschläger commanded Nathan to open his mouth, Nathan said, "'Sir, give me the piece of bread first and after I finish eating the bread, I will open my mouth for your bullet.' I said this very nicely, very politely. He looked at me as if to say, 'Don't you know who you're talking to?' I could see it in his eyes." Startled by Nathan's request, Bartenschläger paused. Then he hit Nathan in the face with the revolver so hard that Nathan fell. A Jewish policeman, Josef Krzepicki, rushed over and began kicking Nathan. "By kicking me, Krzepicki helped me. Can you understand that?" Krzepicki appeared to be beating Nathan, but his kicks were meant to distract Bartenschläger from his original purpose of killing the remaining prisoners.

Although Nathan credits Krzepicki with saving his life, he later learned the policeman was not well-regarded. Prisoners incensed by Krzepicki's abuse of authority killed him a few years later in the Buchenwald concentration camp in Germany. Jewish police were nearly always controversial. Some behaved humanely by trying to minimize mistreatment, but others were as brutal as the S.S. As Krzepicki kicked, Bartenschläger sneered, "You dirty Jew. I wouldn't waste a bullet on you." After that incident, Nathan always went to work.

While dodging conflict contributed to survival, Nathan's ability to diffuse tension was key. Throughout the Shoah, Nathan saved himself by remaining calm and composed. He consciously set aside anger and fear to submit to his captors, making his goal the preservation of life rather than the assertion of ego.

"I didn't answer back. By answering back, there would be a bullet in my head," Nathan said. "I love myself to survive. I loved myself so I could love my enemy. By blocking his anger, he wouldn't do nothing to me. This is the fight for survival. Not to stand up and get killed, but to not stand up and not get killed. If you're drowning, you don't fight the water. By floating, I sustained myself for the time being, until when I can be rescued."

Chapter Thirteen
LEFT BEHIND

Kalman, Sara, and their four remaining children stayed in the Chmielnik ghetto as the Nazis enslaved 1,000 young people in Skarzysko-Kamienna's labor camps and 500 others in Czestochowa. Those crimes preceded Chmielnik's first "liquidation" — the merciless actions to empty a town of Jews — on October 6, 1942. On that day, the S.S. shipped 8,000 Jews unfit for work to Treblinka's gas chambers. The tumultuous days and weeks of late 1942 are a jumble of memories for Regina. Bela also had trouble recalling the sequence of events in chronological order because, during the entire time she spent in Chmielnik, she was grief-stricken over her relatives in Lodz. "For me it was very bad. I was thinking about Golda and my grandmother," Bela said. "I was thinking, 'What if my grandma die? She'll die if I be there or not, but maybe I could be close to her.'"

Bela did not report to Chmielnik's square the day the S.S. abducted Nathan, Sonia, and Helen. Her skin occasionally broke out in rashes, probably resulting from poor nutrition and extreme anxiety. On that particular day, Bela had open sores and boils on her hands and forearms. She knew the Germans rejected, sometimes killed, young Jews who were obviously sick or injured. "I don't know what it was. Maybe it was an infection. At that time, you don't have doctors. You don't have nothing. I have boils. I stay home," Bela said. "The food was very limited. There was nothing to do, just talk about food. Maybe tomorrow is going to be better. Maybe there would be food."

Kalman and Sara did not know the location of Nathan, Sonia, and Helen. "Right away three people left for no reason whatsoever. My parents know they're not going to come back. My parents knew it was very bad. They knew their own lives were going to end," Bela said. "They said, 'Thank God, I have you here.' But I know the Nazis are going to take me because I'm the same age." Shock overtook the household after the sudden disappearance of Nathan, Sonia, and Helen, Regina said, but denial was also present. "Adults were talking about horrible things taking place, that they evacuate people and take them to camps," Regina said. "My father said, 'God is not going to allow something like this to happen.' My mother kept disagreeing."

The Garfinkels somehow avoided the Nazis' first attempt to purge Chmielnik of Jews on October 6. Regina and Bela did not see the selection and transport of people. However, eyewitness Mary Kleinhandler, a Shoah survivor in Los Angeles, wrote about it for the 1993 issue of *Hed Hairgun*, a magazine for former Chmielnik residents and their descendants. Kleinhandler states that Hauptman Mayer and Lieutenant Hugo Haas supervised the crimes. One detail in her account is especially chilling:

"The only person who put up a fight was a six-year-old, the son of Igelnik, a local tailor. When the ill-fated stick pointed at the child, he threw himself on the ground, grabbed his father's pant leg, and held on with all his might." (Helen can hardly bear to read the article, which painfully reminds her of her little brother Fishel.) Kleinhandler continues:

"'Daddy, daddy,' he pleaded, 'don't let them take me away,' as if his father had some power to stop the henchman. I could see his little mouth open in agony. Tears were streaming down his face. At that moment, I felt he was crying not only for himself, but for all of us. The father did not move a muscle. He stood there like a pillar of salt. What choice did he have? Finally the little boy was picked up by one of the Polish firemen. He cried all the way to the wagons, his little arms moving like wings of a bird in flight. He lost one shoe. 'God,' I thought, 'can't you help? Why are you silent?'"

Kalman Mapa heard from some survivors that, on October 6,

the S.S. compelled 8,000 Jews to walk from Chmielnik to Checiny, about 15 miles away. "Half of the people died. They killed people on the way." According to *Encyclopaedia Judaica*, the Nazis conducted a second liquidation in Chmielnik a month later on November 5, 1942. "This time, the remaining Jews, aware of the fate of the deportees, fled into the forests or went into hiding within the ghetto," the reference book states. Simon Wiesenthal records the same information, adding, "Only a small number are deported to Treblinka or murdered."

Treblinka, the dreaded destination of most of Chmielnik's Jews, lies 177 miles northeast. Treblinka was the name of a Polish village, a small labor camp, and a major killing center. Germans established Treblinka I, the lesser-known work camp, in December, 1941, to enslave Poles and Jews. Treblinka II, coded "T.II," functioned as a "death camp" in the true sense of the term. Its first victims, Jews from Warsaw's ghetto, suffocated from carbon monoxide poisoning on July 23, 1942. The Nazis gassed to death an estimated 730,000 to 750,000 Jews there through November, 1943.

Rumors about Treblinka and other killing centers, such as Belzec, Sobibor, and Auschwitz, spread via a handful of escapees and the resistance movement. Consequently, even Jews isolated in ghettos had some notion that the Reich's so-called resettlement camps were not pleasant places; still, they never could have foreseen the magnitude of the killing and suffering.

Saul Jurysta was better-informed. He belonged to the Socialist party and had served as a messenger for the Bund, Hashomer Hazair, and other Jewish organizations in Warsaw. He knew Treblinka's purpose, but he could not coax his family, friends, and neighbors in Chmielnik to resist. "They didn't believe that we go to death," Jurysta said. "They said I was crazy, that I would bring disaster to our town, to the Jews, if I kill a German or start a fire." Jurysta proposed setting a fire to distract the Nazis and to give some Chmielnik Jews time to escape. He figured that killing Nazis would be the best way to alert the world about the plight of

Jews. "I thought maybe the women and children in Germany will hear what's going on here and they'll make noise in Germany. My friends laughed at me," Jurysta said. "I lived with the impression that I'm going to die anyway. I felt we were all lost. I thought, 'If I'm going to die, I should die as a fighter.'"

It angers Jurysta that some thinkers, such as Hannah Arendt, have suggested that Jews went as sheep to the slaughter. He likens the enslavement of young Jews in labor camps to Delilah's act of cutting Samson's hair. Communities like Chmielnik were depleted of their strength before the final deportations to gas chambers, he argues. Those left behind, mostly children, the elderly, and young mothers — all weakened by hunger — could not defend themselves. "Who could be the fighter against Germany when they came with all their ammunition?" Jurysta asks. "If all these workers were taken away, who would be the fighter against Hitler?"

Jurysta's recollection of October and November, 1942, is a remarkable personal account of how he evaded the liquidations of Chmielnik, Klemantow, and Stopnica. When he couldn't get anyone to agree to his diversionary tactics, he tried to outrun the Nazis. His tale of flight began on October 1, when Jurysta bribed his way off one of the trucks bound for Skarzysko-Kamienna. He could not talk his brother, Elia, into joining him. "I'm a gambling man. I take risks. My brother was afraid. He said, 'They're going to kill you.' I jumped down from the truck. I told the German, 'I'm sick. I can't go to work.' I gave him the money. He told me to run away." Two other Jews took Jurysta's lead, but Elia did not budge. In an instant, the two brothers were parted forever. Elia died several months later in Skarzysko-Kamienna's notorious Werk C section. "It bothers my conscience," Jurysta said. "Why didn't I force my brother to come down from the truck?"

Jurysta is the sole survivor of a family of 14. For many Jews like him, the chaotic, desperate scramble to avoid the gas chambers tore apart families and provided no time for farewells.

Usher Tarek, then 17, accompanied his brother and nephew

to Skarzysko-Kamienna, but he sneaked out alone. After only two days, Tarek calculated that his odds of staying alive were slim. On the first day, he endured 12 hours of back-breaking labor, assembling missiles. Then he helped another prisoner carry huge cans of coffee to the barracks. "It burned against our ribs. The guard was a Ukrainian. He started hitting us with the butt of a rifle," Tarek said. "I felt it was no use to being there. I took a chance and got away." Tarek took shelter in a bush in a camp section that was not enclosed. At night, he slipped away, but never set foot in Chmielnik. Nazis rounding up Jews for work assignments apprehended Tarek in Starachowice. Tarek toiled in that city's labor camp until mid-1944, when the S.S. evacuated him to Auschwitz. "You figured one way or another you would be dead," Tarek said. "I lost a family. Before the war, my family consisted of almost 200 people. I was the youngest son from seven brothers and one sister. There were 21 grandchildren." After the war, there were only two grandchildren: Tarek and his brother, Harry.

Saul Zernie reached the same conclusion as Tarek: he would not last long in Skarzysko-Kamienna. Assigned to different sections of the camp, Zernie and his father never saw each other again. His father later died in Werk B. Saul withstood the rigors of Werk A for two weeks. Then, late one night, he jumped the fence and hopped a freight train. Days later, in Chmielnik, Saul could not find his mother and four younger sisters. They had been shipped to Treblinka. He was utterly alone.

Occurring on the spur of the moment, decisions to flee tragically separated friends and relatives throughout Europe.

A moment of panic, a sudden impulse to run, a wave of fear sometimes resulted in a lifetime of heartache and regret. In her own flight from the Nazis, Helen Rozenek Jurysta crossed paths with an uncle in Nowy Korczyn. "My mother found one of her brothers." It should have been a joyous reunion, but Jurysta's uncle was beside himself with grief. "He jumped down from the buggy," Jurysta said, describing a deportation of the town's Jews. "He was mentally sick. He left his wife and two beautiful children. He was mentally sick for what he had done."

The Garfinkels and several other families tried to cling together to dodge deportation from Chmielnik.

Late one night, Sara awakened Regina, Rachel, and Fishel to prepare them to leave home. "My mother put a blanket in the middle of the room, and we put some belongings there," Regina said. The Musial family arrived to collect some of the Garfinkels' prized possessions, including the silver candlesticks and velvet bedspreads. To this day, Regina isn't certain whether the Musials bought what they took, agreed to hold those items, or were paid to protect them. There was no time to think. "When you're fearful, you don't even ask questions because you don't want to know what the answers will be. I wasn't going to ask. I think subconsciously you don't want to know. I just went along. As long as you're with parents, you feel they know best," Regina said. "Looking back, it was ridiculous to think we could escape by going to a town a few miles away."

At the time, however, Regina had no idea where they were headed. With a little food and a change of clothes, the Garfinkels met their neighbors in Chmielnik's outskirts to catch a cargo train. "People laid on the ground to listen for the train," Regina said. The band of runaways assumed the neighboring town of Rakow would be safe — having heard most of its Jews had already been "relocated" to Treblinka. At some point, they got off the train and entered the forest. The journey drained Bela's energy. "We walked and walked and walked in the fields. We thought that Chmielnik was finished and in Rakow that they'll leave the Jews alone," Bela said. "We were tired. It was raining. But there was no place to go. We could hear shooting and killing. We hide and hide and hide." When the group stopped walking, Regina nestled her head against her mother. For hours, maybe days, she sat, not daring to look up. "I just remember being so close to her — me, Rachel, and Fishel — all three of us being so close to her, suffocating her, holding on," Regina said. Sara tried to comfort her little ones by stroking their heads and patting their backs. "I don't think we looked up or down or any other place. You were afraid to lift your head up. We were listening for things to happen." All Regina could hear were gunshots.

Esther Pasternak Tarek, who is younger than Regina, remembers how frightened she was in the melee. She and her older sister, Bela, ran to the Rakow forest, where they were supposed to meet their parents. They found several hundred Chmielnik Jews but not one relative among them. The Garfinkels might have been in the crowd, but that is not certain. The group instructed little Esther to go to the town of Rakow for information. She got lost. "Anywhere I go, it was the middle of the woods," Esther said. "It was raining. I was hungry. I didn't know how to get out from the woods. I was a few days in the woods. Finally, I meet a Polish man. He told me to holler as I walked with him to market. That's how I found the group."

Kalman Mapa and his family also sought refuge in Rakow, but they traveled with another, much smaller group of Chmielnik Jews. Mapa's former teacher, Mrs. Wit, who happened to be the Chmielnik train master's wife, warned him that the S.S. planned to deport all of Chmielnik's Jews. "She said, 'Mapa, you have to run away.' This was a big help. We have to go so nobody should see us. If the Polands see us, not too good for us." The Mapas, the Silverbergs, and a few other families boarded a cargo train to Rakow, Mapa continued, and camped out for several days in the town's synagogue. They decided to return to Chmielnik after learning the S.S. planned to imprison the rest of Rakow's Jews. "On the way back, we had lots and lots of troubles. We went to the small train. The Poles took us. They started to beat us up. They took our money. They took away our things," Mapa said. The families then opted to walk the 20 kilometers to Chmielnik — a difficult journey, given the illness of Mapa's father. "We find a few people dead in the forest. The Polish people killed the Jewish people."

The treachery continued. Mapa saw a Polish man pass on a bicycle. A half-hour later, a pair of S.S. officers arrived on motorcycles. Oddly enough, Mapa and his entourage were allowed to proceed to Chmielnik without interference.

Historian Martin Gilbert describes the Rakow forest not only as a hiding place for Jews but also as a clandestine execution site used by the S.S. For example, in late 1942, the Jewish residents of Piotrkow were forced to dig their own graves in the forest — five long ditches. Then the S.S. shot 560 men, women, and children into those trenches.

Chmielnik's runaways were temporarily spared. Instead of shooting them, the Germans ordered the Jews to hold up their hands and march. They stopped in the orchard, and gunfire ensued. A bullet whizzed by Regina's ear. The Jews walked to Chmielnik's center with their arms raised and their eyes downcast. As they passed the synagogue, Regina realized the guns were no longer aimed at the group, that there was no immediate threat. The Nazis were simply amusing themselves by humiliating Jews. "Our heads were down, our hands were up, but there was no one there," Regina said. "It was the biggest joke."

The Germans confined the Chmielnik Jews in a smaller ghetto. Barred from occupying their own homes, the Garfinkels and several other families shared a house belonging to some acquaintances sent to Treblinka. "It was very crowded. Where you sat, that's where you slept," Regina said. Other relatives joined them in the cramped quarters: Isaac's wife and three children. "She didn't have a chance. She could go to a labor camp, but she didn't want to leave the children," Regina said. "I remember how sorry I felt for them, and I don't know why." Regina credits her parents for masking their anxieties. "They never instilled fears. My mother said, 'This is the way it is. This is temporary.' I had the feeling they knew what it was all about, and it's something that would pass." Despite food shortages and the overriding fear of deportation, people tried to comfort one another and to share what little they had. Saul Zernie met Sara Garfinkel in Chmielnik's ghetto shortly after his escape from Skarzysko-Kamienna. "It was a nice family. She said, 'Why don't you come over?' She gave me something to eat." Then Zernie searched for the relatives he would never find.

Esther Pasternak Tarek and her sister found their home vacant and their parents missing. "It was too late," Esther said. "My entire family, parents, and everyone is gone."

Some of Chmielnik's last Jews clung to the faint hope that the worst was over, but Bela felt overpowered by doom. "Even in Chmielnik, you don't care anymore because tomorrow they come in and kill you," she said. One afternoon, after Regina had left the ghetto to buy bread, the Nazis roused Chmielnik's Jews from their houses. They divided families, separating young adults from children and older adults. Bela stood on the left. Her parents, Rachel, and Fishel gathered on the right, near a long line of horse-drawn wagons. Kalman and Sara tried to give some jewelry to Bela, but there was not enough time. "The Nazis told everyone to throw their jewelry on the ground. If you didn't want to do that, the dogs would take care of it. They put the jewelry in a pail," Bela said. "The Nazis told us to turn around so we wouldn't see the horses and buggies leaving. I wanted to say goodbye. I couldn't because the dog will eat me up. Germans have such big dogs. I am not exaggerating. Those S.S. men, they stood and smile and smoke cigarettes." Mary Kleinhandler, eyewitness to Chmielnik's first liquidation, also noticed the Nazis distributing baskets for the confiscation of jewelry, watches, and money.

On returning to the ghetto, Regina saw her parents, Rachel, Fishel, and other Jews sitting in wagons. The Nazis wouldn't allow in the tow-headed girl. Regina kept telling them her mother, father, sister, and brother were part of the caravan, but the Nazis didn't believe her. She frantically waved to her family, but they did not respond. "I ran in at one point, and they chased me back out. I told the Germans, 'My parents are here.' I was crying. They didn't listen. They didn't believe me."

A Jewish policeman later explained to Regina that her parents and siblings intentionally ignored her so that she would be saved. "There were a lot of Polish people standing on the sidewalk watching. The Polish people didn't seem to care. They were watching what was happening like a circus came to town. Someone said, 'Bela is here.' That calmed me down."

Esther Pasternak Tarek, her sister, and Saul Zernie also sat on the wagons, which, unbeknownst to them, were bound for Treblinka by way of Stopnica. Following their instincts, they jumped off when no one was looking. The Pasternak sisters sought shelter in the basement of their home. Every few days, a kindly neighbor put food on the steps for them. "Of course, we were scared," Esther said. "We had fantasies. We thought about my brother in Israel, that he would come down with a plane, that he's going to take us out."

Bela Garfinkel, meanwhile, felt alone, not knowing the destiny of her parents or the whereabouts of Regina. After Selektion, the S.S. escorted Bela and other working-age Jews to a building guarded by Jewish police.

Regina still couldn't enter Chmielnik's ghetto, so a Polish acquaintance offered to take her home. The woman's husband, a Chmielnik policeman, had known Kalman and Sara well, but he didn't allow Regina to spend the night. He said he was afraid of the risk. Regina re-entered the ghetto in the late afternoon and met Saul Zernie. Together they ferreted out a secret place: the attic crawl space in the building where the Kaufman family formerly had lived.

The next morning, Saul and Regina parted to hunt for new places of refuge. Regina went to the Musials' nearby farm. Years earlier, one of the family's daughters, Stasia, had repeated to Sonia the Catholic priest's "blood libel" defamation against Jews. Although Kalman and Sara had turned over some of their belongings to Mrs. Musial, Regina was shocked, nonetheless, to see her parents' two maroon velvet bedspreads in use. Even more disturbing was the sight of the Garfinkels' credenza in the Musials' home. The Musials had not taken the credenza the night the Garfinkels fled to Rakow.

The Garfinkel siblings debate among themselves about whether the Musials took unfair advantage of their absence. In general, after ridding a town or area of Jews, the Germans seized furniture, silver, art, linens, and other valuables. Neighbors then helped themselves to the remnants — often moving into the abandoned Jewish households.

Although the Musials were sympathetic, Regina said, they were fearful of being caught sheltering a Jew. Consequently, they allowed Regina to sleep in the barn, not in the house. "They took me out to the stable. It was very dark that night. I sat in a corner. I was afraid of getting kicked by the cows and horses." Before dawn, Mr. Musial entered the barn with a lantern. "It was very dark. He apologized. He said it was too risky. I had no place to go."

Regina re-entered the then-sparsely populated ghetto and found Bela. "A Jewish policeman said, 'Bela is here.' It was a relief. I felt like I have got somebody here. I felt like I have somebody to protect me. It's almost like she took over where my mother left. She said, 'We're together. I am here.' I don't think I would have tried or cared without Bela. We leaned on each other after that." A young farmer offered to help the two sisters. "This guy was nice," Bela said, "but I thought his wife was jealous. They were young. We were young. I could see the woman didn't like us. I said, 'It's no good, Regina. She's not going to hold us here.'"

Bela and Regina joined some Jewish teenagers and families in one house. "At this point, everyone felt that we would be safe there, but it didn't turn out," Regina said. "We talked a lot about where my parents might be, but at this time, nobody talked about the death camps. We were told that they went to a labor camp."

To cope, Regina blocked thoughts of her family's plight and the rumors of death camps. It wasn't until after the war that she learned her parents, along with Rachel and Fishel, had been gassed in Treblinka. "In the beginning, we didn't talk about Auschwitz, Treblinka," Bela said. "We know they're building this for the Jewish people, but we don't realize what this is."

Like Regina, Kalman Mapa has a flood of disjointed memories about Chmielnik's various liquidations and his family's panicked flight to Rakow. Mapa, his brother, and two sisters did not budge from the basement the day his parents were taken to Treblinka. Mapa later heard that his father had been killed before reaching the gas chambers and that his mother had cried her heart out afterwards. Mapa's cousin, a Jewish policeman, persuaded Mapa to go to Kielce's work camp. Forced labor, crude shelter, and substandard food rations seemed more appealing, Mapa reasoned, than being without food in Chmielnik's vacant buildings.

Esther Pasternak Tarek emerged from her basement to learn what was happening in Chmielnik: "I went out like a decoy. I saw signs that said whoever was in hiding should give up or they would be shot." She and her sister turned themselves in, and they landed in Kielce's work camp. Saul Zernie surrendered, too. "I volunteered to go to Kielce," Zernie said. "It was November. It was cold. There was nothing to eat. I couldn't put up sleeping one day on one farm and another day on another farm."

The Nazis herded Zernie, Bela, Regina, and other Jews into trucks bound for Kielce's munitions factories. Regina recalls her departure from Chmielnik as uneventful. "It was a very small group. They were all young people, somebody like myself, my friend, Bela, the few Jewish policemen. Nobody resisted. Nobody wanted to stay. It was fairly quiet, no guns, no dogs." Regina and Bela never returned to their hometown again.

The last recorded reference about Chmielnik's Jewish population cites an atrocity several months later, on March 5, 1943: "In Chmielnik, Poland, 1,300 Jews are murdered by the S.S.," Simon Wiesenthal writes in *Every Day Remembrance Day*.

Tosia Fastag Bottner and her sister were fugitives in Chmielnik throughout the cold winter of 1942 and 1943. They moved from one empty house to another at night and slept in cellars by day. Bottner's sister-in-law, imprisoned in Kielce's labor camp, arranged to sneak in one of the girls. That was possible because prisoners occasionally accompanied the S.S. to Chmielnik to gather food and to confiscate valuables. Weary of the harrowing, cat-and-mouse existence, Bottner's sister talked her into going to camp first. Bottner was ill, and her feet were swollen. The sister planned to enter the camp later, but Bottner never saw her again. "There were nine kids in my family," Bottner said. "My sister was killed by the Germans like all my family."

Kuba Zaifman, the young tailor from Kurowenki, was among a handful of Jews living in Chmielnik until July, 1943. The S.S. hand-picked him, a shoemaker, a carpenter, a few housekeepers, and some other personal servants. "I have no idea how many suits I made," Zaifman said. "We remained 10 people only — from a city of (more than) 10,000. It was worse than a ghost town."

Chapter Fourteen
FILLING QUOTAS

Regina and Bela were taken to Kielce, a larger town about 18 miles from Chmielnik. Although murder, mayhem, and slavery marked Kielce during World War II, the city gained notoriety for what transpired afterwards. Most reference books focus on Kielce's post-war pogrom, which triggered a mass exodus of remaining Jews from Eastern and Central Europe. A close friend of Helen and Sonia lost her husband in the attack, an experience so devastating she cannot speak of it.

On July 4, 1946, an unruly mob assaulted about 150 Holocaust survivors, killing 42 and wounding 50. Representing the remnants of as many as 25,000 Kielce Jews before the war, the survivors had returned to rebuild their shattered lives. The ugly crime, reminiscent of the city's 1918 pogrom cited in history texts, culminated the centuries-long pattern of anti-Semitism in Poland and forever labeled Kielce as a place of hatred, bigotry, and violence. Even the horrors of Nazi death camps, which annihilated thousands of Kielce's Jews along with anti-fascist Poles, failed to evoke compassion. Many Poles continued persecuting Jews.

Henik "Henry" Moszenberg Kaufman avoided the bloodletting by a hair. As he traveled with his mother and stepfather from Chmielnik to Kielce, the car radio broadcast news of the attack. On arriving, they hid with some friends. They felt safe, Henik said, because his stepfather had a gun. Henik still owns a Polish document identifying him as a survivor of the 1946 Kielce pogrom.

That incident, entrenched anti-Semitism, and similar post-war murders of Jews in such towns as Biala Podlaska explain why the Garfinkels and many Shoah victims did not stay in Poland.

During the war, Kielce served as a prison to Regina and Bela. To them, the town symbolized a bleak existence of constantly being overworked, underfed, and demoralized. "I was older, and I was taller, so they gave me different work, heavier work," Bela said of her assignment to ammunition. "More production, more intense, and more horrible. If there's something wrong, they make you work more, they give you more hours."

Germany established three labor camps in Kielce during the summer of 1942. The original work force consisted of 2,000 Kielce Jews who had not been sent to Treblinka's gas chambers, according to *Encyclopaedia Judaica*. The Ludwikow camp contained a foundry. The Henrykow camp functioned as a carpentry center. An entry dated August 20, 1942, in Simon Wiesenthal's *Every Day Remembrance Day* pinpoints the creation of Kielce's slave labor site: "During a four-day Aktion, 21,000 Jews are deported from the ghetto of Kielce, Poland, to Treblinka. The ghetto is thus essentially liquidated and the remaining 2,000 Jews are moved to a labor camp."

Bela and Regina toiled in Kielce's Hasag-Granat complex of quarries, workshops, and munitions plants, which included a factory for Granat grenades. Regina's recollection of Hasag-Granat provides impressions rather than a chronology of key events, such as arrival, processing, beatings, and executions. Like Nathan, Sonia, and Helen, Regina and Bela chose top-level sleeping bunks in their wooden barracks. The bunks, made of three shelves, were separated from each other by narrow aisles. The quarters were cramped, Regina said, judging from the ability of 60 women to speak to each other without shouting. Nearly all of their barrack mates were from Nowy Korczyn. The plain barrack offered amenities that the prisoners of Skarzysko-Kamienna could only imagine: blankets, two or three windows, a pot for fetching water, and a steel drum for burning sawdust. The makeshift furnace emitted minimal heat during the winter; Regina and Bela still shivered after piling the royal blue coat sewn by Isaac on their blanket.

Crude shelters outside contained water faucets, showers, and latrines, which were holes in the ground.

In the factory, Regina and Bela were obliged to make two-centimeter bullets. The labor shifts, initially eight hours, were extended to 10 hours and then to 12 hours. At first, Regina, a mechanic, and three women operated eight machines and extracted finished bullets from them. As the shifts grew longer, the work force shrank. Eventually, the responsibility of manning all eight machines fell to Regina, who stood on a box to feed steel rods into them. The S.S. imposed more stringent production quotas, measured in pounds of bullets. "If we made a quota, they would get us a helper," Regina said. "They increased the quotas until it didn't become a job; it became a torture. If you didn't make your quota, you were penalized. You had to work longer, after your 12 hours, or you were beaten."

Regina worked more than 12 hours many times. Like Helen, she wished to transform herself. "There were big windows. I remember seeing a dead dog there stretched out. I was so tired. I couldn't work. I couldn't sleep. It was too much, 12 hours. I remember wishing I was that dog." In better moments, when she lay on her bunk, Regina envisioned living in Chmielnik, sleeping peacefully in a bed, eating and drinking at the kitchen table, observing the Sabbath with her family.

Those visions shielded Regina from Hasag-Granat's terrible reality. Had the guards and S.S. known she was only 12 years old, they would have shot Regina outside the camp or shipped her to Treblinka. Touched by her tender age and look of utter innocence, many prisoners and foremen were sympathetic toward Regina. "I was aware I have to look older. Bela had a lot of people she consulted with," Regina said. "After work some girls had to clean the barracks of the S.S., but the police were warned to never touch me. Once a policeman tried to take me to clean the S.S. barracks. The other prisoners were protective. They gave that policeman hell for it."

The camp's Jewish supervisor, Rozencweig; a Jewish police-man, Motek Pisaz; and Bela brainstormed to save Regina. They procured high-heeled shoes to make her appear taller and scarves, or *babushkas,* to make her look older. Padding inside her clothes added fullness to her figure. During roll call every morning, Bela positioned Regina on a box in the middle of hundreds of prison-ers. Conflicting advice bewildered Regina: "One person said, 'Put your head down.' Then another person said, 'No, that will draw attention to yourself.'"

Other adolescents fearful of being discovered included: Lola Preis Sylman, formerly of Staszow, now in Toronto; Kalman Mapa's youngest sister, Chawa; Esther Pasternak Tarek; and Angelica Druker. Saul Jurysta, also imprisoned in Kielce, describes one hunt for children: "One day there was an order to take out all the kids, ages eight to 12. They didn't say they would kill the kids, but we know. They find some boys hiding in the barracks. They took out about 20 or 25 kids. The fathers saw them taking out their kids. They couldn't do nothing." Kuba Zaifman, transferred to Kielce from Chmielnik in July, 1943, also watched the Germans take away the youngest children. The group included Yosel Friedman, who was only 7 or 8. With adolescents, such as Regina, "They looked away," Zaifman said. "As long as she went to work, she was okay."

Sylman, who was 13 on entering Kielce, regarded Regina as a friend. "Regina helped me just by talking and being friendly. We were closer in age. This kept us maybe closer," Sylman said. "Regina was on the quiet side. She was a very refined girl."

Chawa Mapa, then 12 years old, was protected by her two brothers, Kalman and Chil, and her older sister, Leja. "I was wor-ried about my youngest sister," Kalman Mapa said. "She was young just like Regina. They put her on shoes with high heels."

Tarek, who was only 11, relied on intuition to evade the roundup of children. "I had a terrible feeling," she said, recalling one intensive search. "I didn't go out from the barrack. I must have been hiding under the bed. There was really no place to hide... I was right. They took all the young children. I must have a sixth sense. You learn all these tricks to hide, to survive."

Selektionen occurred routinely. Workers who looked too old, too young, too weak, or too sick were pulled from the group, escorted from the camp, and shot. "Even when we got there, we knew," Regina said of her arrival to Kielce. "We could hear the shots. That's how we knew. Our neighbor, Mrs. Kaufman, was shot. She was in her 40s or early 50s. She was taken away, along with other people."

Getela Kaufman — from one of Chmielnik's rich Jewish families — had bought herself some extra months of life. Knowing she was over-age, she used bribes to get admitted to Kielce's labor camp, but that did not change her fate. It merely altered the circumstances: Getela Kaufman was shot in Kielce instead of gassed in Treblinka. She came to the camp with her daughter, Edie; a friend, Mrs. Lasman of Lodz; and Mrs. Lasman's daughter. Edie survived the war, but Mrs. Lasman was executed with Mrs. Kaufman. The two older women's conscious decision to divert their destination from Treblinka to Kielce repeated itself a million different ways. Many Shoah victims agonized over similar choices, or forks in the road, which, all too often, led to death.

Guidance, support, and protection from others — especially from her sisters later in the war — opened the path of life to Regina. On several occasions, Rozencweig instructed Regina to stay inside the barrack rather than report to roll call. His precautions enabled Regina to avoid major Selektionen, during which her youthful looks might have been noticed. "If I had to fight for myself, I don't think I would have survived. Bela tells me I survived because of her, but I don't remember doing anything. I remember not finishing my food. I would say, 'I don't want to eat anymore,' and I gave my food to Bela."

Despite all of Bela's efforts to save Regina, they never talked about death. Mentally, they existed on a strange plane of denial, and their discussions reflected that. "We kept everything superficial," Regina said. "We never spoke about my parents." If Regina ventured to ask questions, Bela didn't give realistic answers. As their mother Sara had done, Bela masked her own deep-seated worries with a matter-of-fact nonchalance. "Bela — I was always like her baby sister. She made sure that people made sure I ate or went to sleep," Regina said. "Bela said, 'From now on, it's going to be okay. This is what's taking place now, but tomorrow it's going to be different.' Bela never provided any explanations." In accepting Bela's statements, Regina didn't realize the Germans planned to kill all the Jews, yet she sensed Bela's fears. "I remember missing my parents terribly. I was missing everybody but not talking about it," Regina said. "I couldn't bring myself to talk about it, even with Bela." Consequently, loneliness outranked Bela as Regina's closest companion. "I didn't learn the full aspect of what was going on. I went along with everything in my own sad way."

The Jewish leader Rozencweig wielded little power, hampering his ability to help, Saul Jurysta said. "The Germans used the Jewish leaders as puppets." Rozencweig once beat and berated Jurysta to impress the German S.S., but the punishment looked worse than it was. Consequently, Jurysta did not perceive that Rozencweig relished his duties. "As a leader from a camp, he was not bad. If Chaim (Rozencweig) needed to do something bad, he send a Jewish police," Jurysta said. "He got orders to send away these kids. Another time, he got an order to send away people to another camp, Pionek. They send away my wife's mother because she was older. Forty-five was old already. Chaim made the list. He was sometimes the decider of life and death. Can you imagine?"

Helen Rozenek Jurysta painfully remembers her mother's departure. She knew her mother was in trouble from the start of entering Kielce. "My mother was between 39 and 40 years old. She wasn't as fast. I have to make a little more. We had a quota. We each had to make 10 or 12 plates. If not, we couldn't go home. We were all oily, on our faces and our clothes. The conditions were impossible." What's more, Jurysta and her mother endured numerous beatings. "They said we sabotaged some bullets because some bullets weren't right. They took us to a room. We had to take off all our clothes. He took a whip. He beat us up. The next day we couldn't even sit. We had to work standing up 12 hours. This wasn't the first time. It was many times." Within two months of their imprisonment in Kielce, Helen Rozenek Jurysta and her mother were brutally separated. "All of a sudden, a truck shows up. The Gestapo looks around. They took out all the women who are the same age as my mother. They took them on the truck. I start crying. My brother said maybe we can go with my mother. One of the Germans hit us with something so we wouldn't go near the truck." It wasn't until after the war that Jurysta learned her mother had been taken to Pionek.

Two sisters, Evelyn Szczebakowska Cala and Regina Szczebakowska Zalcman, originally from Lodz, now in Brooklyn, New York, credit Rozencweig with trying to do good. "I said, 'Please don't separate us! Let us be together,'" Zalcman recalled. "Chaim Rosencweig tried not to separate families. He said he would try to keep families together." Cala said, "If somebody is a leader in a camp, you'll always find something against them, but I can't say one word against Chaim Rozencweig." His opposite, a German officer called Kirshbaum, distinguished himself through sadism. "He was a very mean man. He was an older man. He was real S.S. He walked around with a whip," Regina said. "Just for the fun of it, he took people at random and whipped them."

Another German, Milke, also beat workers. Saul Jurysta was one of his victims. "I heard about this. He chose five or six people every day to beat for no reason," Jursyta said. "He called me to a room full of barrels of oil. I had to pull my pants down. He gave me six lashes. A man in my barrack had 25 lashes. He begged us to kill him." Milke's sadism backfired, Jurysta said. "The machine run while he beat. After this happened a few weeks, the machines start breaking. They took Milke away. The Germans wanted production."

In contrast to Milke, Kirzner showed some compassion. The German officer caught Saul Jurysta dozing while seated on a wooden box. "Kirzner pulled my hair and lifted my head. Could you imagine what I thought? I knew I would be killed." Gozzinski, a Jew who had accompanied Kirzner into the factory, stammered, "All the machines are working." Unlike most of his colleagues, Kirzner turned down a chance to punish or kill. "Kirzner was not bad as a person," Jurysta concluded. "If he were here today, I would take him out to dinner."

The two Szczebakowska sisters developed a strong friendship with Regina and Bela in Kielce. They shared the same barrack, and Cala worked in the same factory as Bela. "We sat together arm-by-arm. We were very close," Cala said. "If I wasn't feeling well, Bela would sing. She had a beautiful voice. Bela was always singing." The songs, some Polish, others Yiddish, animated other prisoners. Cala and Zalcman each said Regina's sweetness and cheerful demeanor made her a favorite in the barracks.

Yet Regina felt empty. Intimidated by the brutality of camp existence, drained from long workdays, and weakened from deficient rations of bread and soup, Regina was vulnerable. One day, Regina's hair became tangled in the wires of a bullet-making machine. Moving parts battered her skull and cut her scalp before the mechanic turned off the assembly. The near-fatal accident caused bleeding and swelling. Even after her bruises healed weeks later, Regina suffered headaches for many months.

"Isn't it amazing, there was no infection?" Regina marveled. "A couple of incidents like this happened to other people. They were supposedly taken to the hospital. They never came back." For that reason, Bela and Rozencweig rejected seeking medical help. First, Regina's age might be exposed. Second, the camp "hospital" had little, if any, medicine, bandages, or other supplies. Bela and Rozencweig considered cutting Regina's hair to accelerate the healing, but they were afraid that would attract too much attention to her injury.

To endure the hardships and perils of Kielce, Regina blocked out thoughts. "I started working and thinking like a zombie. I was never thinking. I never complained. I never said anything to anybody. I went around like a robot. My mind was like a blank. That's the only way I could survive. I don't remember asking, 'Why are we here? Where are we going? What's going to happen?'" Some thoughts seeped in, nonetheless. "I remember crying myself to sleep every night for my parents."

Chapter Fifteen
A REAL MENSCH

Bela also felt numb to feelings, but she devoted herself to Regina's welfare. She begged the Jewish policeman overseeing the barracks to help protect her baby sister. "I said, 'I don't care about myself. I don't want anything. Just help me take care of my Regina. She's too young. They'll take her away.'" The policeman, Motek Pisaz, a Jew from Nowy Korczyn, suggested that Regina would attract less attention during Selektionen if she stood behind Bela. Motek also provided some small, but life-saving favors to the two sisters.

When Bela and Regina ended their shift late at night, Motek unlocked the showers so they could bathe. The accumulation of toxic oils from the bullet-making machines caused many prisoners to become weak and ill, so Bela made showering a priority, even over food. "You have to put oil on the machines in order to work," Bela said. "Everything was full of oil — our feet, our hands. We have no hot water. At night, there was no lights. There was a war going on." Motek guided them to the showers. Sometimes he gave Bela and Regina leftover soup. They ate the extra rations in the showers so that other inmates would not see, ask questions, and develop jealousies. "He did a big favor," Bela said. "If they catch him at night to come to the camp where the girls are, they shoot him."

On the pretext of checking the fuse box, Motek entered the sisters' barrack to hide bread in their bunks while they worked. If Motek was on duty as a guard, Bela knew she wouldn't be frisked. She could then risk smuggling bread to her barrack from the munitions factory. Her Polish foreman sometimes hid bread and rolls at her bullet-making machines. "He was a human being. He saw our problems," Bela explained. "When I looked in the cabinet, the package was there. I knew this package was for me." Bela doesn't recall the foreman's name, but she is grateful to him. The S.S. rotated the Polish foremen, however, so they would not bond with Jewish prisoners. Bela remains most indebted to Motek Pisaz.

"Until the last minute, Motek helped me," Bela said. "I liked him a little. I know he liked me. He always did me favors." The flirtation terrified Bela, however. "Motek had a special office. He always watched me when I go to work. He was always there when I come back from work. I am afraid of him like I am afraid of a German. I was afraid he would ask me to sleep in his barracks. I had to be careful with him. I know what is cooking. I said, 'Bela, play cool.'"

Jews appointed by the S.S. to police their own people received extra food and other rewards, such as private sleeping quarters. Bela feared being compromised. Having sex was a crime punishable by death, and pregnant women were executed. At Skarzysko-Kamienna, Sonia and Helen knew a Jewess who was pregnant on entering the camp, about the same time they had arrived. That woman gave birth in the latrine and let her baby drown in the sewage; otherwise, she would have faced a firing squad. Also in Skarzysko-Kamienna, a Jewish policeman and his wife delivered a baby in secret and killed it to avoid being killed themselves. Such incidents reveal the hideous evil of the Shoah: the Germans and their collaborators devised a system that sometimes forced the victims to become criminals. Another prisoner, a friend of Gutka, paid the ultimate price for her pregnancy. When her condition was discovered, she was shot, Helen said.

In Kielce, "Motek was always friendly. But I was always afraid he would ask me to go to his barrack. I would be afraid to say no. He never ever, ever asked me. That shows me he was a person," Bela said. "If Motek would be alive when we were liberated, I would have told him, 'Thank you.' I would say, 'You're a real mensch. You're a real person.' Motek was not proud of his job."

Regina remembers Motek as being protective, never calling on her for extra work. Although he did not abuse his authority, Regina said, he shouted at his fellow Jews in the presence of S.S. "He had a very good reputation. He was very nice," Regina said. "Sometimes he brought extra firewood for the stove to keep the barrack warm." Motek could not be friendly and helpful all the time. The S.S. expected him to play the disciplinarian. Bela saw him beat other prisoners. "He hit people, too. They could not go to work. They were half dead," Bela stated. "One time I saw it. I saw him hit a neighbor of mine from Chmielnik."

Even the best of Jewish police evoke controversy. "I personally didn't have anything to do with him," Kuba Zaifman said diplomatically of Motek Pisaz. "It's hard to judge. Some people say he was good. Some people say no. It's the same thing today with police in a city. Some policemen will give you ticket. Others, no."

The role of Jewish police was one of compromise and favors, Kalman Mapa said. "There are things that are very touchy." If Motek Pisaz beat his fellow Jews or committed crimes, it was not of his own accord. "Motek wasn't such a bad guy. He didn't do by himself. He was told what to do," Mapa said. "His brother was my best friend in camp." Mapa's cousin worked as a policeman in Kielce, too, but Mapa never sought his help. "He didn't do me favors, but I didn't need favors," Mapa said. "People say my cousin did bad. This was a very bad situation. It wasn't normal."

Saul Jurysta was not fond of the camp's Jewish police or leaders because they confiscated his shoes to give to the Germans. "I wore beautiful boots into the camp. Then I had to wear wooden shoes. It took me months and months to get some money to get some shoes."

Helen Rozenek Jurysta, originally from Lodz, credits Motek with rescuing her in 1942. She had been hiding in a cellar in the town of Nowy Korczyn. "It was a hole with 30 people. There was no air. We were laying there. They gave us some food and some water every now and then. We were there about five or six days.

We were very hungry." Jurysta's mother left the cellar to search for food. After more than three hours had passed, Jursyta crawled out of the hole to look for her mother. She found her at the home of an acquaintance, but a Gestapo official intercepted them. "We were white like a sheet. He said, 'From where are you?' He knew we weren't from this town (Nowy Korczyn). We didn't answer. We were so scared, we couldn't talk. He said to me and my mother, 'Come outside. Give me your rings.'" Quaking with fear, the two women peeled off their jewelry for the would-be executioner. He shouted, "Turn to the wall!" Certain she was drawing her final breaths, Jurysta began hyperventilating. "He took off his gun, ready to shoot us."

From nowhere, as though from heaven, a Jewish policeman intervened. Motek shouted, "Stop! Stop!" He persuaded the Gestapo that the two women might be useful for Hasag's work camp in Kielce. Their lives spared in an instant, mother and daughter almost welcomed imprisonment and slave labor over their hand-to-mouth existence as fugitives hiding in barns, haystacks, cellars, and huts.

Regina Szczebakowska Zalcman considered Motek to be a good friend. She had known him in the Lodz ghetto and in Nowy Korczyn, where she and her sister, Evelyn Szczebakowska Cala, tried to outrun the Germans. Their paths crossed again in Kielce. "Motek helped me," Zalcman said, "but he could not help everyone."

Conditions in Kielce were less harsh than those in Skarzysko-Kamienna. Nathan, Sonia, and Helen refer to Kielce as a "good camp" based on comparisons discussed with Bela and Regina. "If Regina be with me in Skarzysko, I don't know if she would survive," Sonia said. "In Skarzysko, there wasn't enough food. There was a big difference in our camp." Good, however, requires further definition. In Kielce, the food rations were more plentiful, clean uniforms and blankets were distributed, but Jews still died there. Bela noticed some newcomers to Hasag's factories could not endure the long work shifts, scant rations, and perpetual discomfort.

"There were people from rich neighborhoods in other cities. How long they survived? Eight days. They couldn't last. They couldn't sleep on the floor. Forty years at that time, you look 60. You don't go to the beauty shop. You don't go to have your nails done or a pedicure." Bela envied Mrs. Kornblum, a prisoner from Nowy Korczyn, who worked in the kitchen. "She was like my mother's age. When I look at her, I think, 'How lucky can she be? Why can't my mother come here and work in the kitchen?' I said to her, 'How lucky you are. You have so much food.' She said, 'It won't last forever.' I think she was taken away in the third selection." The grim surroundings made Bela treasure her royal blue coat, trimmed in fur, that much more. "I don't want to separate from this coat." It was Bela's connection to Isaac. She hoped to find him after the war.

Esther Pasternak Tarek is one survivor who can compare the work sites of Kielce and Skarzysko-Kamienna based on personal experience. She and her sister, Bela, were transferred from Kielce to Skarzysko-Kamienna's dreaded Werk C. "I really wasn't transferred. My sister was. I was hiding. Then I stepped forward," Tarek said. "I didn't want to be separated from my sister." Tarek's physical health diminished in Skarzysko-Kamienna, and she was shocked by what she saw. However, the emotional support from her sister — her only link to family and Chmielnik — strengthened Tarek's morale and may have, ultimately, saved her life.

Hearing of Skarzysko-Kamienna's bad reputation made Kalman Mapa value his relatively privileged job in Kielce. He unloaded steel and other supplies outside the camp. The work was dirty, but contact with civilians enabled Mapa to buy bread, which he smuggled to his three siblings working on the assembly lines. "If they catch me, they put me on a chair, and they gave me 30 or 40 lashes. I still have good signs," Mapa said, referring to his scars. "Of course, this happened often. I was young, I could take." The four Mapa siblings lived through the Holocaust despite many brushes with death. They, like the Garfinkels, are rare among survivors. "We are one in a million," Kalman said. "My brother and I always stayed together, and my two sisters stayed together. We are one in a million."

Kuba Zaifman said his job as Kielce's tailor was preferable to that of factory worker. His sewing skills were tested in such a way, however, that his barrack mates thought he would be executed. Once, a German officer, General Shlicht, demanded that Zaifman finish a gray leather coat. Apparently, Shlicht had seized the garment, which lacked sleeves, from a Jewish tailor's shop in Kielce. "I said, 'How can I finish this? There is no material. I have no material,'" Zaifman recalled. "He said, 'I don't care.'" Although Zaifman had never sewn leather, he procured a cowhide in town. He tried dyeing the skin, but he couldn't duplicate the coat's medium shade of gray. "I had an idea. I took a piece from the back — it was a pleat — and made sleeves from that. Then I took the new leather and made a new back pleat," Zaifman said. "Everyone said, 'You're not going to come back alive. He's going to kill you. He's going to shoot you.'" Pleased and confident with his handiwork, Zaifman delivered the coat. Shlicht offered a cigarette and said, "It is good."

Prisoners again predicted the tailor's demise after Shlicht gave him some suede to make gloves. They were to be a Christmas gift for Shlicht's brother-in-law. Zaifman had never sewn gloves, so he persuaded a housekeeper to lift a pair from Shlicht's quarters. Ever so meticulously, Zaifman took apart the gloves to make a pattern, and then he re-stitched them. His barrack mates did not expect to see Zaifman alive after he crafted new suede gloves. Proud of his finished product, the tailor walked tall to Shlicht's house. "They were amazed. They were happy. They gave me some soup," Zaifman said. "There were lots of tailors, but me they picked. I was the only one working as a tailor. They said (about me), 'Don't do nothing to him. He has gold hands.'"

Zaifman saw Bela and Regina in camp, but he rarely talked with them because he was preoccupied with survival. "You didn't care what anybody was doing. There was no time for that." Despite his comfortable job and the S.S.'s praise of his talents, Zaifman felt insecure. Kielce's poor conditions and violence appalled him. "Every day there were people dying from dirt and hunger. When people were a little bit sick and they couldn't work, they were shot," Zaifman said. "I lived with ammunition workers. At night they came home full of oil and dirty and not much to eat. It was crowded. It was impossible to describe." In contrast to the fancy attire he sewed for German officers and their families, Zaifman patched the worn and threadbare clothing of his fellow Jews. To this day, Zaifman isn't sure what prevented him from succumbing to despair. It is as inexplicable as the survival instinct. "We lived from day to day. We lived from hour to hour," Zaifman said. "Everybody wanted to live. We were young people, in the teens, and hoping for a better tomorrow. We were thinking to survive maybe a day."

Saul Zernie functioned best by keeping to himself. "I never talked to the Garfinkel sisters," he said. "Everybody had their own problems. I used to work 12 hours a day on the machinery. Then I would go to sleep." Tosia Fastag Bottner described the same tedious routine: "You lived from day to day. We worked in the ammunition. We came back for soup and bread. You laid down. There was nothing. We slept a few hours and start over again." Tragedy punctuated the monotony. "There was accidents every day. There was oil spills from the machines. It was a terrible time."

Evelyn Szczebakowska Cala almost severed a finger in the bullet-making machines, but she was able to get stitches and to continue working. Kielce's so-called amenities, which included rudimentary medical treatment, were deceiving. Cruelty and random violence erupted. A friend of Cala was chosen for transfer to Pionek. As Cala's friend boarded the bus, her mother followed to give her a coat. A guard shot the mother. "This was my very close friend. Her mother was handing her daughter a coat, and the soldier shot the mother for no reason," Cala said. "Each of us can write a different book, but it all comes to the same suffering."

Hot oil lubricating the machines scarred the skin. "I used to have little holes on my arms and legs and on my elbows and knees," Regina said. Tiny pits dotted Saul Jurysta's face. A mechanic, Jurysta maintained and fixed the bullet-making equipment he called *Stahlkern*. Assembly-line workers, mostly women, fed thin, steel rods 14 feet to 18 feet long through each machine, which spit out bullets within five minutes. "Everyone had eight machines to run, not just one. The machine ate up the rod so fast. If I was a good fixer for the machine, I didn't have much to do. I wasn't under the gun like the women," Jurysta explained. A terrible accident, similar to Regina's, befell his future wife, Helen Rozenek. "She put a rod into the machine. She bent down, and this rod catch her hair. Two rods pulled the hair from her head," Jurysta said. "It happened to a few people. The trouble was if you couldn't work, then you would be killed."

That is why Bela was so anguished when Regina's hair became enmeshed in the machine. "I see this, and I scream," Bela said, noting the German guard merely smiled at the accident. He could have stopped the machine, she said, but did nothing. The Polish foreman cut the electricity. "She bent down, and her hair got caught," Bela said. "She was too young. It was a very, very hard job. You have to work so fast. I said, 'Maybe Regina should work in a different place.' But Motek and Rozencweig couldn't do anything. They have no power." With no access to medicine, they could only douse cold water on Regina's head; she resumed working.

Regina tried to fend off thoughts and feelings. "I think, at the point where I was separated from my parents, I expected everything without fear," Regina said. "People said to be careful, safety first, but I didn't care. In camp I was not surprised by anything.

When they came in and took somebody out and shot them, I wasn't surprised. I thought, 'That's the way it is.' I never even stopped to think what could happen next, could they kill me or shoot me. The shootings were like an everyday thing."

The pressure was constant. "This was a regular torture to keep your eyes on the machines, 12 hours a day. If you didn't do it right, something would be wrong with the bullets. They watch to see if you make sabotage. The machine shouldn't be empty," Bela said. "You have to concentrate. Inside you're hungry, you're tired. I don't know how many times I wished I would be killed today. Every day, the same. Every day, the same. You're so preoccupied with your life, your piece of bread, you can't be concerned about anyone else. You don't know what you're doing yourself."

Despite its oppression, Kielce was what Bela called a "resort" compared with subsequent camps. It actually had a kitchen, where prisoners lined up for their rations of bread and soup twice a day. "I was lucky. I had enough food." Bela believes prominent Jews, such as Rozencweig, paid the Germans to get adequate rations. Saul Jurysta is also under the impression that wealthy Jews from Nowy Korczyn and other towns arranged their deportation to Kielce and paid some of the camp's expenses. "Kielce was something to grab like a straw in the water," Jurysta said. "People wanted to go to Kielce because they wanted to avoid Treblinka." Regina cited additional reasons for Kielce's more tolerable conditions. "The German leader of that camp was extremely fond of Rozencweig," she said. "I remember people talking, saying we are blessed." The soup and bread sustained energy but did not satisfy. "It was thin soup," Regina said. "The joke going around was: you have to make a dive to find a noodle." Bela remembered craving food: "I said after liberation I wanted to have a whole bread, not just a little."

The prospect of the war's end enabled some Jews to continue. "Why did we live so terrible?" Jurysta asked. "It was the hope. We knew the Germans would lose the war. We thought the Russians would come. Every Jew that went to death knew the Germans would lose the war. We didn't know if they would kill us all."

Motek tried to persuade Bela to escape, and he offered to include Regina in the plans. He explained the Soviet army was advancing west, that the S.S. would shut down Kielce's munitions factory and send Jewish prisoners to Germany. "He said, 'If you go to Germany, it will be very bad for you.'" Like her brother, Nathan, Bela reasoned that fleeing would be futile without a specific destination, hiding place, or outside contacts. She thought the risk was too great, and she was right. According to Bela, Jurysta, Mapa, Zaifman, and other survivors of the Kielce work camp, Motek was caught escaping and was killed.

"I didn't want to go with him. I don't care for him. Who's he? I want to go with everyone else," Bela said. "What's the difference? He was shot anyway. At that time, you have to be selfish. You don't think about anybody. They have their own problems."

Zaifman said his barrack mates had urged him to escape when he had a chance to do so while searching for the cowhide. Unescorted, the blonde Zaifman clutched an S.S. pass to enter the town of Kielce. "To the Germans, I looked like a Jew. To the Polacks, I looked like a Jew. They had a way of finding out," Zaifman said. "To the Jews, I looked like a German. They all said, 'Run away!' I said, 'Where am I going to go?' There was no place to run away. Where would I go? What would I do?" Zaifman, like Bela, wanted to face his destiny with his fellow Jews.

Chapter Sixteen
LIFELINES

Germans confined the Garfinkels to separate camps during much of World War II, from October, 1942, until mid-1944. Nathan, Sonia, and Helen toiled without a break in Skarzysko-Kamienna, while Bela and Regina labored non-stop in Kielce. As slaves condemned to death by Germany's policy of *Vernichtung durch Arbeit*, or "extermination through work," the Garfinkels arrived at their respective prisons with no more than the clothes on their backs. In an environment lacking decent food, shelter, and medical care, such items as pens, paper, money, and stamps were unobtainable luxuries. Needless to say, writing letters was not allowed — even if prisoners had the energy for correspondence. Jews learned of each other's whereabouts from one another and from the few guards and Polish foremen who were somewhat humane.

Trains and trucks carrying raw materials, machine parts, and supplies traversed the 22 miles between Skarzysko-Kamienna and Kielce. By talking to workers assigned to those shipments, some Jews located relatives, friends, and other loved ones. After all, Hasag operated several camps besides Skarzysko-Kamienna and Kielce. Whenever Nathan met outsiders, he asked about Chmielnik and the fate of its Jews. One of Nathan's contacts was Schreiber, a Jewish prisoner from Kielce, who helped deliver goods to Skarzysko-Kamienna. Schreiber told Nathan that Bela and Regina were alive.

Within a few weeks of entering Skarzysko-Kamienna, Nathan figured Sonia and Helen were in Werk B, and they found out he was in Werk A. The sisters began seeing Nathan on Sundays, when they and other Werk B prisoners bathed in Werk A's showers, a few kilometers away. Skarzysko-Kamienna's squalor was so intolerable, prisoners looked forward to cold showers once a week. Monday through Saturday, Sonia and Helen cleaned themselves in Werk B's washroom, a crude wooden shed with several sinks. "For animals, they would build a nicer thing," Sonia said. "There were thousands of people and only a few sinks." Hundreds of women waited each morning to use the washroom and to splash their faces with cold water before reporting to work. In the winter, after Sonia washed her hair, it froze into icicles as she walked to the barracks. The washroom provided the prisoners with their only source of drinking water.

When they reported to the showers on Sundays, Sonia and Helen brought Nathan potato flakes and bread, which contributed greatly to his survival. "It was in the Nazis' interest to have people take showers for health reasons. It gave me an opportunity to be together with Sonia and Helen, to get more to eat, and to help other people," Nathan said. "When I saw Sonia and Helen, they looked tired. You could see this in them. You could see stress, worry."

Sonia and Helen were upset to see Nathan give away the food they had so painstakingly saved for him. They were angry to see other prisoners preying on their brother's kindness. The generosity they had so admired in Nathan at home was an all-too-obvious handicap in camp, where hunger ruled. After several months, it gnawed at Nathan, too. Slowly, Skarzysko-Kamienna's adverse conditions crushed his big heart and high ideals. Nathan began depending on the rations his sisters accumulated. Every bit of food was precious — even to prisoners working in the mill with its seemingly endless supply of potatoes. The daily allotment of two pounds of bread for eight people, or four ounces per person, was insufficient to sustain life. Helen's preoccupation with food motivated her to devise survival strategies. "If you stood in the front of the line, the soup was watery. But, if you were too far at the end of the line, there wasn't enough soup," Helen said. "Once

I found a bandage in my soup. I showed it to the foreman, but he didn't care. He said, 'So what?' I squeezed out the bandage and drank the soup. This is hunger."

Starvation and death climbed to alarmingly high rates — even for labor camps. While statistics in history texts shock readers, they don't capture, as eyewitness accounts do, the complete desperation of Jewish prisoners. Each day, the haggard munitions workers walked near the potato mill's dump site. Mounds of peelings and other waste, set aside to feed livestock and to make fertilizer, were off limits, but hunger drove some individuals to break the rules. "Sometimes people would throw themselves on the piles of garbage to look for food," Sonia said. "The guards would hit them, and they would scream."

The ammunition workers straggling past also troubled Etka Raitapfel Baumstick. One day, a boy ran from the group to beg in the potato mill, and Etka handed him some dehydrated potato flakes. Guards caught the boy rejoining his co-workers, and they thrashed him. Etka watched in anguish from the factory window. "This I will never forget. To see him being beaten, I suffered. He wouldn't tell who gave the potato chips. We saw the punishment he took for not telling. He knew what would happen to me," Etka said. "I didn't know the boy. It was the one time that he came in for chips. I don't know what happened to him. He was not from Chmielnik."

Saving food for Nathan presented special challenges to Sonia and Helen. Theft among prisoners made hiding rations in their bunk impractical. The sisters needed a secure storage place. They asked a Jewish carpenter to make a wooden box, and they paid him with a week's worth of bread rations. The sisters spent another week's bread supply on a lock. "People stole food from each other," Helen said. "Once they broke the lock and stole the bread in our trunk."

Stealing was common, said Mania Poper Cherston. In the beginning, she saved part of her bread for the next day. "You have to be strong to have will power to keep this half slice of bread for breakfast. Sometimes I couldn't sleep knowing this bread was under my head." Several mornings Cherston woke to find her bread missing. "It's unbelievable. People become animals over food. These are good people, these are nice people, but they were hungry. When you're hungry, you see something, you grab." Cherston relinquished her self-imposed discipline of saving part of her rations. "I learned to eat my bread with my soup. I didn't want to worry at night what would happen to the bread." Nathan reached the same conclusion near war's end.

Besides food, the Garfinkel sisters smuggled paper sacks from the potato mill to the barracks. Prisoners fashioned shoes and sleeping tunics from the bags, which were several layers thick. The S.S. sporadically distributed clothing as the prisoners' garments fell apart, but they rarely passed out shoes. On entering Skarzysko-Kamienna, Helen and Sonia owned plain leather shoes with straps, similar to Mary Jane-style flats. "How long could those shoes last? We exchanged our bread for old shoes," Sonia said, noting the replacements never fit. Even European civilians who were not imprisoned had difficulty procuring shoes because the war economy depleted the supply of leather and other basic goods. The importance of shoes in camp can never be underestimated, said Israel "Ira" Kaminsky. His were stolen by a prisoner who then escaped from Skarzysko-Kamienna. "I was devastated," Kaminsky said. He begged his Polish foreman and the Jewish police for a pair. They gave him wooden clogs, which hurt his feet. Eventually, Kaminsky got some leather replacements that fit, but he could never forget the thief. "After the war, I wanted to ask him why he wanted to kill me by stealing my shoes. He wanted to save his life. At the same time, he jeopardized my life." Sonia said, "There were times in Skarzysko I didn't have shoes. Sometimes we had rags on our feet. I made paper shoes." Sonia cut slits in other sacks to make nightgowns that she wore while her clothes dried. Sonia gave potatoes to another prisoner in payment for washing her clothes. Thus, services were also bartered.

For Nathan, information proved as vital as bread. Knowing about the war's developments formed an invisible lifeline. Without it, Nathan said, he would not have nurtured the will or hope to continue. "Maybe, if I would know by 1942 that Germany will succeed, I would give up," Nathan said. "We saw Nazi Germany was terminally ill. We knew that Nazi Germany would die."

A kindly supervisor who fixed bullet-making machines, Jan Zawacki, gave Nathan a window to the world. He was among Polish employees allowed to go home after his shift. Nathan describes Zawacki as one of the few foremen with whom he could talk. Zawacki, in his late 20s, lived with his wife and children in the town of Skarzysko-Kamienna. "He was a nice person. He was not anti-Semitic." The Polish patriot loaned Nathan underground newspapers featuring the latest on battles, the partisan movement, railroad explosions, and other acts of sabotage.

"This give me courage and strength," Nathan said. Reading about current events once or twice a month reinforced what he had absorbed from history classes. "My teacher taught us that no enemy ever won a war on Russian territory." The publication also contained devastating news, corroborating Nathan's worst premonitions. He read that Chmielnik had been "liquidated" and its Jews sent to Treblinka. "From 1935 on, I was on death row," Nathan said, referring to the year Germany enacted the Nuremberg laws abolishing Jews' rights. "In 1935, I didn't know it, but by 1942, I knew I was on death row." Updates about the war inspired Nathan to outlast the Nazi regime. "Time was the main objective. I wanted to live to tell."

The underground newspaper circulated secretly, and Nathan did not inform his sisters about its existence until after the war. The one-page publication, printed on cigarette paper, could be folded and hidden in one's mouth behind the gums. After reading in the privacy of the Jewish latrine or his barrack, Nathan always returned the newspaper to Zawacki. "If I were caught, I would get tortured," Nathan said. "Zawacki was afraid, but he trusted me."

The S.S. eventually ferreted out the illegal printing operation and ruthlessly squelched subsequent issues. "A leader of the underground paper was caught," Nathan said. "They brought out all the prisoners in all the barracks. This person had been beaten beyond recognition." The S.S. made a spectacle of the publisher's execution by scheduling it for late afternoon, when thousands of prisoners changed shifts. The publisher, either a Pole or a German, resembled a businessman with his suit, dress shirt, and tie. Hanging him from a tree would discourage others from resisting fascism. "This is what can happen if you don't obey the rules. He was hung, but the branch broke. Everyone shouted, 'Let him live!,' but Nazi tanks surrounded the camp. They picked him up by his necktie. Then they shot him. Every time I put on a necktie, I am reminded of this man. After that, I didn't see an underground paper."

Mandzia Wajchendler Mapa remembers guards rounding up workers to watch the hangings. "They did this to scare everyone." Once, Mandzia recognized the victims, a young married couple, Hinshinka and Zwatka. They had bribed a Ukrainian guard to help them escape, but he betrayed them, Mandzia said. "It was a story without end. Everything you hear, you don't hear enough. What my eyes saw is without end. What I saw. What they did." Killing was simply part of the daily routine in Skarzysko-Kamienna, according to Fay Skrobacka Goldlist. "All the time, they were shooting people. I witnessed executions, but I didn't look. I didn't see them. I hide my eyes. I couldn't take it." Israel "Irving" Buchbinder observed Ukrainian guards killing escapees in Werk A. "One girl was hanged, and three guys were shot right in the back of the head," Buchbinder said. "Escape never entered my mind. My family was shipped to Treblinka. Nobody was there. I didn't have where to run." Buchbinder also witnessed the execution of a Polish factory worker who had been caught smuggling ammunition to anti-fascists.

The underground publisher's murder disrupted the flow of conventional war bulletins. Zawacki, however, provided another glimpse beyond the barbed wire by allowing Nathan to use his home as a mailing address. Supplied with pen and paper from Zawacki, Nathan wrote the Musial family a letter asking what happened to Chmielnik's remaining Jews and to his family's possessions. He asked them to send food.

Mrs. Musial's reply verified what Nathan had read: Chmielnik's Jews had been shipped to Treblinka. Mrs. Musial wrote that the Garfinkels' velvet bedspreads were the only items she had. Kalman and Sara had exchanged the covers for food with the understanding they would retrieve them after the war. Mrs. Musial sent bread, cheese, and hard-boiled eggs for Nathan to Zawacki's home. Zawacki brought Nathan food each day — a little bit at a time — in his lunch pail.

The Nazis forbade letter writing but occasionally exploited it as a deception. An instance of this practice occurred in the Skarzysko-Kamienna camp, according to Volume VI of *Yad Vashem: Studies on the European Jewish Catastrophe and Resistance*. The S.S. ordered 20 young men from Kielce to write to their relatives about the camp's good conditions. Teenagers who refused were tortured and killed.

Letters from death camps such as Sobibor and Belzec served as propaganda. *Yad Vashem Studies* state some new arrivals were well-treated, given a continental breakfast, and encouraged to send postcards home. The correspondence, the S.S. figured, would convince non-Jews as well as Jews that deportations were to resettlement camps, not to gas chambers. The Germans also used the postcards to obtain the addresses of other Jews.

The letters between Nathan and Mrs. Musial weren't the only evidence that Chmielnik was *judenrein*, or free of Jews. Confirmation came from additional sources within Skarzysko-Kamienna. Mr. Friedman, a Chmielnik Jew in Werk B, was always networking for the latest news. Friedman asked his boss, Kowalczyk, about the fate of Chmielnik's Jews and offered to pay for information. After accepting Friedman's money, Kowalczyk dispatched his son to Chmielnik; he reported what the others had heard. Friedman was older and more savvy than the Garfinkel sisters. By establishing a rapport with Jewish policemen within Skarzysko-Kamienna and by paying a few bribes, Sonia said, Friedman landed a job in the camp's garden. Jan Laskowski oversaw the garden, but Kowalczyk was its hands-on manager. Friedman's position there gave him access to food and to frequent contact with Polish workers who brought word from outside the camp.

Inside the barbed wire, constant violence made life unbearable. Nathan seriously considered escape, a big temptation offset by the low odds of success. The penalty for getting caught — torture, then death — dissuaded many inmates from trying. The S.S. used fleeing prisoners they had apprehended to set examples. A Volksdeutsch commander, Paul Kuehnemann, demanded that the runaways kneel; then he shot them in the backs of their necks. The bullets usually exited through an ear or the top of the head. Kuehnemann, described in history texts as a sadistic camp deputy, is called "Kellerman" by Nathan and other survivors. Relying on what they had heard in passing, Jewish prisoners didn't always know the exact names of their oppressors. For the most part, the S.S. and guards loomed as anonymous thugs who didn't speak in a normal tone of voice. They shouted ultimatums and threats. Nazis viewed Jews as non-human and, therefore, unworthy of conversation. "His face was so nice," Nathan said of Kuehnemann. "He was smiling when he killed people."

The idea of dying with dignity, while fighting or escaping -- as opposed to languishing in the camp -- appealed to Nathan. What made leaving so dangerous was not knowing where to go, Nathan said, or whom to contact to reach anti-fascists. One group of partisans -- *Armia Krajowa*, or the Nationalist Army, was anti-Semitic. The other resistance organization, *Armia Ludowa*, or Populist Army, accepted anarchists, communists, socialists, Jews,

and anyone who defied fascism. Ironically, discrimination as well
as political ideology prevented the two armies from combining
resources to repel the common enemy. Anti-Semitism actually
superseded anti-fascism. Jews who crossed paths with the wrong
group of Polish patriots were murdered.

"From Skarzysko, I could have escaped very easily. It was
very easy. Dig a little deep under the fence and crawl." Nathan
discussed such a plan with two Werk A prisoners from Jedrzejow.
"I didn't escape for two reasons. To escape, you needed to have
someone outside. You needed to communicate with someone from
the outside. The other reason I didn't go: I didn't want to rescue
myself and leave my sisters here. I couldn't do that. I couldn't
rescue myself and leave my sisters." That decision most likely spared
Nathan's life. His two friends did break away, but Nathan never
heard from them or of them again. After the war, he asked other
survivors in vain about them. Nathan assumed they were captured, died of exposure in the forest, or were mortally wounded
with partisans.

Helen and Sonia, like many prisoners, were only vaguely aware
of partisans in the countryside and of resistance within the camps.
For them, forced labor constituted a miserable, monotonous existence. "Not to know an hour or a day. We didn't know what day
it is. If it is cold, it must be winter. If it is hot, it must be summer.
We didn't know what time it is. If it is light, it must be day. If it is
dark, it must be night," Helen said. "We didn't talk about books.
We didn't talk about songs. We talked about when are we going to
get a piece of bread. Or when are we going to be free."

Chapter Seventeen
THE KAISER ROLL

Inquiries from students, teachers, and interviewers about beatings perplex Helen, Sonia, and Nathan. Physical punishment — whether for an alleged violation of the rules or for no reason at all — was integral to camp existence. Once an S.S. caught Helen taking vegetables from the garden. On another occasion, guards spied Sonia lugging extra soup rations from the potato mill to the women's barracks. For each of these "offenses," Helen and Sonia received 25 lashes from a whip, a strip of leather attached to a wooden stick. Beatings usually took place in a station in the forest.

"The first few lashes you scream. Then you don't feel nothing. Then the skin breaks," Sonia said, echoing Nathan and Helen. "I couldn't survive 75 lashes. The lashes I got once, but I was beaten many times. Everybody got used to the beating. They looked to beat us. You didn't have to do nothing. If you were Jewish, that was enough." Guards caught Miriam Pasternak stealing potatoes, and they escorted her outside the camp. When she returned to the barrack later, half of her face was scarlet, the other half was white.

Mandzia Wajchendler Mapa trembled when she sensed the presence of a sadistic German supervisor, Meister Georg Hering, in the munitions plant. "He hit me once. He stays behind me. He hit me with steel. He throw at me. He hit me on the back and the back of my head. I worked. It hurt me. For no reason why he did this," Mandzia said. "Every time when I was working, I always saw his shadow. I thought he was after me. When I saw him, I was afraid of his shadow. Everybody was afraid, actually."

Beatings rendered one unable to work. Fighting aches, pains, illness, and fatigue, Sonia and Helen prodded each other to go to the mill. "You had to work," Sonia said. "You couldn't stop working. If they find you in the barrack not working, they would take you in the forest and shoot you. We were afraid to stay in the barrack." When the desire to sleep longer tempted Sonia, she thought about Pearl Osia of Chmielnik. Osia became sick and failed to show up at the ammunition factory. A Ukrainian guard with a rifle strapped to his back burst into the barrack. From the potato mill's window, Sonia watched the guard drag Osia outside. The two disappeared into the forest. One shot rang out. "So many they shot," Sonia said. "Her name stands out because I saw it."

Nathan, who was almost executed for remaining in his bunk, never forgot the importance of reporting to the assembly line. Yet any Jew, despite his or her best efforts to follow rules and to avoid confrontation, could become the target of abuse at any moment. Consequently, lessons Nathan learned during his early weeks of captivity — making oneself inconspicuous and toiling diligently — offered no consistent protection against violence.

The civilian director of the Shuhe-Abteilung building distinguished himself through cruelty. He wore the enemy's badge, a red armband with a black swastika. "I don't know his name," Nathan said. "We hardly ever saw him. If we saw him, we walked away to let him by. This director was not just mean, but looking at him you could see he didn't want to see you."

Inattentiveness nearly cost Nathan his life during one of the director's rare visits. Preoccupied with loading steel into his bullet-casing machine, Nathan didn't notice that other prisoners stood erect and silent as the director passed. Still absorbed in his task, Nathan bent over a dolly to activate a lever that would raise the crate of steel. Nathan was kicked so hard in his back he fell. A voice, the director's, boomed, "Clean my shoe. You dirtied my shoe." Angry, Nathan stifled his first inclination to talk back. He crawled on his hands and knees to wipe the director's shoes with a rag used for cleaning the machines. The director thundered, "This is dirty." He pointed to the rag and spit in Nathan's face. Furious and humiliated, Nathan did not move. Remaining crouched at the director's feet, Nathan pulled a handkerchief from his pocket, spit directly on the director's shoes, and proceeded to polish.

Incredulous, the director demanded, "Why did you spit on my shoe?" Nathan replied, "To clean better," and continued rubbing. As in previous conflicts, Nathan swallowed his rage and chose his words carefully. To do otherwise — to lose his temper, to say what he really thought, or to properly defend himself — would have been fatal. Yet Nathan retained his dignity. He groveled at the director's feet, but he also spit back. "It was a passive retaliation," Nathan said. "I think this helped me survive."

The director stomped away, but the encounter had not ended. Before Nathan could resume filling his machine with steel, one of the director's assistants beckoned Nathan to follow him to a small room near the office. No more than 10 feet by 10 feet, the room contained a chair in each corner and a phonograph against the wall. "As soon as he opened the door, I know what it was because people talked about it," Nathan said. It was the *Musikstube*, or music room, a torture chamber devised by the S.S. to thrash Jews. "People who went there, I never heard from again."

In the Musikstube, four Nazis each donned boxing gloves and stood in the corners. To amuse themselves, they punched their defenseless captive so he would fall from one corner to another. Music blared loudly from the phonograph to drown out the victim's cries. The director, the foreman, Alfred Wagner, and a fourth individual hit and kicked Nathan repeatedly. "Ride of the Valkyries" from Richard Wagner's opera *Ring of the Nibelungen* played during Nathan's boxing session.

"If they couldn't hit me strong enough to knock me over, they kicked me. When I fell down, I made a point to fall in the middle, not to anyone else." After a few minutes and several falls, the Nazis released Nathan. With swollen ears and a bloody nose, he returned to his machines. "For some reason, I was lucky. They boxed most people until they were unconscious. The idea was to beat people until they couldn't work. Then they were shot."

The fear of injury, not pain, lurked in the minds of Jews. The prospect of not working, as much as the beatings, contributed to mental strain. Nonetheless, some individuals acted on their need to help others and engaged in what Nathan calls "passive retaliation." By taking risks no matter how small, Jews asserted their will to live amid death, maintained their sanity in a world gone mad, and reminded themselves they were human beings under the yoke of barbarians.

That is why Helen, Sonia, Cesia Zaifman, Etka Raitapfel Baumstick, and others regularly smuggled potatoes from the mill. Sonia often hid potato flakes on her bunk's second shelf, where Bela Strauch and her sister, Frymet, slept. "Bela used to come to visit us in Chmielnik to play cards on Saturdays. She was more Nathan's friend than my friend. Somehow I felt obligated to her." Sonia often persuaded her co-workers in the mill to let her distribute extra soup rations to the ammunition laborers who were more desperate for food. "At night it was horrible to look. The bunks looked like — like caves," Sonia said, visualizing the many times she carried the precious soup can. It was midnight. The women stared listlessly at Sonia from the shelves where they lay. "Those big eyes. They haunt me. Every time I looked at those eyes, they were pleading for help. The eyes don't shrink. The face shrinks. The eyes stay the same."

The short distance between the mill and fence surrounding the wooden dormitories made stealing potatoes feasible, Cesia Zaifman said. "One person would watch to see if there was a guard. It was two or three seconds from the door to the gate." Zaifman dropped little potatoes inside her coat's lining; big potatoes would make noticeable bulges at the hem. "We tried to steal, to take out to help somebody. We tried to help others. But you couldn't do that every day."

Etka Raitapfel Baumstick perceived Sonia as gentle and kind-hearted. "Everybody liked Sonia. Most people under the circumstances, they didn't care for others that much. Everyone was suffering. Everyone had their own problems," Etka said. "Sonia, regardless of her own suffering, she cared about others. She gave away to other people more than anyone else did. I cannot say I was as generous as Sonia." Fay Skrobacka Goldlist credited the Garfinkel sisters with helping her combat starvation in Werk B, where she swept floors, dusted machinery, and cleaned buildings before her transfer to Werk A to make bullets. "Every day they came and gave us potatoes," Goldlist said. "They gave me a lot of times potatoes. It helped. A lot of girls worked in the (potato) factory, but not everyone brought potatoes. Sonia was a good-hearted person."

Not having enough to eat wasn't the only concern. The most minor of illnesses and accidents seemed menacing, given the absence of drugs, bandages, and other medical supplies for Jewish prisoners. The camp's "hospital" merely held the sick and injured a few days until the S.S. could kill them. "Some people lost their fingers in those presses," said Israel "Irving" Buchbinder, who produced ammunition in Werk A. "There was always accidents. They send to a hospital, and you never see them again. Sometimes I cut myself by shavings," he said, referring to steel fragments on the assembly line.

Zosia Kalmowiez Kiman considers her survival on Werk B's assembly lines, under the evil Meisters Laidek and Meshner, nothing short of miraculous. Once, as she noticed some of the bullets emerging crooked, one exploded in her face. Pieces of bullet grazed her forehead and neck, and a chunk of metal lodged in her thigh. Burning powder singed her eyelashes and eyebrows. The impact pushed her so hard against a machine she still bears a scar on her back. A co-worker grabbed a package of white cotton gloves used for the finishing line, dipped them in water, and pressed the bundle against Zosia's neck. "Blood was spurting. I thought I would be dead, but it was not deep."

Although Zosia limped for several weeks after the accident, she tried to be inconspicuous during roll call and while reporting to work. She stood in the back surrounded by taller women. Her hair covered the wounds on her neck and forehead. "I was a strong girl to went through this," Zosia asserted, attributing her survival to a love of sports. Like Helen, Zosia had been a tomboy. She had learned to ride a bicycle, and she had played soccer with boys. For all her exterior toughness, Zosia had a tender heart. "I was scared. Every night with my sister I was praying to die because we never believed to survive this what we went through. We didn't want to live," Zosia said of herself and her sister, Chana. "We saw how they were killing people and hitting. At least to die normal, to go to sleep, not to wake up. This was every night praying not to wake up."

The anxiety of staying alive in such a hostile environment caused mental illness. The older sister of Sonia's best friend, Lola Warszawska, suffered a nervous breakdown in the potato mill, but fellow prisoners helped her through the crisis. "She lost herself," Sonia said. "We had to clean her every day and wash her clothes. I gave her potato flakes. We watched her. She came to herself." The older sister survived the war, but Lola, who was left behind, was gassed in Treblinka.

"It's unbelievable," Sonia said, echoing other Shoah survivors. "At nights when I can't sleep, I think it was a dream. How can it be possible that we lived through this? I see many dead people in front of me. Many times I thought it was the last day for me." Sonia nearly died twice during her early imprisonment in Skarzysko-Kamienna.

One day while she ate her soup and bread in the mill, someone moved the iron table where she sat. The rough bottom of the table leg ripped the nail from her big toe. She couldn't walk — her left foot hurt so badly. Jan Laskowski, the unconventional Nazi, saw Sonia hopping, and he ordered her to stay in the barrack two days. After resting, she limped back to her job. "If I had worked in the ammunition factory and this happened, I would have been shot." As her foot healed, Sonia evaded some S.S. inspectors by hiding in the lavatory. "If they saw me with something wrong, they would have killed me."

Later, Sonia succumbed to fever — probably stemming from typhus, which is extremely contagious. Lice, overcrowding, and unsanitary conditions catalyze the disease. Throughout mankind's history of warfare, typhus epidemics have sometimes surpassed combat as the leading cause of death among soldiers. During World War II, the squalor of Nazi death camps provided an ideal host — increasing the odds of dying well beyond the average rate of one death for every four infected patients. Jewish prisoners perished in greater numbers because they did not receive proper medical treatment. In addition, they were executed for not recuperating in a few days — and typhus rages for two weeks or longer. Mandzia Wajchendler Mapa's mother, Cyrla, was stricken shortly after she was transferred to Skarzysko-Kamienna. "She came to us sick with typhus," Mandzia said. "She was with us a few weeks. Then she died in camp — the 17th of January, 1943. She was 43 years old. This I remember."

Few recovered from typhus. Zaifman did not notice Sonia's illness or injury. "People were scared to tell. If somebody took ill, they hide it, because they would take you away, they shoot you. They didn't want sick people," Zaifman said. "Everybody was worrying for themselves. Everyone was crazy about their own thoughts."

Sonia was so sick, she fainted. When she came to, she was lying next to two other women in a horse-drawn wagon. She passed out again. She awoke in the women's hospital near Nathan's section of camp. "In the hospital they didn't give us anything." Physically, Sonia hovered between life and death. Mentally, she alternated between lucidity and delirium. "I saw how they took out people. They were half-dead." She saw an acquaintance, a dark-haired Jewess from Skarzysko-Kamienna, also stricken with typhus. Sonia cannot recall Sophie's last name, but she will never forget Sophie's big, soulful, black eyes. One day, Sophie lay next to Sonia. The following morning she was gone. "I was happy because I knew I would be next. I was so sick. I was happy it would be the end of the misery," Sonia said. "My father had told me we would reach a point where we envied the dead."

Nathan countered Sonia's wish to die. To visit his sister, Nathan volunteered to carry soup from Werek A's kitchen to the hospital. That job, arranged by his foreman, brought Nathan daily to Sonia. The stench of excrement, the sound of deranged screams, and the sight of women lying on the filthy floor appalled Nathan. "At least in the barrack, some people clean it. They used a broom to clean it. They didn't bother to clean the hospital. It was dirty, neglected," Nathan said. "The Nazis called it a hospital, but it was really a warehouse for the disabled." If Sonia could walk to the doorway, Nathan made sure she ate her rations. Otherwise, he gave her food to the Jewish nurse. By befriending the nurse, Nathan learned the S.S. killed all the patients as soon as the hospital became full. "Those who cannot work, those who cannot produce, the Nazis said, 'Forget it. We don't need you.' Hitler did this to his own people. Disabled people and the mentally ill were killed," Nathan said, referring to Germany's "euthanasia" program of killing "undesirable" citizens in the 1930s. The S.S. exploited their handicapped and retarded countrymen as guinea pigs to test the lethal gasses later used to annihilate Jews.

Forewarned by the nurse, Nathan carried Sonia to a women's barrack in Werk A. During the designated liquidation, on a Sunday, he watched guards lift patients by their arms and legs and throw them onto a truck. After the vehicle disappeared in the forest, Nathan carried Sonia back to the hospital.

Once, Sonia opened her eyes to see an attractive, blonde, camp official leaning over her. "She asked me in beautiful Polish, 'How do you feel?' Right away it hit me, that my Laskowski must have sent her. If not for Laskowski, I would have been taken in the forest and shot."

What Sonia remembers most distinctly about her illness was seeing her brother in the clinic's doorway. Despite its clarity, Sonia thought the image was a vision or fever-induced dream, but Nathan verified what she saw. "I remember this like yesterday. Once I saw Nate in the door. I saw a kaiser roll in the palm of his hand. I didn't see a kaiser roll since I went from home. I know he didn't eat for days to exchange his bread for a kaiser roll." Nathan bought the roll from a woman prisoner who worked in the garden. He paid for it with the potatoes and potato flakes Helen had given him. "I wanted the kaiser roll. It was more luxurious," Nathan said. "Because it was something different, it was like a medicine."

In a week to 10 days, Sonia's fever subsided. Guards sent by Laskowski escorted her to Werk B. Too weak to stand, she sat to peel potatoes and to fill paper sacks with dehydrated flakes. Laskowski looked the other way. Prisoners urged Sonia to lie down behind some sacks of potato flakes. No one would notice during the night shift, they said. "I wouldn't lay down because I was afraid they would beat me. I knew I couldn't stand a beating." Sonia often wonders why she lived when, deep down, she wanted to die. "I prayed to die. I know if I died, I would be with my father, I would be with my mother. In the camp, I didn't see any future there. I was looking for a way to die. I am sure there are plenty who prayed to live and they died."

She didn't realize it then but, by living, Sonia would be able to rescue her siblings. Injuries and illnesses befell her at the beginning of imprisonment — as though to prepare her for the more horrible weeks at the war's end. Sonia later had strength when her sisters were at death's threshold. She later gave them her rations without feeling hungry. At critical junctures months and years later, Sonia saved her sisters.

Chapter Eighteen
SAVING NATHAN

As 12-hour work shifts and malnutrition sapped his energy, Nathan depended more and more on the food Sonia and Helen smuggled to him on their weekly treks to Werk A's showers. In the beginning, Nathan eagerly greeted his sisters, hugged them, and asked about their welfare. Distressed by their shabby clothes, he wept upon seeing how thin and anxious Sonia and Helen looked. The bread and potatoes they delivered were secondary, and Nathan often gave away the food, Sonia said. "We didn't eat the bread. We saved it for Nate. I used to get mad to see him give the food to others."

Nathan's generosity eventually diminished, and he grew more desperate for his own survival. One Sunday, the food interested him more than his sisters. "I think my brother went off his rocker," Helen said. "I went to see him. I remember my brother acted like a wild man. He grabbed the bread and put it in his mouth." On her return to Werk B, Helen discussed Nathan's uncharacteristic behavior with Sonia. They were worried. The next week, a friend of the Garfinkel family visited Nathan on her way to Werk A's showers. She reported that Nathan, who previously was emaciated, looked chubby. Sonia subsequently saw for herself but couldn't believe it. "Nate was all swollen. He was all puffed up — his feet, his fingers, his toes. I couldn't understand it." While Sonia walked back to Werk B, it dawned on her. "I remembered that once I read in a book if people don't eat, they swell up." Sonia realized her brother was starving. "Hunger is very, very painful," Sonia said, speaking from personal experience. "You feel like your body is shrinking. Hunger is like a disease." In her barrack, Sonia heard women crying in pain from hunger. "I visualized and dreamed about food. I got filled up with dreams."

At times Nathan felt as though he were losing his mind. The atrocities he had witnessed were as much to blame as was his deteriorating health. The recurring image of his beloved mentor, Mijer Gorlicky, dying of hunger depressed Nathan. The two rarely saw each other in Werk A because they were assigned to different barracks and ammunition plants, and they often worked opposite shifts. On one evening they crossed paths, but Nathan barely recognized his former teacher. Mijer, reduced to skin and bones, could hardly walk. Nathan helped him to his barrack. Mijer crawled onto his shelf next to the floor. As Nathan sat nearby, Mijer said, "Tell this, what took place in the 20th century in a civilized society." When Nathan returned the next day, prisoners told him Mijer was dead. "I was afraid he had died. I expected him to die. He was dehydrated from starvation," Nathan said. "I assume they took him to a mass grave and buried him."

Nathan would have suffered the same fate if not for Sonia. Driven by the awful realization that her brother was starving, she tried to procure him a job in Werk B's potato mill. "I asked the foreman to help my brother. I begged him," Sonia said. "This I could do better than Helen. I told him my brother is a good worker, my brother is a nice guy, he needs help." That Polish foreman, by the name of Galczynski, suggested that Sonia put her request in writing, and he gave her a pencil and paper. Sonia wrote a letter in Polish, that, she said, "would break your heart." The letter follows, to the best of Sonia's recollection:

"Dear Mr. Laskowski: I have a brother in Werk A, and we would like very much if you could bring him to us. His name is Nathan Garfinkel. He is an excellent worker. You are not going to be sorry. Please, we beg of you, please bring him to us. We would love to be together. From the two sisters who admire you a great deal. You are like a father to us. Sonia and Helen."

Galczynski promised to deliver Sonia's letter and to talk to Jan Laskowski about reassigning Nathan. Helen considered

Galczynski, the day supervisor, and Visniewsky, the tall night boss, to be "nice guys," which requires some elaboration within the context of the Shoah. Galczynski and Visniewsky did not go out of their way to rescue Jews or to share food, but, unlike the Ukrainian guards, they did not beat or murder their workers. Helen appreciated the fact that both foremen, like Laskowski, pretended not to see the pilfering of potatoes. Galczynski and Visniewsky also ignored the times Helen and Sonia could not stand because they were ill or weak from beatings.

Although their actions were neutral rather than heroic, the foremen occasionally provided a human touch to the assembly line, showing that not all Poles were rabidly anti-Semitic. Helen noticed that Galczynski, who was married and had children, subtly flirted with a Jewess he liked by bringing her little gifts.

Nathan arrived at Werk B within a few weeks of Sonia's emotional appeal to Galczynski. Etka Raitapfel Baumstick, who had observed Sonia and Helen stockpiling food for Nathan and faithfully visiting him every Sunday, recoiled at his ghost-like appearance. "He looked bad. He looked like a skeleton. He had very hard work and very little food, but when he came to work for Laskowski, he got better," Etka said. "Laskowski did that transfer. You see, no other one (boss) would do that." Sonia and Helen believed the relocation saved Nathan's life. Nathan agreed with that assessment: "We weren't getting enough to eat in Camp A. I wouldn't have survived. The population in the barracks was decreasing. People were escaping. People were getting ill. People were dying. People were getting executed."

Nathan's physical and mental health gradually improved after his transfer in 1943. He had less contact with guards and the cruel Fritz Bartenschläger and Paul Kuehnemann. He could snitch potatoes to supplement the insufficient rations. "Good things you can see right away about a person," Nathan said. "If Laskowski saw you eat a potato, he looked away. If he saw you take a potato, he looked away." Laskowski also sounded the alarm when necessary.

After working in the factory for several months, Nathan decided to carry as many potatoes as possible to the men's barrack. The night shift was ending. He tied his pants at the ankles and filled the legs with potatoes. Nathan figured he could pull off the caper undetected. It was still dark at 7 a.m., and he would march surrounded by other men. He proceeded, stiff-legged, to the barrack. Inside, to everyone's astonishment, he unloaded the contraband. The prisoners couldn't stop laughing to think Nathan had stuffed his pants full of potatoes. Humor masked the terrible risk he had taken. Had the guards discovered Nathan smuggling potatoes, they would have killed him.

"I didn't know this, but Laskowski was watching me through the window. The next day, he came to the factory at quarter to seven. He said to me, 'I know you are stealing potatoes. Don't do it. If a guard catches you, I can't protect you. I know your sisters are taking potatoes. I know that other people are stealing potatoes. I can't protect you if you're caught. Inside the factory, I am in charge. Outside, the guards are in charge.' He gave me a warning. After that, I only put a few potatoes in my pockets."

Still determined to help others, Nathan again tried to get more food to the ammunition workers in his barrack. Late one night, he threw a sack of potatoes over the barbed wire fence. The bag burst, scattering evidence of theft throughout the yard. A guard began interrogating prisoners to learn the culprit's identity. Leon Kanarek, a Jewish policeman, figured Nathan was responsible but kept his hunch to himself. Grim-faced, Kanarek confronted Nathan privately saying, "You created a big problem here." Nathan didn't deny or confirm Kanarek's accusation but took it as a warning. "I kept it secret," Nathan said. "This was the first time and the last time." Nathan returned to his old method of slipping a few potatoes in his pockets.

Chapter Nineteen
A MOUND of CLOTHES

The lives of Nathan, Sonia, and Helen hung by a thread despite their relatively more bearable circumstances in Werk B. *The Encyclopedia of the Holocaust's* reference to Skarzysko-Kamienna describes the enormous obstacles the Garfinkels faced each and every day:

"The prisoners were led to work by factory police and Jewish police and were compelled to fill quotas that were beyond their strength. The camps (A, B and C) were mixed, with men and women together, but they slept in separate huts, on bunks with two or three tiers of wooden shelves, without blankets.

"Sanitary conditions were intolerable." Here the *Encyclopedia* generalizes about the latrines, which were just holes in the ground requiring the women to squat, according to Mania Poper Cherston and the Garfinkel sisters. A crude, wooden shelter enclosed the latrines, located the equivalent of two city blocks from Sonia and Helen's barrack. Lacking paper, the women used leaves to wipe themselves. The urge to defecate occurred infrequently, Sonia noted, because the prisoners received so little to eat. However, diarrhea afflicted many prisoners, and they had to run a good distance to reach the latrines. "At night there wasn't even a bucket to urinate in," Sonia said. "When women got sick sometimes they had to use the pot for food. Don't ask." Farmers arrived every few months to empty the latrines to make fertilizer. The stench was perennial, Sonia said, but it worsened in the summer.

The Encyclopedia of the Holocaust continues: "The food rations consisted of seven ounces (200 grams) of bread a day and about a pint (0.5 liter) of watery soup twice a day... The prisoners had to work in the same clothes week after week, and when these disintegrated — as they inevitably did, particularly in Camp C — they wrapped themselves in paper bags." Israel "Ira" Kaminsky witnessed his fellow Werk C inmates covering themselves with paper used for packing ammunition. The paper helped insulate against the winter's bitter cold.

More excerpts from the *Encyclopedia:* "In all three camps there were epidemics of dysentery, typhus and a disease caused by weakness, called hasagowka by the prisoners after the Hasag company... Periodic Selektionen took place, and the prisoners who were singled out in this way were killed by a 'shock troop' (*Stosstruppe*) made up of factory police."

The grim conditions were worse than what the *Encyclopedia* describes, Sonia said. "Soup twice a day? No. It was once a day between 11:30 and 12. I wish we had soup twice a day. They make lots of mistakes in the *Encyclopedia.*" When discrepancies arise between history texts and people's memories, Sonia and other Shoah survivors offer a simple explanation: "The books are wrong."

Etka Raitapfel Baumstick echoed Sonia: "You get a little soup. It was next to water. You get a slice of bread. That was for a whole day. We were young. We needed a lot of food. We didn't get it." Mania Poper Cherston also remembered the mid-day distribution of bread with thin soup and the morning coffee she calls *Ersatz,* which means replacement or substitute in German. The focus on food superseded everything else, she said. "If we get a plate of soup, everybody look to see if someone got more." Sometimes on Sundays, the S.S. served a slightly thicker soup made from white beets. Sonia called it "sweet soup," and she vowed to eat sweet soup every day after liberation.

In Werk A, Israel "Irving" Buchbinder received coffee made of burned corn in the morning, a portion of thin soup at midday, and a slice of bread at night. "On Saturday you get two slices of bread: one for Saturday and one for Sunday," Buchbinder said. "I saved it. They stole it from me. That's the way it goes. Everybody is hungry. You barely survived." Buchbinder's Holocaust experience disproves the notion that blood is thicker than water. Once, when he was ill, Buchbinder entrusted an uncle to collect his rations. Instead of saving the bread as agreed, the uncle sold it for personal gain. Buchbinder never forgave his uncle and shunned him long after World War II ended. "That's why I didn't talk to him. I didn't want to bother with relatives like this."

The Garfinkels' jobs in the potato mill under the neutral Jan Laskowski gave them an edge on survival but no guarantees. They were by no means sheltered from the camp's brutality. Although Nathan regarded Werk A as more dangerous than Werk B, he once received help in Werk A. He also nearly lost his life in Werk B.

When potatoes were not available, the S.S. employed the mill workers elsewhere. Nathan and about 55 other prisoners were dispatched to dig the foundation for a new hospital wing in the town of Skarzysko-Kamienna. A fence enclosed the construction site, but a gate opened to the street. The view of a bakery and the aroma of fresh bread tormented the starving prisoners. Nathan and three others sneaked out to beg for food. Some Polish civilians gave them bread, and they returned.

A guard, Hermann Lachmann, stepped from behind the gate where he had concealed himself. Nathan sensed there would be reprisals because Lachmann was a known killer. Nathan had heard the story of Lachmann chasing Feingold, a Chmielnik Jew, to Werk A's fences. Lachmann then shot Feingold for supposedly trying to escape.

At the hospital expansion site, Lachmann accused Nathan and his three companions of fleeing. "He said, 'You tried to escape, didn't you?'" Nathan recalled. "We said, 'We could have, but we didn't. We came back.' He spoke to us in German. We spoke to him in Polish. He started beating us. I was the worst one, I think, because I had the biggest piece of bread. He beat the hell out of us."

Lachmann hit Nathan with the butt of his rifle until Nathan

fell, unconscious. Nathan awoke to a German officer reviving him with some water and coffee. Nathan thought he was dreaming. A Nazi was helping him? But Nathan knew he was awake. Through piercing pain, he felt loose teeth. They sounded like marbles. He spit out four teeth. In a rare gesture of decency, the officer took Nathan and the three other bruised and bleeding prisoners inside the hospital.

The contrast between that Nazi and the guard, Lachmann, underscores the wide range of behavior among oppressors. Survivors — including Nathan, Sonia, and Helen — often say the Polish and Ukrainian guards were more bestial than the German S.S., but each individual, each situation differed. Lachmann was a Volksdeutscher, born in Poland.

Worried about loosing his teeth, Nathan consulted a Jewish dentist nicknamed *Kaczka*, the Polish word for duck. The dentist advised Nathan that, with proper nutrition, his gums would heal and his remaining teeth might stabilize. That prognosis was wishful thinking, given the camp's inadequate food rations and lack of sanitation. By war's end, Nathan had only two or three teeth left. Later, in 1949, he testified against Lachmann in a war-crimes trial in Leipzig, Germany.

"There was friction between guards and Nazis," Nathan said. Otto Schnitzler, a German officer, defied the stereotype of Nazi tyrants within Werk A. On one Sunday, Nathan was picked to load crates of bullets onto train cars, potentially hazardous work because one defective bullet could ignite an explosion. Schnitzler, who supervised the task, barred the guards from entering the warehouse. If guards beat the Jews, causing them to drop boxes, the entire building could go up in flames. Outside, of course, the guards abused Jews to entertain themselves. They kicked and hit prisoners as they lugged heavy crates to the railroad platform. Upon re-entering the warehouse, Nathan found a sandwich — a discovery that evoked fear, surprise, and delight. Helen would have a similar experience a few years later. "I found a sandwich.

That could be a provocation. If I eat the sandwich, he might tell me I stole the sandwich. Schnitzler made a sign to me to eat the sandwich. He brought his fingers to his lips, and then he put his hand in his pocket. He was signaling me to keep the sandwich. I couldn't believe it. There were tears in his eyes." Buchbinder remembers Schnitzler as a nice, good-natured man who occasionally gave him half of a sandwich. Prisoners dubbed the S.S. officer "the little rabbi," Buchbinder said, because they thought he looked more Jewish than German.

"How can we judge?" Nathan asks. "I saw Schnitzler later (after the war) testifying against other Nazis." During that chance encounter at Lachmann's trial in 1949, Schnitzler told Nathan he had left out sandwiches for other Jewish prisoners. "I attribute my survival to people like that." Nathan's gratitude aside, Schnitzler and Laskowski cannot be called heroes. They did not take big risks or endanger their lives to help Jews. However, they stood out among S.S. officers because they did not overstep their authority by mistreating prisoners. Their apparent neutrality, lack of cruelty, and occasional small favors helped some Jews. Nathan benefited psychologically; it gave him hope in humanity. The decency of Schnitzler and Laskowski emerged all too rarely during World War II — especially inside the death camps.

Alfred Wagner, a German engineer in Werk A, was more typical. He routinely ordered Jews to clean his office and always left some bread, wrapped in paper, on his desk. If Wagner returned to find the bread missing — which usually was the case — he could execute the janitor for stealing. "Word had gotten around about this," Nathan said of the S.S. premise of "justifiable killing" or "killing by provocation." When he cleaned Wagner's office, Nathan put the bread in the trashcan. "Wagner goes around saying, 'Where's my bread?'" Nathan recalled. "I picked it up from the wastebasket. I said, 'Oh, I think it's here.'" So great was his hunger, Nathan discarded the bread in hopes Wagner would allow him to keep it after retrieving it from the garbage. "He said, 'Get out of here!' I run as fast as I could. He might put a bullet in my back. I risk sometimes to have a piece of bread."

Each day, each situation held potential torment for prisoners. "Laskowski disliked me sometimes," Nathan said. "He tried to make me night foreman. I told him, 'No.'" Nathan did not want to be in the position of disciplining others. The late Primo Levi expressed similar sentiments by writing about "the gray zone of morality" in *The Drowned and the Saved*. Repulsed by the prisoners' self-created caste system within Auschwitz, Levi shunned opportunities to assume authority. Like Nathan, Levi feared the possibility of compromising himself and loathed the idea of castigating fellow Jews to please the S.S. A Chmielnik Jew, Jakubowicz — Bela Jakubowicz's uncle — took the night foreman job that Nathan had refused. "Laskowski punished me for not being foreman. Once he made me unload by myself." Steel, coal, oil, and potatoes were among the goods shipped to Skarzysko-Kamienna's labor camps. Sonia, too, was offered a supervisory role, that of *Stubenälteste* in her barrack. That individual was responsible for cleaning and monitoring the lights: one dim, overhead bulb. Sonia did not have the heart to order any of her barrack mates to do chores, so she often swept the floor herself. "I couldn't point to anybody. You look at the girls. You see how they look." Much to Sonia's relief, someone intervened to appoint a tougher individual to serve as Stubenälteste.

One summer, the S.S. sent Helen and Sonia to Georg Hering's munitions plant, where they struggled to move crates of bullet casings. "If we worked there all the time, we wouldn't survive," Sonia said. To conserve energy, they dragged the boxes across the floor when foremen and guards weren't watching. There, they saw the unreasonable production quotas. A female prisoner inspecting each batch for defective bullets was shot after the S.S. accused her of negligence. That particular individual might have been deliberately careless. Despite heavy restrictions and the lack of resources, some Jews formed an underground network to thwart their captors. Making and packing defective bullets qualified as resistance.

Sonia and Etka Raitapfel Baumstick remember a Jewess who gave her life to the cause. Lola, a redhead from Lodz, sang Polish songs every night in the Garfinkel sisters' barrack. "She had a beautiful voice," Sonia said. Stationed at the finishing line, Lola slipped new bullets in her pockets. She gave the precious ammunition to Leon Kanarek, a Jewish policeman with underground connections. "Lola was caught. She was shot and killed," Sonia said. At the time, Sonia knew Lola had been accused of sabotage, but she did not learn all the details until after the war.

The Encyclopedia of the Holocaust cites several underground movements within the Skarzysko-Kamienna complex. They included: *Zydowska Organizacja Bojowa*, known as ZOB, the Jewish Fighting Organization; and the *BUND*, or "Federation," which communicated with Jewish leaders trapped in Warsaw's ghetto. "Jewish prisoners smuggled arms out of the factory and handed them over to Polish partisans belonging to the Armia Krajowa (Home Army)," the *Encyclopedia* states. "Links also existed with the Polish Communist underground, the *Polska Partia Robotnicza* (Polish Workers' Party)."

Few participated in the resistance, but heroism manifested itself daily in much simpler actions. Courage lay in prisoners' attempts to overcome the camp's misery by integrating some normalcy in their lives. Cyla Perlstein, a Jewess from Chmielnik, exemplified that. Her death reveals how prisoners were constantly subject to the whims of madmen and criminals. Guards saw Perlstein kissing a Jewish policeman, so they broke her jaw and shot her. "I remember this," Sonia said. "It was terrible to live there. Life wasn't worth nothing." Although Sonia had no energy or interest in cultivating romance, she understood why other prisoners craved such relationships. "Some girls were starving, so they got a boyfriend to get a slice of bread. Maybe men wanted a girl for a kiss, for a kind word. Where could they have sex? There was no place."

Work assignments alone doomed some Jews. The Applebaum sisters, whose parents had operated a grocery store in Chmielnik, were chosen by Georg Hering to make bullets. They slept on the bottom shelf of Sonia's bunk. "These two girls came back with oil all over them. They had no way to wash," Sonia said. To compound their problems, dysentery kept the Applebaum sisters running to the latrines all night. "Every day, they were shrinking, dying," Sonia stated. "They died in a few months from hunger and exhaustion."

On several occasions, Sonia and Helen pulled weeds and hoed in the garden. The chance to eat raw vegetables, no matter how unripe, made farming and yard work the most coveted jobs in camp. "Some girls washed the carrots and ate them," Sonia said. "I couldn't. I felt sorry for the carrots. They were so little, so thin. It was like a little stick. I put them back in the ground." Etka Raitapfel Baumstick savored biting into the garden's tomatoes and cucumbers.

Although Sonia and Helen welcomed being outdoors amid the greenery and fresh air, they could not escape the horror of Skarzysko-Kamienna. The garden overlooked Werk C's explosives center, where blank-eyed, emaciated prisoners could barely drag themselves around. "I saw people. They were yellow," Sonia said. "I thought, 'I don't see good. My eyes, maybe — something wrong.' I looked, and I looked."

The sight of Werk C's jaundiced prisoners distressed Sonia and Helen. They later learned that Polish laborers exposed to the plant's toxic powders worked only a few hours, during which they wore protective overalls and masks. To offset their contact with lethal chemicals, the Poles ate foods rich in fat and protein: eggs, milk, meat, and ham. The S.S. did not extend the same precautions to Jews, who were, literally, worked to death.

"Werk C belonged to the filling plant (*Fullanstalt*)," according to *The Encyclopedia of the Holocaust*. "This was the harshest and most notorious camp, on account of the deadly nature of the work there: producing underwater mines and filling them with picric acid." The *Encyclopedia* continues: "In late 1943 and early 1944, mass executions took place in Camp C. The victims were prisoners of different nationalities who had been brought in from the Gestapo jails in the Radom district."

Etka Raitapfel Baumstick witnessed some of those murders while she tended the garden. From a distance, she saw stick figures of men and women being led to the execution site. "Not far from the garden, there was this place where they were shooting people. My stomach was turning. I turned away. I didn't want to look. I saw them being shot. I still have nightmares."

Kaminsky viewed one of Werk C's first executions at what he called the shooting gallery, or *strzelnica* in Polish. A well-dressed Jew was killed there for not turning in his valuables on arrival. "He gave them some money, but he still had some money, so they shot him. This scared everyone." Facing death daily, Kaminsky handled the picric acid and troilite, a white mineral, for one-and-a-half years. He started on the assembly line, where he pressed out the metal halves of underwater mines, poured in troilite, and welded the parts together. Inhaling the powders caused prisoners to choke. After several months, Kaminsky was promoted to supervise production in Halls No. 51 and No. 53. For each press, there was one woman to measure the troilite and four men to operate the machine.

To ease the workload, Kaminsky persuaded a Polish foreman with underground connections to accept 14, rather than 15, boxes a day from each press. Kaminsky tested the foreman first by mentioning the *miecz*, or sword in Polish, and *plug*, or plow. By the glint in the foreman's eyes, Kaminsky knew he was familiar with the underground publication entitled *Miecz i Plug*. "I took a chance. I said, 'Maybe you can help me. You see how our people suffer. They can't produce their quota. If we produce less, the occupiers will have less.'" He cannot remember the foreman's name, but Henryk Kopecki was the production supervisor who approved the plan. After the war, Kaminsky learned that Kopecki had smuggled some of the ammunition in Hall No. 15 to Poland's underground. In her book, *Death Comes in Yellow*, Felicja Karay confirms that Kopecki maintained connections with the Polish underground. Although Kopecki did not physically abuse Jews, he made his viewpoint clear by saying he was fighting for "a Poland without Jews." Professor Ringel, another Jewish supervisor, begged Kaminsky to help reduce the workload in Hall No. 13, which made picric-filled mines. On discovering the lower production via a Jewish informant, the Nazis punished Kaminsky and Ringel by forcing them to join the picric assembly line. Kaminsky was relieved of that deadly work after the arrival of 1,000 Jews from Krakow's Plaszow labor camp. Werk C's Jewish police commander, Henek Eisenberg, arranged for Kaminsky to work as a barber. "I was accused of sabotage. I was a candidate to be shot," Kaminsky explained. "They gave me a job in the barracks. This was the way I was saved." Six months later, he still bore traces of yellow on his body.

To Esther Pasternak Tarek and her sister, Bela, Werk C's hellish conditions made Kielce's camp seem like a haven. Eyewitnesses quoted in Karay's book make similar comparisons. "Werk C wasn't a pretty camp. There was a lot going on," Tarek said. "In Skarzysko, men and women could mingle. There were babies born. They died, or they were killed. I didn't take any interest in this. Maybe it's not nice to say these things. There were some Jews who didn't behave right. There were more good things going on. Thank God for that." For example, Tarek recovered from typhus thanks to the kindness of some Werk C prisoners who took turns replacing her on the assembly line, doing what she calls "the yellow work" of filling metal shells with powder. "Every day they pulled us down from the bunk bed," Tarek said, outlining the routine for sick women in her barrack. "We were there for the count, and then I went back to the bed. Other girls worked in our place. We did this for each other."

Yet another danger pervaded Skarzysko-Kamienna. The Germans used Selektionen to remove and to kill the sick and weak prisoners. During roll call, or Appell, Helen and Sonia stood in the middle, toward the back, where they wouldn't be as conspicuous. "We would pinch each other's cheeks," Helen said. They bartered with Polish workers to get red tissue paper, which they moistened to spread the dye on their faces. "We traded the bread for the red tissue paper," Helen said. "Ah, red tissue paper was like gold." Sonia said: "Many girls put pebbles in their mouths to fill out their cheeks. They picked people who could hardly move, who were skeletons. People cried. People screamed. People throw themselves to the Germans. They pleaded. Nothing. We stayed still. There's no way you can fight or say anything."

Selektionen terrified Mandzia Wajchendler Mapa who, like Helen, was still an adolescent. "I was scared because I was very skinny. I was afraid that I didn't look enough mature. I looked even younger than I was. My father worried for me very much."

Sonia noticed the evil Meisters Georg Hering and Wilhelm Leidig, clad in their cloaks of death, overseeing the proceedings. "They wore black silk overcoats over their uniforms. You were afraid to lift your eyes." The S.S. pulled "unfit" Jews from the group, Helen and Sonia said, marched them into the forest, and shot them. "We knew. We heard. We knew it was happening," Sonia said. "They did this every few months, usually before a new transport is supposed to come," she said, referring to the arrival of more prisoners. Sometimes the S.S. locked the sick, injured, and exhausted prisoners in a small barrack for several days before execution. "They told us they gave these people more food because they were sickly," Helen said. "We could see the people in the little barracks through the window. I didn't see any killing, but we knew what was going on. During roll call, we heard shots."

Prisoners toiled under sadistic masters, who fabricated reasons to kill one minute and to grant pardons the next. Sometimes the mercy bestowed was perverse, as Esther Pasternak Tarek can attest. "One tray came back. They said that one explosive was chipped. They said I made a sabotage," Tarek said. At that instant on Werk C's assembly line, she was certain she would be killed. "I didn't make sabotage. The German called me in the office. He said, 'You better start running before I start shooting you.' He let me run, and he didn't shoot... I can say a German did something nice for me once." Kaminsky also endured the whims of an unpredictable boss in Werk C. Philich, the Nazi overseeing the production of underwater mines, mercilessly beat Kaminsky in the factory. Then, a few days later, he promoted Kaminsky to supervise the presses. "This Philich, he almost killed me, and then he made me in charge of both halls."

One evening, as Israel "Irving" Buchbinder trudged from Werk A's ammunition factory to his barrack, the Germans directed him to the right side. Knowing that destined him to the shooting range, Buchbinder bolted. He ran as fast and as far as he could, weaving around buildings. As though the hand of God opened to protect him, Buchbinder spied a hole under a barrack. Burrowing inside was easy. Buchbinder was only skin and bones. He spent the night there and reported to work the next day. The Volksdeutsch commander, Paul Kuehnemann, asked, "'Who is this fox who run away?'" Because he was a hunchback, Kuehnemann was nicknamed *der Hojker* by the prisoners. "They couldn't believe I could fit in such a small hole," Buchbinder said. "He said if I could do that, I could live. Because I have the nerve to run away, he give me a change of clothing. He give me a piece of bread." Like Esther Pasternak Tarek, Buchbinder found that his life depended on his captor's mood.

Some selected prisoners died in Treblinka's gas chambers, according to Simon Wiesenthal's *Every Day Remembrance Day*. For example, on October 30, 1942, within a month of the Garfinkels' incarceration, the S.S. deported about 2,200 Jews from the Skarzysko-Kamienna labor camp to Treblinka. Earlier that month, they had sent more than 2,000 Jews trapped in Skarzysko-Kamienna's ghetto to Treblinka.

In *Holocaust*, Martin Gilbert records an especially disturbing massacre of Jews too weak to work in Skarzysko-Kamienna, which he calls "...one of the most ferocious of all the labour camps in German-occupied Poland." On November 16, 1943, the Ukrainian guards promised double soup rations to some sick and exhausted ammunition workers whom they had isolated in a special barrack. As they emerged for the soup, the condemned prisoners were gunned down. Some were forced into trucks bound for the execution site. Guards threw bread in the vehicles just to watch the prisoners fight. Roza Bauminger, the eyewitness quoted by Gilbert and also by Felicja Karay in *Death Comes in Yellow*, testified: "It suddenly dawned on me what hunger really was... At that moment when they were being driven off to their deaths, they fought... The piece of bread was more important than the thought that they were going to be killed."

Mania Poper Cherston beheld equally pathetic scenes. When the S.S. accumulated 20 to 30 sick and exhausted Jews, Cherston said, they marched them to the forest behind the barracks. "They shot people there. We heard the noise from the guns," she said. "When they took the prisoners out to be killed, they were begging for a piece of bread. They know they're going to be killed, but they still begged to be given a slice to eat." Esther Pasternak Tarek also watched executions in Werk C. Once, during Appell, "They hung five people," she said, remarking that some memories are unshakable. "Sometimes you forget for a minute. Then you remember."

Even Sonia felt life had been reduced to a bowl of soup and a piece of bread. "We got the soup in the factory. We got the bread in the barrack," Sonia said. "We were thinking all day about the slice of bread. The hope for a slice of bread kept us alive."

Anxiety, a constant companion of Skarzysko-Kamienna's prisoners, intensified during Selektionen. "Every time we were always afraid," Sonia said. "Maybe I'll be next. If a German didn't like how I looked, he would pull me to the left."

Early in their confinement, before they had encountered all the evils of Skarzysko-Kamienna, Helen and Sonia stopped menstruating. The sisters speculated that something in the soup caused them to miss periods because all the other women experienced the same symptom. The real explanation is that the women's bodies were simply responding to extreme duress and lack of nutrients. Regina, who was only 12 years old in 1942, had not started menstruating when she was taken prisoner. She had one period in Kielce's labor camp, she said, and then her menses ceased until after the war. Other Shoah survivors, including Tess Wise of Orlando and Regina Rosenzweig of Tampa, said they did not menstruate during their incarceration. Regina Rosenzweig believes the S.S. poisoned the food to sterilize Jews, while Tess Wise thinks stress was the culprit. In her memoirs, *Playing for Time*, Fania Fenelon recreates a debate among her barrack mates over why they no longer had periods. Some women blamed "something in the soup," while others, including Fenelon, contended it was the lack of food. Fenelon, a French cabaret singer, survived the Birkenau-Auschwitz death camp by performing in the women's orchestra.

"In the beginning, I prayed a lot," Sonia said. "I cried a lot. I cried myself to sleep, and I prayed. Later I stopped praying. I held the prayers out of anger." Sonia visualized scenes of being at home in Chmielnik and of lighting the candles for Shabbat. She also dreamed of singing and eating with her family on holidays. "I tried to live in a dream world until I woke up, and I saw the reality that was still there." If she awakened in darkness, she heard that reality in sounds. Women cried with homesickness, they groaned in physical pain, they coughed from illness, they screamed during nightmares. Sometimes, women who shared bunks didn't get along, and they fought. Despair overtook Sonia, but Helen played a pivotal role in animating her older sister. At times, Helen stuffed

Sonia's pockets with potatoes and potato flakes. "The most important thing is to steal," Helen said. "I stole."

Cesia Zaifman noticed the Garfinkel sisters were opposites. "Sonia was very bad with the soup. We begged her to eat. She wouldn't eat her soup," Zaifman recalled. "Helen was tougher. She was more the organizer. She was more active." Mandzia Wajchendler Mapa also described Helen as lively and energetic.

When the guards dumped a mound of clothes in Werk B for the women to use, Helen elbowed her way through the crowd. Disinterested, Sonia stayed inside the barrack. "Those clothes, the Nazis took from dead people," Sonia said. The garments belonged to Jews gassed in Treblinka, Majdanek, Auschwitz, and other killing centers. "The prisoners throw themselves like animals on the clothes. To this day, I feel guilty that Helen brought me clothes. I felt ashamed that I could help myself but I didn't. I didn't care. I couldn't take it. What if I remember clothes from somebody? I was the only one left in barracks. Helen knew I was afraid. Helen knew I lost the lust to live." Sonia was 20 years old.

Greedy, Helen grabbed as many items as she could, so many that the guards beat her. Initially, she didn't consider the source. "Not right away. I didn't think about it," Helen said. "But later we used to talk about it, that these clothes came from murdered Jews." Although Sonia lacked the motivation to get clothes, she was happy with what Helen had brought. By then Sonia's green coat was filthy, its lining shredded. The garment, a sad reminder of comfortable, carefree times, tenuously linked Sonia to Bela and her boyfriend, Isaac. "It was like a tweed with gray in it. There was a belt with a hook and snap," Sonia said. "Isn't it funny, how I remember this?"

In Nathan's barrack, a Jewish policeman distributed used clothing to the men every three or four months. "The policeman would try to match the clothes to the individual," Nathan said, "or the prisoners traded among themselves." Once, David Krawczuk, an acquaintance from Chmielnik, found a $50 bill, U.S. currency, inside a pair of trousers. Nathan ripped apart the pants he had received but didn't find a zloty. "That $50 bill helped David survive. He gave the money to Polish people. They brought him back food," Nathan said. "Every time I saw David after the war, I said, 'David, you owe me $25.' It was hard to accept that these were the clothes from somebody who died, but the fact is there that we needed these clothes."

Both Nathan and Helen sustained a burning drive to live — unlike Bela, Regina, and Sonia. Helen's younger age, 16, and lack of fear helped her concentrate on the task at hand: survival. "I was very ambitious," Helen said. "I always pushed myself." Sonia felt that Skarzysko-Kamienna's remaining Jewish laborers would share the fate of her parents and younger siblings in Treblinka, but Helen kept such thoughts at bay. If Helen did think beyond her immediate struggles — ever so fleetingly — denial helped her retain a tad of optimism.

"I still thought I would see my parents. The Polish foremen would tell us that they took the Jewish children and old people away in trains. It never registered in my head," Helen said. "When you're cold and hungry and you're living a miserable life, you don't think about it. Maybe because I was young. Later, in Germany, I didn't think at all about my parents. The only thing I was thinking about was food."

Helen marvels that Sonia survived the Shoah. Yet she credits Sonia with saving her several times — at the war's end, when Sonia was the healthiest of the Garfinkel sisters. "I remember telling Sonia, 'If you're not going to steal, you're not going to survive.' Sonia was more of a softie. I thought, 'Sonia is not going to survive because she is a softie.'"

Chapter Twenty
AN UNLIKELY REUNION

A s the eastward tide of battles reversed in 1944, the once-victorious German army retreated from the Soviet Union. That prompted the S.S. to eliminate evidence of their crimes at such killing centers as Treblinka and to move entire work camps farther west. In the summer, the S.S. compelled the prisoners of Skarzysko-Kamienna to dismantle the ammunition plants, including the potato mill. Most of the machinery, supplies, and prisoners were relocated to Czestochowa, where the Hasag company operated other slave labor camps.

Known for its rich ore deposits and steel manufacturing, Czestochowa is a famous pilgrimage destination in Poland. Devout Catholics journey long distances to glimpse the black Madonna enshrined within the *Jasna Gora*, or "Bright Mountain" church. In the Madonna's shadow, thousands of Jews suffered and died. Czestochowa's Jewish residents, including relatives of British historian Martin Gilbert, were subjected to pogroms, firing squads, and overcrowding before their deportation to gas chambers.

In *Every Day Remembrance Day*, Simon Wiesenthal documents the atrocities — similar to those of other Polish communities — in chronological order:

"September 3, 1939. The Wehrmacht murders 150 Jews in Czestochowa, near Warsaw, Poland.

"September 4, 1939. In the history of Jewish martyrdom this day is known as Bloody Monday... The Germans organize a pogrom in the course of which some hundred Jews are slain.

"December 25, 1939. The Germans round up the Jews of Czestochowa, Poland, and carry out a pogrom. The synagogue is burned down.

"August 23, 1940. The Nazis single out 1,000 young Jewish men between 18 and 25 in Czestochowa, Poland, and send them to a forced labor camp in Ciechanov, Poland. None of them will survive.

"April 9, 1941. A ghetto is set up in Czestochowa. The Jews are crammed into the ghetto, where for lack of space and provisions they suffer from hunger and epidemics.

"September 23, 1942. A large-scale Aktion — lasting for the following 12 days — begins in the ghetto of Czestochowa. The Nazis send 40,000 Jews to the Treblinka extermination camp.

"October 5, 1942. The Aktion that began on September 23, 1942, is completed. The S.S. has shot 2,000 Jews and deported 25,000 Jews to the Treblinka extermination camp. A small number of Jews remain in the 'Smaller Ghetto.'"

Wiesenthal also writes of bravery amid the terror:

"January 3, 1943. In the ghetto of Czestochowa, Poland, an armed group of Jewish resistance fighters under the leadership of Mendel Fiszlewicz takes on the Nazis who want to enter the ghetto. In the fighting, 20 Nazis are killed and 25 resistance fighters die. As a retaliatory measure, the S.S. shoots 250 Jews.

"March 20, 1943. The S.S. executes 127 Jewish intellectuals.

"June 25, 1943. After a Jewish armed resistance in Czestochowa, Poland, in which many Jews are killed, the Nazis deport 1,000 Jews to Auschwitz.

"June 26, 1943. The liquidation of the small ghetto begins, although the Jewish resistance tries to fight. Several hundred Jews are murdered on the spot by the S.S., about 1,000 Jews are deported to a camp, and 4,000 Jews are deported to the Hasag labor camp, where they work in a factory.

"July 20, 1943. From the Hasag camp, 500 Jews are killed in the Jewish cemetery in Czestochowa.

"July 27, 1943. The last Aktion takes place in the ghetto of Czestochowa."

The city's remaining Jews toiled away their lives. Hasag's industrial complex included the Rakow steel mill and foundry and the munitions plants of Apparatexbau, Czestochowianka, Pelzery, and Warta. Nathan, Sonia, and Helen rode in trucks to the camp's Czestochowianka section. They scarcely recall the 97-mile trip. Much later, after the war, they learned that Soviet soldiers had liberated some of the prisoners left behind in Skarzysko-Kamienna.

Other prisoners — Mania Poper Cherston among them — were taken by train to Germany. "The same way they send people to Auschwitz," Cherston said. "We didn't know where we were going. We were eight days traveling. Don't ask. This was terrible. No food. No water. No sanitary facilities. Nothing. They open the doors (after eight days) and say, 'Get out.' We could hardly walk." Cherston arrived in Leipzig, Hasag's headquarters city. The munitions plants there were larger, enslaving more than 10,000 people, including Russian prisoners-of-war and Jews from France, Hungary, and other nations. Ironically, Cherston never fell ill in the more primitive conditions of Skarzysko-Kamienna, but she almost died of a mysterious virus in Leipzig. "They took me in the sick room. I knew they would kill me. I said, 'I am well. I can go back to work.' The will power of life is unbelievable. It is strong." Cherston not only outlived the illness, but she also endured a three-week death march in Germany. Soviet soldiers liberated her. "My son, Larry, asks me how I survived. I tell Larry, 'Ask God.' I don't know. You couldn't survive being smart. What if you got sick?"

Many of those left in Skarzysko-Kamienna died, according to The *Encyclopedia of the Holocaust*'s account of the summer of 1944. The S.S. assembled a special unit of inmates to excavate Werk C's mass grave and to cremate the corpses. Several hundred Jews tried to flee Werk C, but most were gunned down. In the process of emptying the Skarzysko-Kamienna complex, the Nazis shot more than 600 prisoners.

Esther Pasternak Tarek and her sister, Bela, joined the runaways, but Tarek's recollection is hazy because she was so worn down and exhausted. "In the camp there was an uprising. From Werk C we run away in the middle of the night. We ran, I don't know where. People were shot." The Germans transferred Tarek and her sister to Leipzig. Like Mania Poper Cherston, they spent several months making bullets and then withstood a grueling death march before Soviet soldiers freed them. "I couldn't survive without help," Tarek said. "I didn't have what to eat. Twenty-three days without food. I couldn't walk. They dragged me. They were schlepping me."

The day after the breakout, Israel "Ira" Kaminsky heard that about 60 Jews got away. Years later, he learned of their fate. "The escape was successful, but the end was very tragic." The group fled to the mountains to join Polish patriots, who killed them for being Jewish. A handful of stragglers managed to survive, Kaminsky said. "It was at night. At night it was much easier to escape." Shortly afterwards, the S.S. removed many of Werk C's prisoners. Kaminsky and his brother, Harry, landed in Buchenwald, and their sister, Rachel, went to Leipzig.

The S.S. detained some Jews in Skarzysko-Kamienna as late as January, 1945, according to Simon Wiesenthal's *Every Day Remembrance Day*. He writes: "The labor camps of Skarzysko-Kamienna, Mielec, and Plaszow (all in Poland) are liquidated. Of the total of 15,000 Jewish internees, 10,000 of them are shot, 5,000 transported by train to the Buchenwald and Ravensbrück concentration camps in Germany."

Nathan, Sonia, and Helen were shipped with more than 6,000 Skarzysko-Kamienna prisoners to Czestochowa in the summer of 1944. Anxiety ran high because they did not know what to expect. They thought they might be killed, so they almost welcomed the miserable, but familiar, routine of bone-tiring work, substandard shelter, and insufficient rations.

As it turned out, Nathan, Sonia, and Helen were relatively fortunate in their new prison — having been reassigned to Jan Laskowski's potato mill. As they contemplated the advancing Soviet army and the consolidation of camps, they wondered whether Bela and Regina were alive and, if so, whether they were still in Kielce. Nathan, Sonia, and Helen began asking other prisoners where they were from and in which camps they had worked. Sonia heard that some inmates had come to Czestochowa from Kielce, about 70 miles east.

"I asked around. Not everyone knew Bela and Regina." Sonia sought Rozencweig, a Jewish leader from the Kielce camp. Unbeknownst to Sonia, Rozencweig had protected Regina by hiding her during Selektionen. "It wasn't easy to see Rozencweig. The chills go over me now that I remember I asked Rozencweig," Sonia said. "I went in and asked about my sisters in Kielce. He said, 'Regina and Bela are your sisters?' He couldn't believe it. He told me they're alive. I asked him, could he bring my sisters to Czestochowa? He said they would be coming. Word went around through the whole camp that two sisters found two sisters. Even a guard from the Ukraine in broken Polish said, 'You found two sisters? I bring them tomorrow.'"

With each delivery of prisoners and equipment from elsewhere, Helen asked about Bela and Regina. "I remember these trucks coming," Helen said. "I would ask, 'When will they come, Bela and Regina? When will they come?' They said they would come later, later."

In Kielce, what Motek Pisaz, the Jewish policeman, had predicted, occurred. The Germans began relocating the prisoners. Some, including Bela, Regina, Tosia Fastag Bottner, Saul Jurysta, and Helen Rozenek Jurysta traveled by trucks northwest to Przedborz. There, near the Pilica River, the Wehrmacht forced them to dig anti-tank ditches. That particular episode of their captivity was so deplorable, Regina and Bela couldn't bear to recall it, let alone talk about it. They each shuddered as they described as briefly as possible their memories of wielding shovels that chafed their hands, digging as it rained, sinking to their knees in mud, and buckling under the blows of guards.

"I was digging in the wet. I was so underwater. Lots of people fell in. They didn't come back. I fell down. I fell in. I couldn't do it. I didn't care anymore," Bela said. "Regina's feet were so swollen. I don't know if she's going to be alive. That time I was very sad."

Regina's feverish condition caused prisoners to debate each morning whether to risk leaving her in their temporary sleeping quarters, a barn. They always opted to carry her to the trenches. Regina's attempts to work were feeble. "I remember lifting the shovel and having nothing on it. I couldn't dig. I think I passed out several times." Sometimes when Regina opened her eyes, she was lying in the mud. At other times, she awakened to beatings. "There, we had a lot of German women. They were *Kapos*," Regina said, referring to camp police. "They were horrible. They were much worse than the men. They pulled people out at random for no reason to beat." She repeated the criticisms they barked: "You're not holding the shovel right! You're not working fast enough! You're not moving the dirt!" A few times when she opened her eyes, prisoners were pulling Regina from what easily could have become her grave. "I remember being very, very weak then."

The ditches looked like a huge burial pit, according to Saul Jurysta's details. "It was 10 feet deep, maybe more, and 15 feet wide. It was made so the Russian tanks fall in. It was very hard. We were half-naked. If you didn't work so fast, they beat us. We dig the ditches. Sometimes it rained. Rain is nothing. If you're near death, rain is nothing."

Lola Preis Sylman felt as though the enormous trenches had swallowed her. "You had to throw the sand very high. It was twice as tall as I was. I had to do so much. My brother used to help me do my part." Sylman says she would have perished without assistance from her brother, Zyga Preis. "This place (Przedborz), from there they divided us." Sylman was taken to the Ravensbrück concentration camp in Germany, where the Swedish Red Cross rescued her. Her brother ended up in Czestochowa and, later,

Theresienstadt. "What people tell me, he died the day before liberation or the day after liberation," Sylman said. "I think I was in
Sweden when I heard about the Garfinkels. It's like a miracle for
every survivor. It's a book about them, but every one of us has a
book."

Kalman Mapa and his brother, Chil, parted with their two
sisters, Leja and Chawa, in Przedborz. The ever-resourceful Kalman
Mapa tried bribing German officers to make sure the girls stayed
together. The sisters took the same route to Germany and Sweden
as Lola Preis Sylman, while Mapa and his brother ended up in the
same camps as Zyga Preis. Mapa's impression of Przedborz is one
of filth. The barns where the prisoners were forced to sleep were
as dirty as the ditches. "It was very bad. Bad isn't the word," Mapa
said.

Evelyn Szczebakowska Cala and Regina Szczebakowska
Zalcman also struggled to dig. Steeped in their own misery by
then, the two sisters had lost track of Bela and Regina Garfinkel.
"It was hell. The whole summer we were working. It was raining.
It was near a cemetery," Zalcman remembered, noting that the
German army distributed food rations in the graveyard. "We were
crying over the graves for people to help us." In a strange fluke,
Cala was pulled from the awful chain gang. Someone accidentally
threw dirt on Cala's head; during the meal break, she begged some
Polish people to let her wash her long, black hair. A German of-
ficer, observing Cala's plight, picked her to clean his house, a dramatic contrast to ditch digging.

Any change of events was unsettling. Just when the Jews
thought things couldn't get worse, they were thrust into more pun-
ishing situations. Therefore, any improvements — even a slight
abatement of suffering — seemed miraculous. Bela and Regina
simply could not believe the news that they would be reunited
with Nathan, Sonia, and Helen. "They told us, 'You're going to
meet your sisters.' I didn't believe them," Bela said. A Selektion
preceded the move to Czestochowa, at which point Bela aban-

doned her royal blue coat. That final reminder of Isaac had been reduced to rags, and Bela feared never seeing him again. The future looked bleaker than ever. "I kept that coat until the last minute," she said. "Every time there was a Selektion, we thought, 'That's it. They send us to Treblinka now.'"

That easily could have been the outcome. In *Every Day Remembrance Day*, Simon Wiesenthal summarizes August 1, 1944: "Several hundred Jews, who earlier marched on foot from the Lublin labor camp to Kielce, Poland, are deported from Kielce to Auschwitz. Upon arrival 200 of them are gassed by the S.S." For August 25, 1944, Wiesenthal writes: "The remaining Jews in the camp at Kielce, Poland, are sent to Auschwitz and the Buchenwald extermination camp in Germany. Kielce is officially declared 'free of Jews.'"

Earlier that month, of course, Bela and Regina had been sent to Przedborz' ditches and then to Czestochowianka's bullet factories. Although breaking down and rebuilding work camps made no sense and seemed like futile busy work, Jurysta said, it spared the German officers from serving in the Wehrmacht and from facing most certain death on the Russian front. What sustained Regina through the hardships of forced labor was her vision of being with her family in Chmielnik. Even not having anything to eat for the Sabbath meal formed fond memories. "I remember thinking I was so stupid for thinking those times were bad." Regina held onto the image of her parents. "In the back of my mind, it was the hope of recapturing those memories, that security, someday. I couldn't say that hope in words, but in my mind it was what I imagined. That's why I could go on."

In the transfer from Przedborz to Czestochowianka, some prisoners talked of their hopes: reaching a better camp, getting easier work, or more food. A few even speculated about the war's end, a victorious Soviet army, liberation. Others spoke of their fears: being shipped to gas chambers. Barely aware of the conversation and chatter, Regina felt nothing. "Emotionally I was in a trance." Bela strained for a glimpse of their new camp. She was skeptical of ever seeing her other siblings again, yet she could not suppress that wish deep inside her heart. Bela cried out that she could see Nathan, Sonia, and Helen; Regina didn't believe her.

Bursting with anticipation, Sonia and Helen waited near the camp gates, where new prisoners arrived by truck and train. Each afternoon between work shifts, they joined the crowd of people gathered there to search for loved ones. Nathan sometimes tagged along. He figured Bela and Regina would, eventually, be evacuated west, but he thought the odds of meeting them were slim. "We knew they were going to come somewhere, somewhere, somewhere. We didn't know which camp. Even Czestochowa had three camps." Consequently, Nathan was amazed to see Bela and Regina huddled in the flatbed truck. "It was unbelievable happiness to see them. We knew the war was coming to an end." As Nathan put his arms around his sisters, fellow inmates, guards, and soldiers took notice and were touched. "We cried and hugged. Even the Werkschutz said the family got together," Helen said. "We were so happy, people were envious."

Alternating waves of disbelief and joy overwhelmed Regina, who was at the center of embraces. "Just seeing them alive, that's the only way I could believe it was real." Yet the unlikely reunion, amid dozens of onlookers, had a strange, surreal quality. Her brother and sisters looked different than Regina had remembered. They look haggard and worn, tired and sick.

Sonia felt a strong undercurrent of sadness. "We were mostly crying. We had forgotten how to laugh," she noted. "We were crying. The whole camp was crying. It was happy that we were united, but it was five skeletons together." Sonia wondered whether they could possibly outlast the war.

More feelings began to penetrate Regina's trance. "Naturally, we were overjoyed at the time. That was the part that was most unbelievable, that I was with my brother and sisters. That's what brought hope to me. I thought, 'Maybe my parents are someplace else in a camp.' That's what went through my mind, that we would still be together."

Although the guards and other prisoners said Jewish children and older adults died in gas chambers, Helen and Regina pictured their parents working in another camp. "I knew my parents were old but not so old. They were not like grandparents," Helen said. "Somehow, when I was in Skarzysko and Czestochowa, I still thought I would see my parents."

Like many prisoners, Kuba Zaifman was aware of, yet oblivious to, the Garfinkels' reunion. "For them it was happy." In retrospect, it was amazing they found each other, Zaifman said, but, at the time, it didn't seem so amazing because what was abnormal masqueraded as normal. "Nothing was possible. Nothing was impossible. Nothing surprised anybody. One day could be good, but the next day they could take you out and shoot you," Zaifman said. "Nobody knew what the day would bring, what was going to be tomorrow."

Chapter Twenty-One
IN THE MADONNA'S SHADOW

The Garfinkels' reunion represented an exceptional moment of joy during their long, grim struggle to stay alive amid physical hardship and psychological strain. The S.S. reassigned Bela and Regina to the munitions factory, but they slept in the same barracks as Sonia and Helen. Czestochowa's living quarters were more primitive and crowded. Each women's barrack accommodated more than 300 on planks of raw wood. Offering no separation or space between prisoners, the bunks were simply two long shelves on the wall. Without windows, the buildings seemed like tombs. Czestochowa's washrooms and latrines were as disgusting as the facilities of Skarzysko-Kamienna.

Their work schedules coincided so that the Garfinkels could eat together in the evenings. When the siblings figured out that the Jewish policeman who distributed food had pilfered their bread, they confronted him. Each loaf, weighing four to five pounds, contained five rations, but the policeman cut six portions to keep one for himself. Nathan demanded the entire loaf. The policeman agreed, provided the five siblings identify themselves to him simultaneously.

After getting a whole loaf to divide as they pleased, the Garfinkels always tried to give more bread to each other, Helen said. Most often the sisters insisted that Nathan take pieces of their bread. "All my sisters said, 'You're a man. You need more to eat.' My sisters were pushing me to eat more," Nathan said. "Bela said, 'I don't need much. You eat the rest of my bread.' Sonia was the worst. She said, 'I already had a slice of bread. You eat mine.' I ate the most of the bread. I felt bad about it, but I was forced into it."

Such preoccupation with food indicated the daily routine had not changed. Czestochowianka resembled the Garfinkels' previous camps: after 12 hours of back-breaking labor, the prisoners collected their meager rations and rested a few hours on hard, wooden shelves. Sleep deprivation plagued everyone. Not only were the work schedules unreasonably long, but the S.S. also disoriented Jews by rotating them between day and night shifts. "I am suffering of sleepless nights since. That was left with me. I have had a hard time during the years being able to sleep enough," said Etka Raitapfel Baumstick. "Twice a week I take sleeping pills. The doctor said he wasn't going to give sleeping pills if I take them every night. If you look at me or Helen or Sonia, when you look at us, you can't even imagine what all of us went through." Alternating workers between night and day shifts every week or two had occurred in Kielce and Skarzysko-Kamienna, too. Apparently, the S.S. preferred tormenting prisoners to increasing production. "You might get used to sleeping during the day. It wasn't so easy," Regina said. "By the time you get used to one shift, there would be another shift. That part wasn't to their benefit."

Shoes remained a critical source of concern and trouble for prisoners. Nathan had worn leather shoes with laces the day he left Chmielnik. As the soles deteriorated, he placed straw inside; as the soles separated from the shoes, he wrapped cloth, string, and sometimes wire around to hold them together. At some point while working in the potato mill, Nathan procured replacement shoes and access to a shoemaker, but his shoes were always in bad condition. "Shoes was the biggest problem," he said. "We didn't receive shoes. We received clothes."

Fay Skrobacka Goldlist made bullets in Czestochowa's Warta section, where prisoners hung on to hope. "It was unpleasant all the time. Nothing to sleep on, just a board. We imagined that the Russians were nearer to the border," Goldlist said. "What we talked. We hoped to be out in freedom and to have enough bread to eat and maybe we find somebody from our family after the war. That was our talk all the time. That was our hope and prayer: to find somebody from the family."

Common sense and wild speculation, rather than hope, enabled Bela Garfinkel to continue. "I know you can't kill everyone in one day. We thought there would be a miracle. We thought maybe Hitler would die. We didn't know what was going to happen tomorrow. I never have hope," Bela said. "We were like animals. That time your mind was just on a piece of bread. That's it."

Monotony served as a thin veneer to the constant threat of being punished or killed. Every now and then, terror jolted every prisoner. Cesia Zaifman became deathly ill for several days in Czestochowianka, where she made ammunition. She awakened in a room full of other sick prisoners. "I didn't think I would make it. I was afraid I was on the list for people who couldn't work," Zaifman said. "My foreman said, 'No, she's a good worker.' He saved me." Such help came unexpectedly and all too rarely.

Toiling long hours with heavy equipment made the prisoners susceptible to accidents. "They told us to wear scarves. If the machine caught one hair, it would take all the hair and you were bald. That's what happened to me," said Helen Rozenek Jurysta. During night shift in Czestochowa, she bent down and was scalped. One moment of carelessness resulted in months of excruciating pain and headaches. "I thought I would never have hair again." Jurysta's hair did not grow again until after the war.

Bela's most vivid recollection of the Czestochowianka camp includes the finishing line, where she tested and packed bullets. "This was worse than Kielce. I worked like a horse." A cruel woman, a Volksdeutscher, supervised production by watching for mistakes and then beating the prisoners. Once, the forewoman hit Bela for not seeking permission to eat some bread she had saved. She also struck Bela sharply on the back of the neck if Bela nodded off from exhaustion in front of the machines. "And then she gave me two more hours. She was such a rough, horrible woman." Although Bela made a point of remembering the woman's name, she eventually forgot it. Instead, she remembered the incident.

"This woman hit me plenty. She hits everyone for no reason. She used the whip. She was so proud of herself when she hit people. I wanted to tear her hair out," Bela said, expressing an uncharacteristic violence. Like Nathan, Bela knew survival depended on controlling her emotions and masking her anger. "I was afraid to look at her. You could imagine how I felt. I felt if I have something, I kill her. I said, 'God help me if I am going to be free.' Me, I won't hurt a fly, but I would kill her after the war."

The guards almost executed Helen several times as she continued taking risks by stealing potatoes and bartering. "If you're hungry, you don't ask any questions; you don't think about the consequences. Even after that beating for stealing potatoes in the garden," Helen said, referring to Skarzysko-Kamienna, "I would steal again. I wanted that my brother should survive. I would steal socks or a jacket or something for my brother so he should survive."

In Czestochowianka, Helen worked several weeks sorting clothes in a large warehouse. Some of the garments were new, and others were the uniforms of Polish and Soviet soldiers. Once Helen put several pairs of socks on her feet, to smuggle to Nathan. Then she couldn't squeeze into her wooden shoes, so she removed some of the socks. On another occasion, Helen put heavy socks under her arm, but a German soldier saw her. As he started hitting her, Helen threw down the socks. She was lucky she wasn't shot. In yet another incident, guards suspected Helen, Etka Raitapfel Baumstick, and Helen Hiutka Rayfer of stealing clothes. "At that time we were innocent," Etka said. Usually, "...we all tried to take whatever we could; but this time we were beaten — that was the only time we didn't take clothes. We were taken and beaten half-dead. For three weeks I couldn't lay on my back. I was just sick after the beating. I had to get up and go to work. I was afraid to stay in the barracks. It is so hard to talk about it. It's so many years passed, but I still have nightmares from this ordeal."

The beating was so severe, Helen said, that she cried. Jan Laskowski tried to animate her by saying, "Keep working. You'll be liberated soon." Despite all the physical abuse she endured, Helen feels grateful she didn't die. "Laskowski knew I was stealing clothes," Helen said. "He would talk to me in Polish and tell me not to steal. He would shake his finger at me. I had a good boss. If he wasn't good, he would have taken me and have me killed."

Chapter Twenty-Two
NATHAN'S PRAYER

The prisoners of Czestochowa sensed the war was concluding, but, of course, they remained enslaved. "We fought within ourselves psychologically, how to survive another day," Nathan said.

The S.S. announced the camp would be dismantled and evacuated, the same way Skarzysko-Kamienna and Kielce had been a few months earlier. "When they told us we were going to move out of Czestochowa, the fear was bigger," Nathan said. "Then we would not know what was going to happen tomorrow. Maybe there was going to be a battle. Maybe we were going to be separated again. We knew we would remain in their (the Nazis') hands longer. We wanted to be liberated there."

Prisoners who were dispirited or apathetic did not view the possibility of the war's end with as much hope, fear, and dread as Nathan did. Nathan felt more hope because his four sisters were alive, so his determination, endurance, and willpower strengthened. At the same time, he felt more fear because he had more to lose.

Nathan considers himself a believer in humanity despite the atrocities he witnessed and suffered in submission to the S.S., the Nazis, and the guards. Having rejected his father's practice of, and devotion to, Orthodox Judaism, Nathan is a self-proclaimed agnostic.

Yet, one night, in the barracks of Czestochowa, Nathan found himself talking to God. He lay in his customary place, the top bunk. "I still think I was dreaming, but I know I did not. I look at the ceiling. I saw a little spot. It looks like a fly sitting on the ceiling." His memory of looking at the ceiling indicates Nathan was awake, rather than dreaming. Yet he mentions another possibility: "I dreamt with open eyes." That he would even address an entity called God is so uncharacteristic of Nathan he wonders whether he was in some altered state.

"Whatever it was — coincidence or miracle — it happened. It wasn't a prayer. It was a plea bargain. It was a little negotiation with God. 'Please God, I give you something. You give me something.'" Nathan made his unlikely but irreverent proposal under duress and in anticipation of the war's final days. Anxiety about the outcome added to his fear and exuberance.

Nathan said, "God, if I have two of something, take one that my sisters might live. I have two eyes. Take one that my sisters might live. I have two legs. Take one that my sisters might live. I have two ears. Take one that my sisters might live. I have two hands. Take one that my sisters might live."

The next day, Nathan was ordered to disassemble machinery in the potato mill to be transported to another location farther west. He cleaned first. Nathan wrapped a rag around his left hand to wash and dry the rollers for compressing steamed potato slices. The rag snagged between the spinning rollers, and Nathan's hand was crushed between them. Steam heat burned the flesh.

With his hand trapped, Nathan managed to kick open the door and to yell for help. Jan Laskowski rushed in and turned off the machine. Nathan's mangled hand was not broken because springs made the rollers flexible, but the top of his hand was raw down to the ligaments. The rag had protected his palm.

Laskowski took Nathan to the barracks and later brought bandages and salve. Nathan believes Laskowski had access to medical supplies through his son's girlfriend, a nurse. Had the more typical, tyrannical Nazi or S.S. supervised Nathan, he would have been shot. Helen and Sonia screamed in anguish and cried when they learned of the accident. They knew their brother was doomed. Past executions of ill and injured prisoners convinced the sisters they would not see Nathan again.

"Laskowski said a few days later I would be shipped out, but he didn't know where. He said, 'I can't help you anymore.'" Nathan couldn't sleep, his hand hurt so badly, but the salve helped. After resting for two days, Nathan was herded with other prisoners into train cars heading west. "I was shipped to Buchenwald. My sisters were shipped somewhere else, where I didn't know. I didn't find out until the end of the war."

Sonia and Helen assumed Nathan was dead, but that realization did not emerge in their conscious thoughts, so great was their own struggle to survive during the war's last hellish months. They did not know their unconventional brother had made a deal with God — what most people would call a prayer. So they did not recognize his injury as an answer.

Chapter Twenty-Three
WESTWARD BOUND

The three-day train ride from Czestochowa, Poland, to the infamous Bergen-Belsen concentration camp near Celle, Germany, proved to be one of the Garfinkel sisters' most terrifying experiences. From the onset, they did not know the specific destination, only that they would be shipped west, away from the advancing Soviet army.

On the day the S.S. evacuated Czestochowa's labor camps, in early 1945, Bela received a warning. Another prisoner, Mrs. Zwirkowa, suggested the Garfinkels stay behind with her and her daughter. Mrs. Zwirkowa preferred the unknown risk of waiting in Czestochowa for liberation rather than being transported to another camp or killing center. Mrs. Zwirkowa proposed they all hide in the building housing the latrines. The plan tempted Bela, but she could not persuade her sisters to follow Mrs. Zwirkowa's advice. "We didn't listen to her. We saw her after the war. She was liberated the next day."

Sarah Frydman Goldlist, formerly of Chmielnik, now in Toronto, was freed with Mrs. Zwirkowa. "Women were marched out, I remember," Goldlist said. "I was left behind. This is another chapter. I write myself a book. I am writing it for years." After World War II, news that the five Garfinkel siblings survived the train rides, death camps, and forced marches in Germany seemed miraculous, Goldlist said. "It was miracles that any one of us survived. We do believe in miracles. It was miracles or luck."

Mandzia Wajchendler Mapa was also spared the nightmarish train ride to Germany. As a forewoman decided which prisoners to send west and which to keep, Mandzia's sister, Rose, pleaded that they not take Mandzia. Consequently, the two sisters remained in Czestochowa. "It was a split of a minute," Mandzia recalled. "My sister started to beg. She pulled me back. The same night we were liberated. Some people who went away, they never came back."

Fay Skrobacka Goldlist was freed in Czestochowa through a mishap. A bridge had been damaged in a bombardment, and the prisoners could not cross town. "They took us back to the barracks. We were liberated that night. That was our luck."

The Garfinkels, like most prisoners, proceeded to the train station, where the battle already raged. "All of a sudden, we saw Germans running. They were bleeding," Sonia said. "I remember seeing a man drop his machine gun." The four sisters were dazed after more than two years of forced labor, poor nutrition, threats, beatings, exhaustion, and psychological strain. In retrospect, Bela, Sonia, Helen, and Regina realize they could have escaped. The melee and confusion provided a rare opportunity to slip away unnoticed. Years later, Helen heard about prisoners who did just that, including a man who hid on the tracks under a parked train. Etka Raitapfel Baumstick said, "You know what happened there as we were standing? There were two Polish people. They passed by. They saw us. They said, 'The Russians are on the other side of Czestochowa. Why don't you run away?' We didn't believe the Polacks. Some girls ran away. We went on the train. We were packed like sardines."

The possibility of escape seldom entered the Garfinkel sisters' minds. When it did, questions accompanied it. Where would they go? To whom could they turn for help? In the moments they waited on the train platform, the notion of fleeing was absent. "They gave us, when we came in the train, a slice of bread," Sonia said. "We even joked among ourselves that we run to the train like a herd of animals because they give us a slice of bread."

A tremendous amount of shoving nearly lifted Helen from the ground. German soldiers and guards continued pushing the women into train cars designed for livestock, not people. "That train ride," Helen said and shuddered. "I think that was a death sentence." So many women jammed the Garfinkels' cattle car, they could not sit, much less lie down. Other than the initial slice of bread, they received no food during the entire 500-mile journey. They had no water, either. There was no toilet, not even a bucket. Because the women could not move, they urinated and defecated where they stood. So the rustic cattle car became unsanitary and smelly, too.

"We were all quiet on the train," Sonia said. "We didn't know how long we have to live, or what. We didn't know where they were taking us, to the gas chambers, to the ovens." With no room to maneuver, the women dozed on their feet. The extreme discomfort clouded their ability to think clearly.

For Regina, who had sustained herself in Kielce's bullet factories by not thinking, the events following Czestochowa are a blur, so much so she listed subsequent camps in a different order than her sisters. Regina remembers succinct details, but substantial chunks of time remain blank to her, so horrible were the final months. "When they evacuated us, we were all together," Regina said. "The Germans were running back and forth. We could have probably run away at that point. We were so vulnerable. They pushed us into the train. We went along. That's when the torture really started."

The deplorable train ride made Kielce's grueling work camp and Spartan barrack seem civilized — the same way the camp had made Chmielnik's impoverished and starvation-ridden ghetto seem like heaven. Regina would have given anything to regain the sense of security she had with her parents on Friday evenings. "During the war, my father emphasized learning. He said, 'You know, possessions can be taken away from you, but what you have up here, what you've learned, can never be taken away. It cannot be destroyed.' He must have known something already then. At the time I couldn't understand why he is saying, 'Everything can be taken away,'" Regina said. "While I was in camp and after the war,

I realized what he meant. But then I was thinking, 'Well, your mind can be destroyed, too.' And a lot of people's minds were destroyed after the war." Regina lost consciousness in the train.

Sonia kept vigil. A small opening at the top of the cattle car enabled her to discern whether it was night or day. At night, she saw the glare of bombs. "We didn't have any air. It was winter. It was freezing weather outside," Sonia said. "A girl stood on my shoulders. She tried to look out the window." At one point the train stopped, and Sonia saw the name of a German town, Würzburg. The train stayed there all night.

Bela, for her part, silently berated herself for not heeding Mrs. Zwirkowa. "I have in my mind: 'Why didn't I hide with Mrs. Zwirkowa?' But I wouldn't hide for myself. I wouldn't leave my three sisters. I have guilt my whole life that I left my grandmother in Lodz. I couldn't leave my sisters," Bela said. "Then I thought, 'We deserve this punishment because we did what they told us. We got on the train.'"

Cesia Zaifman, on the same train bound for Bergen-Belsen, tormented herself with similar thoughts. While she had walked along Czestochowa's streets, "Neighbors called out saying we shouldn't go on the train because the Russians are coming. People were calling in Polish: 'Run away!' We didn't want to listen to them. We didn't believe it was true. The mind was brainwashed. We didn't care what they do to us. They pushed us in, more than the train can take." As the train lurched and rattled that first night, Zaifman was alone with her regrets about not sneaking away when she had a chance. "We couldn't see nobody. It was dark. It was closed up. No food or water. Quite a lot died on the train."

Helen struggled to breathe. "I wanted to go to that little window. I needed air, and I needed water." After two days, Helen and Sonia estimate, the train ground to a halt and the doors opened. The women tumbled out, stunned. German soldiers ordered the healthier looking prisoners to pull out the corpses of women who had died from thirst, hunger, fatigue, and exposure.

Soldiers with guns allowed the prisoners to relieve themselves at the forest's edge. The Garfinkels later learned that some women disappeared into the woods during that break. Helen heard gun blasts, but she didn't see anyone running away or being shot. "I never thought about escape," Helen remarked. "I was never thinking about escaping. I saw the guns. I was afraid."

The Germans gave the women water before cramming them into the cattle cars. The removal of dead bodies did not necessarily create more space, Helen said. "It was just as crowded and horrible as ever."

Chapter Twenty-Four
LOGS OF WOOD

Nathan, like his sisters, also suffered a grueling train ride from Czestochowa, Poland, to Germany. By keeping the Jews prisoners, the German government could continue exploiting them as a labor source and maintain the goal of genocide — even in the face of military defeat.

Guards and soldiers pushed Nathan and other male prisoners into trains meant for livestock. So many men crowded the boxcars, that sitting and lying down were impossible. "We were squeezed in like standing sardines." The 400-mile journey to the notorious Buchenwald concentration camp lasted 10 days. The train stopped often, Nathan said, yielding to passenger trains carrying German soldiers from the eastern front. The doors of Nathan's cattle car never opened, so the prisoners received no food, water, or fresh air.

Israel "Ira" Kaminsky also traveled by train to Buchenwald, but his transfer, directly from Skarzysko-Kamienna, had occurred a few months earlier. "This was the worst experience of my life," Kaminsky confessed. "We were four-and-a-half days without water. They threw a little bread into the wagon. We were hungry, but we couldn't eat the bread without water." At a stop, the Jews paid a Ukrainian guard to fetch some water, but he simply pocketed the money without reciprocating. They succeeded in persuading another guard to bring water. "Everyone around me took a little drop of water to wet their throat," Kaminsky said. "We came out dehydrated, terribly. Everyone told me that my lips were completely black. I don't like to talk about it." In the chaos of multiple evacuations, prisoners were scattered.

Israel "Irving" Buchbinder also went directly from Skarzysko-

Kamienna to Buchenwald, but his subsequent stops, Schlieben and Mauthausen, differed from those of Kaminsky and Nathan Garfinkel. The final months were so torturous, Buchbinder said, some prisoners committed suicide by throwing themselves on electrical fences and in front of moving trains. Buchbinder attributed his physical survival to instinct and his emotional survival to hope.

"Any animal in the wild wants to survive. The human being is the same thing," Buchbinder asserted. Even though he heard that his mother and siblings had been gassed in Treblinka, "In the back of my mind, I thought maybe somebody survived. I had a strong will. I wanted to see what happened, to see if somebody else survived — maybe one of my brothers or my only sister."

Saul Jurysta may have been on the same train as Nathan. Jurysta chastised himself for not escaping while the Soviet army invaded Czestochowa. "I got sick on the train. I beat my head on the wall. I was so disgusted. Oh, you fools, you run away from the Russians!" After about an hour, the train stopped, and the prisoners in Jurysta's car drank water from the locomotive's steam engine. He passed up another chance to flee. "Again, you were always afraid if the Poles catch you, they give you away to the Germans or they kill you." Kuba Zaifman felt similar frustrations during his transfer from Czestochowa to Buchenwald. "Lots of people were smart. They hid. They remain free. They were liberated," Zaifman said. "We were sitting on the train. We heard the shots from the Russians. We couldn't escape."

The evacuations west were so indescribably cruel, some Holocaust survivors cannot talk about the train rides and forced marches they endured. Those who do, speak with great trepidation. Many prisoners died. Some were stricken with diarrhea, including Kaufman of Chmielnik. Nathan cannot remember the teenager's first name, but he was not related to the Kaufmans who had been the Garfinkels' neighbors. In the train, the young Kaufman asked Nathan to hold him so he could defecate through the small window near the top of the boxcar. Vibrations made this task difficult, so they waited until the train stopped.

Nathan lifted Kaufman. Within seconds, soldiers outside fired their guns. Kaufman cried, "Take me down. Take me down. I'm shot." Horrified, Nathan dropped Kaufman to the floor. "It was quick. When I laid him down, I tried to talk to him. I said, 'What's the matter? How are you doing?' But he didn't answer." Kaufman was dead. Nathan rarely cries while describing his ordeal of the Shoah. When he does, his tears flow for others. He cries for the teenager from Chmielnik, for whose death he feels responsible. "If I didn't hold him up, he wouldn't have died," Nathan said. "This is the guilt-complex of survivors."

Kaufman's odds of survival would have been remote even if he had not been murdered.

Once, during a stop, prisoners shouted for water. The Germans responded by aiming a hose at the boxcars' small openings. The water drenched the prisoners. Being wet accelerated their exposure to cold, and some men froze to death. They also perished from starvation, dehydration, illness, and exhaustion. Nathan estimates that about one-third of the prisoners died en route to Buchenwald. The living stacked the corpses to one side as though they were logs of wood, Nathan said. "We were satisfied that more people were dying in the car. When people died, there was enough room for us to move around."

Chapter Twenty-Five
BERGEN-BELSEN

Before the Garfinkel sisters arrived, Bergen-Belsen had already exceeded its capacity. The concentration camp, originally built for 10,000 prisoners, had absorbed more than 15,000 by November, 1944. Its population ballooned during the winter as the Germans raced to conceal their crimes from the approaching Soviet forces. In April, Bergen-Belsen held 60,000 inmates, mostly Jews evacuated from camps farther east. To say conditions were inhumane is an understatement. "Bergen-Belsen is hell on this earth," Sonia said. "I am not afraid of hell. I have been there."

In a perverse paradox, the S.S. required newcomers to bathe before stepping into Bergen-Belsen's filth. The twisted intent of disinfecting, however, was to terrorize and to dehumanize prisoners. Not knowing what would happen next heightened the Garfinkel sisters' state of panic. They felt the end was near. German S.S. officers, guards, and soldiers herded the women into a large, empty warehouse and ordered them to disrobe. Sonia and Helen prepared to die — having already heard about gas chambers from their captors in Skarzysko-Kamienna and Czestochowa. "We thought for sure this was gas," Helen remembered and shuddered. "We cried. We prayed to God that we should not feel the pain."

Sonia persuaded her three sisters to hang back with the final group of 50 women. That decision may have marked the difference between life and death at some later point. For whatever reason — haste, inefficiency, laziness — the S.S. did not shave the heads of the remaining naked women. "It was a big plus to have your hair," Sonia said. "You looked different, and it was warmer."

Etka Raitapfel Baumstick huddled with that final group, too, and her long, dark-blonde braids were spared. Likewise for Cesia Zaifman's short, blonde hair. "Some people were lucky," Zaifman said. "I don't know why. We didn't ask questions. You never understand why." An S.S. woman pushed Evelyn Szczebakowska Cala onto a chair and towered over her, peering at her head, poking a pencil in her braids. "She said if my hair was dirty, filthy with lice, she would cut my hair." Cala passed inspection. Once again, her long, black hair made her stand out in the crowd.

Besides profiting from the sale of human hair for use in wigs and bedding, the S.S. cut off hair to weaken and to dispirit the Jews. As a result, the women were indistinguishable from each other as well as from men. The minutes seemed like hours. "Waiting there not knowing and not seeing anyone coming back," Sonia said. "We didn't know. We didn't know if they killed them."

Terror gripped Helen in the shower room. She screamed in fear and then cried in disbelief as water gushed from the showerheads. "We felt relief when the water was running," Sonia said, "but we learned not to trust the Germans. They fooled us many times." Had they foreseen the misery awaiting them, the sisters might have wished for gas. Sonia would commit suicide rather than relive the Shoah, she said. Bergen-Belsen is one of many reasons why.

Bela felt the same. "I would commit 50 times suicide, but I didn't have a pill," she said. "When we arrive to this place, I thought we did a mistake, but now it's too late. It was bad. I thought they take us to the death chamber." Bela wished she and her sisters had stayed in Czestochowa with Mrs. Zwirkowa.

What Regina remembers most vividly about the shower room was a big tub, where the women were forced to immerse themselves, one at a time. Regina placed one foot in the murky, cold water. Her other foot stuck like glue to the icy floor. "We had to wash our hair. My hair was freezing."

Bergen-Belsen's showers represent the Garfinkel sisters' last bath until liberation four months later. Soaked and shivering, the women donned wooden clogs and gray, striped garments resembling long nightshirts. Etka Raitapfel Baumstick remembers standing naked under dripping water all night before being handed a long, gray nightgown and a coat without buttons. Etka tore a strip from the gown's hem to use as a belt to close the coat. In a measure calculated to degrade women, no underwear was distributed — the absence of which Bela found to be unsettling. "I said to Sonia, 'They should kill me now.'" To exacerbate the discomfort and cold, the S.S. did not provide socks. The clogs hurt. "These shoes never fit right," Sonia said. Thus inadequately clothed, the women proceeded to their so-called barrack, a huge, wooden warehouse. It contained no furniture, bunks, or shelves to sleep on, so hundreds of women, many of them sick and dying, lay on the floor.

That sight appalled the Garfinkel sisters even though they had tolerated sub-human living conditions and their guards' cruelty for many months. "These girls looked like skeletons. I didn't want to go close to them. I never knew that I was going to be like one, too," Helen said. "There were so many girls, that we couldn't even stretch out our legs. I thought, 'Once we are liberated, I'll sleep and stretch out my legs.'" The women lying on the floor were so weak and ill, they did not have the energy to go outside to the latrine. "I don't want to bring this up," Bela said, "but in the barracks, the floor was full of urine. Actually you don't have to go to the bathroom (defecate) because you don't eat nothing."

Sonia is certain there were no latrines in her section of Bergen-Belsen. Women afflicted with dysentery ran outside the barrack and relieved themselves in the snow — if they had the strength. "They were running on people's heads, on people's hands, on people's feet," Sonia said of the scramble to exit the barrack at night. "It wasn't just diarrhea. There was vomit. How can anyone describe Bergen-Belsen? There was no gas chambers, no ovens in Bergen-Belsen. It was a living hell. At least in Auschwitz, when you cannot work, they take you out and kill you." Unbeknownst to Sonia, there was a crematorium at the camp's edge. It was so small, however, it could not handle the high volume of corpses.

Even in those hideous conditions, the Garfinkels were lucky to have a roof over their heads. The camp could not accommodate the tens of thousands of prisoners streaming in from Poland and eastern Germany during the winter spanning 1944 and 1945. An estimated 20,000 women were forcibly marched to Bergen-Belsen from the Auschwitz, Buchenwald, and Gross-Rosen camps. Male prisoners also populated Bergen-Belsen. "I remember there was a fence, and we were told there were men on the other side," Regina said. "I was pretty much out of it by then. I didn't care. I didn't look around." Without rudimentary shelter, many prisoners died from exposure, while others perished from the lack of food and water. The squalor resulting from such overcrowding bred disease. In addition, there were bedbugs, what Helen calls a *wanze* or *vantz* in Yiddish. "They bit in the skin. They left red marks. It itched. We were weak. We were lying there, and suddenly they would bite. This is from filth."

Other eyewitness accounts of Bergen-Belsen ring with the same shock and despair expressed by the Garfinkel sisters. Violette Fintz, a Rhodes Jewess interviewed in 1985 by Martin Gilbert for *Holocaust,* said: "Many people talk about Auschwitz, it was a horrible camp; but Belsen, no words can describe it. There was no need to work as we were just put there with no food, no water, no anything, eaten by the lice. From my experience and my suffering, Belsen was the worst. I came to a point where everyone was saying, 'Violette is dying.'" Fania Fenelon, the French cabaret singer, also was relocated from Auschwitz to Bergen-Belsen — an awful ordeal she outlines in her book, *Playing for Time.*

Bergen-Belsen's most famous inmate was Anne Frank, whose posthumously published wartime diary has touched readers around the world. Nazis discovered the teenager and her family hiding in Amsterdam in August, 1944, and shipped them to

Auschwitz. Several weeks later, Anne and her sister, Margot, were transferred to Bergen-Belsen, where they died in a typhus epidemic that killed more than 18,000 prisoners in March, 1945.

Each morning, guards roused the women and forced them to march outdoors to be counted. "They came very early to get us. They didn't care how many of us there were. They wanted us to die," Sonia said. "During the count, some women couldn't stand any longer. They fell down and froze."

The count, known as *Appell*, was a meaningless exercise. No names or identification numbers were called aloud. The S.S. insisted on Appell whether it was raining or snowing, and the extreme cold during the winter of 1944 and 1945 made roll call a torture. Bergen-Belsen's hierarchy of S.S., guards, and soldiers were all German, Sonia observed. "Sometimes we stood for hours in the cold. Our hair got so stiff from the frost," Helen said. In the mornings, "When we heard the siren, we didn't want to get up. We just wanted to lay there. But we never tried staying in the barrack. We didn't know what would happen."

The Garfinkels ran outside quickly because the guards whipped the last women to exit. Women too weak to rise were also flogged. "I never saw that the women were killed," Helen noted. "I don't think in Bergen-Belsen they had to kill. They (the S.S.) knew the girls were half-dead." Unnerved, Bela ran her hands up and down her uniform to brush off the lice. "I said, 'Please God, let something fall from the sky and let me die.' I believe in God, but I said, 'Those S.S. men are stronger than God.'"

Already dangerously thin, the sisters soon became emaciated from the lack of food. Prisoners received bread only two or three times a week. The war disrupted supplies, they were told, and Bergen-Belsen no longer functioned as a work camp. It was merely a concentration camp — by 1945, a place to die. Helen said they got soup in the barrack, but Sonia and Bela recall only the sporadic distribution of bread. When asked about rations in Bergen-Belsen, Sonia responds, "Food? What food? There was no food in

Bergen-Belsen." Even more critical was the lack of water. There were no washrooms or faucets in the Garfinkels' section of the camp, according to Sonia. The women depended on liquid in the so-called soup and coffee — rations that Sonia claims were never distributed. To satiate their thirst, the women pounced on freshly-fallen snow. Old snow was putrid from human waste and corpses. "I was afraid of the snow," Sonia said. "In Bergen-Belsen, I was thirsty. You swallowed your own saliva."

Helen Rozenek Jurysta remembered the occasional distribution of so-called coffee. "It wasn't coffee. It was a chemical that looked black... The women used the coffee to wash their hair. No human being can understand the conditions that were there. It was unbearable. I don't know how we survived if I look back and think about it. I don't believe that we're here."

Women fighting for food and snatching bread from each other were disturbing, but common scenes. "Sometimes it happened to Sonia. They steal bread from her," Bela said. "We save portions for tomorrow. When you sleep, they take the bread from you. I was holding the bread so tight," Bela said as she crossed her arms over her chest.

Helen sought out the kitchen. "I went through the garbage and ate the peels of potatoes. I ate leaves. I ate paper." She also used paper and leaves to insulate her feet. "Sometimes I dug some leaves from under the snow and put them in my shoes," Helen said. She also wrapped her feet in paper. "It was so cold the paper dissolved," she said. "I ripped my uniform and wrapped the threads around the paper around my feet. If your feet are cold, your whole body is cold. When you're hungry, you're even more cold."

Regina shudders to think of the ill-fitting clogs she wore in Bergen-Belsen. "When wooden shoes were in style in the '50s and '60s, I couldn't believe it," she said. At various points during her imprisonment, Regina walked barefoot. Sometimes she wrapped her feet in rags. "I don't remember when, where. I really don't."

Shortly after Etka Raitapfel Baumstick arrived at Bergen-

Belsen, her shoes were stolen as she slept with them tucked under her head. Confronting the thief was impossible in the dark, congested barrack. Etka tore more strips from her gown to wrap around her feet. "I was without shoes. It was January. I had no shoes. Germany is quite cold in January," Etka said. Months later, a Polish Kapo helped recover Etka's black leather, lace-up shoes from a Russian prisoner. Etka's proof of ownership was German marks sewn inside the lining. "By then, it was April. It wasn't so cold anymore. When I needed the shoes, I didn't have them. It was amazing I didn't get frostbite."

She was so ill, Regina has difficulty recalling Bergen-Belsen. "I got sick. I was in a semi-conscious state most of the time." One day, Regina awakened in the camp hospital with corpses surrounding her. The knowledge that people were taken there to die barely registered. Regina could not think clearly, and, when she did, she wanted to die. The sight of Sonia peering through a window was no coincidence or miracle as far as Regina is concerned. "By us it was different. We were not a selfish family. We all looked out for one another," Regina said. "Someone lifted me, and Sonia pulled me out. Sonia has no recollection of this." Regina is the only one who remembers being pulled through the window of Bergen-Belsen's infirmary. Regina is certain that incident was not a dream, hallucination, or product of delirium. Being saved by her sister is real. It happened. It is a memory, Regina's memory, that her rescuer, Sonia, cannot remember.

The lack of food, the constant exposure to cold, and the proliferation of lice made many women susceptible to dysentery, typhus, and other diseases. "Girls fell like flies when they entered this camp," Helen said. Worst of all, the prisoners became insensitive. "In Bergen-Belsen, it's a living death. In Bergen-Belsen, you give up altogether your life. In Bergen-Belsen, do you think there was anything left of me? There was nothing. I was a body," Bela said. "They make you feel like you're not a person anymore. You wake up in the morning, this girl dead, that woman dead, another one dead. I kicked dead bodies with my feet. Everybody dead. I didn't give a damn. I want to die like them. I was sick like them, but my time wasn't up."

Desperation made Helen resort to what she now recoils to think of: scavenging among corpses. "I took off clothing from dead people. Before Bergen-Belsen, I couldn't do this," Helen said. "Nobody pushed me to go do these things. I did it on my own."

As they languished, the Garfinkel sisters concluded the best course of action was no action. They concentrated on conserving energy, doing nothing, and lying among the dead and dying. "Many children in schools ask me, 'Do you still believe in God?'" Helen said. "I say, 'Yes. In concentration camp I slept next to dead girls, and God let me live. I believe there's a God.'"

Dying in peace, much less existing without harassment, was impossible at Bergen-Belsen or any other camp. The S.S. enjoyed devising tasks to wear down the weak and dying prisoners. "They take me to sweep the streets," Helen said, referring to the walkways between buildings. "They take me to pick up leaves, to pick up stones. It was not work." Etka Raitapfel Baumstick also noted: "You know what they did to us? There was a huge bunch of stones. They ask you to take it from one place to another. The next day we moved the stones back. This was useless work. This was just to wear people out, to kill them."

Sonia's features — high cheekbones and above-average height — gave her an appearance of health and vigor relative to others. Once, the S.S. commanded Sonia and Regina to carry a wrought iron headboard — of all things — from one end of camp to the other. Regina distinctly remembers lugging the headboard through the snow, begging Sonia to leave her alone, to let her die. The responsibility of caring for Regina weighed heavily on Sonia. She did not want to disappoint their parents.

"Regina's hands froze to the headboard. She pleaded with me to let her die. I cried to Regina. I said, 'Please, please, no.' I took her hands and put her fingers in my mouth. I took a piece of cloth from my clothes and wound them around her fingers." Some-how, the two sisters managed to drag the headboard across the camp. They staggered back to their barrack, which can only be described as a warehouse of death. Sonia's concern for Regina made her frantic.

"I knew I had to look for some food for Regina. I ran out. I saw a pile covered with snow. I thought it was potatoes. I thought I found potatoes. When I came near, I saw a hand sticking out. I ran so fast. I was afraid of the snow from the ground because of all those dead bodies. In Bergen-Belsen, everywhere there were bodies. There were mounds of bodies."

Chapter Twenty-Six
BLOCK NUMBER 65

Buchenwald, one of Germany's largest concentration camps, contained about 63,000 prisoners in November, 1944, before Nathan's transfer there. The population swelled to more than 86,000 by March, 1945. Despite its heinous reputation, Nathan considered Buchenwald a "good" camp — "good" assuming another definition in an environment dominated by evil. "It was the best camp I had ever been in. There was nothing to do," Nathan said. "For me, compared to the previous camps, Buchenwald was a haven: to do nothing, die, starve, freeze. They let you die."

Germany's industrial infrastructure had deteriorated by the time Nathan arrived. Little work remained in Buchenwald or its 130 satellite camps outside the town of Weimar. An estimated 238,980 political dissidents, Soviet prisoners of war, and Jews passed through Buchenwald from 1937 to mid-1945. Tens of thousands met their deaths in nearby quarries, armament factories, and other work sites. The most infamous auxiliary camp was Dora-Mittelbau, also known as Nordhausen. Within Buchenwald, German doctors maimed and killed Jews via pseudo-medical experiments.

Nathan concealed his injured hand upon reaching Buchenwald. When the S.S. compelled newcomers to clean the trains, Nathan kicked out the bodies instead of lifting them. The men went through a disinfecting process, shedding their tattered clothes to shower. Nathan got his first camp uniform bearing blue and white stripes. The S.S. assigned him a number, 115117. Instead of joining his Jewish camp-mates from Czestochowa, Nathan mingled with non-Jewish prisoners who had disembarked

from other boxcars. The S.S. led non-Jews who were ill and injured to the camp's medical clinic. Nathan followed to get treatment for his hand. Remarkably, during this entire process, he
managed to keep the bandages given him by Jan Laskowski.

The *Revier*, Germany's version of the Red Cross, operated
Buchenwald's makeshift, poorly-supplied hospital. It was a re-
spite contributing to Nathan's survival. He got soup and bread.
For the first time in years, he slept alone in a "bed" — a cot lined
with a sack of straw.

While he recuperated, two Polish prisoners approached
Nathan. They were non-Jews who had formerly prospered as merchants in Lodz. Poznanski came daily to visit Galarus, the hospital's
caretaker. The two asked Nathan to witness a spoken agreement
that obligated Poznanski to give Galarus an entire block of buildings in Lodz after the war, provided Galarus gave Poznanski bread.
Galarus collected the rations of prisoners who were dead or too
sick to eat. Such pacts to enhance survival were common among
the wealthy — be they Jews or non-Jews — but few lived to fulfill
their promises. Both Poznanski and Galarus died before World
War II ended.

A patient in the adjacent cot befriended Nathan and supplied
him with underground newspapers similar to the publications of
Skarzysko-Kamienna. Nathan suspects, however, the young Polish patriot denounced him as a Jew, resulting in his eviction from
the hospital.

Nathan was sent to Block Number 63, a long, wooden building for 1,500 to 2,000 Jewish teenagers and youngsters. Later, upon
learning he was 24 years old, the S.S. moved Nathan to Block Number 65 for adults. After the war, Nathan read that Elie Wiesel,
renowned author, lecturer, and Nobel Laureate, was confined in
one of the barracks for youngsters. The *Encyclopedia of the Holocaust* identifies Block No. 66 as a special tent barrack for an estimated 600 children and teenagers evacuated from Auschwitz. A
ravine separated the even- and odd-numbered buildings, so Nathan

never saw the infamous "Children's Block 66." The ravine served as a latrine. Weak and ill prisoners sometimes fell and drowned in the sewage, Nathan said.

Like his sisters in Bergen-Belsen, Nathan endured the agony of Appell. The men stood outside for two or three hours each morning and evening, regardless of the weather. The rations of bread and soup were so meager, prisoners died of hunger by the hundreds each day. Nathan's gruesome memories confirm the descriptions of starvation in history books. "The morning was the worst," Nathan said. "Not everyone came out of the barracks. People died. People were sick. We piled the dead bodies outside the barrack." The bodies were counted and later picked up by trucks for cremation.

The instinct to evade death sometimes elicited the most bestial behavior from the living. One night, while resting in his bunk, Nathan heard scuffling and shouting. A prisoner was searching the pockets of a sleeping inmate for food. The man awoke and reached behind his neck for the piece of bread he had saved. Realizing he would probably lose it during a fight, the man popped the bread in his mouth. Not to be denied, the thief grabbed his victim's throat and squeezed. Unable to breathe or swallow, the victim opened his mouth. The partially chewed and saliva-laden bread fell out. The thief ate it.

"Starvation hasn't got any law," Nathan observed. After that incident, he ate his entire ration of bread as soon as he received it. Before, Nathan had consumed half in the evening and saved half for the morning, when he would need some energy. He, too, had hidden bread under the back of his neck while sleeping.

Buchenwald's extreme conditions drove some individuals to act in ways they never would have imagined, which, again, underscores the evil of the Shoah. Similar to Bergen-Belsen, Buchenwald was littered with cadavers, and Nathan witnessed things he could not believe. He saw prisoners sharpening pieces of wood with stones. They were making implements to carve flesh from corpses.

Cannibalism had crept into the camp.

Although he was faint from hunger, Nathan could not eat dead bodies. He and some other prisoners walked by the Scandinavian barrack, isolated from other buildings. The Swedes, Norwegians, and Danes threw pieces of bread through the windows to Jews. Apparently, Scandinavian inmates were better treated and got more food. In early 1945, representatives of the International Red Cross in Geneva, Switzerland, inspected the Scandinavian barrack. Jews aware of the visit shouted, "Come see us. Come see our block," Nathan recalled. He still wonders, "Why didn't they come to my barrack?"

Chapter Twenty-Seven
FROM CAMP TO CAMP

The chance to leave Bergen-Belsen presented itself in March, 1945, as the Garfinkel sisters wasted away on their barrack's filthy floors. German soldiers burst in to gather some women for a work assignment outside the camp. "We ran like crazy people. Everyone wanted out of Bergen-Belsen," Sonia said. "They opened the gates to the camp. Lots of people pushed us out. The Germans pushed us back in. They beat us in. I got separated from Bela and Helen. I hung on to Regina."

Etka Raitapfel Baumstick was pushed back inside the gates. She gave up trying to maneuver her way out because she feared getting crushed by the mob. Etka was left behind. "I cried my eyes out. I wanted to be with them together." Cesia Zaifman was somewhere in the melee. "We were called again. They needed workers," Zaifman said. "They picked whoever was a little healthy-looking." Outside the gates, the women walked four abreast. Sonia and Regina traded places with other prisoners, row by row, to reach Bela and Helen. With hundreds of women marching, the soldiers did not notice that four sisters wanted to be together.

As in past transfers, the Garfinkels did not know their destination. Their long and nearly fatal journey took them to various German concentration camps, including Burgau, Türkheim, Dachau, and Allach. They covered most of the 375 miles by truck and train, but, in the final weeks, they were forced to go on foot. Like many other Holocaust survivors, the four sisters endured a death march, one of many that crisscrossed German-occupied territory at the war's end. The marches, typically associated with the evacuation of camps, were yet another means to weaken and to kill Jews. Anyone who fell behind or fell down was shot. Regina could barely walk, so her three sisters took turns supporting her.

"This I always remember," Sonia said. "Regina pleaded with me that I should let her die. I said, 'Please, Rechu, maybe a little bit longer.'"

On April 15, 1945 — several weeks after the Garfinkel sisters began their torturous route — the British army entered Bergen-Belsen. Photographs and films of the 60,000 prisoners on death's threshold and of the 13,000 corpses strewn throughout the camp were the first glimpse Americans and Western Europeans had of the Shoah. The news reports shocked the world. Whether the Garfinkels would have lived by staying in Bergen-Belsen is questionable. Some of the prisoners were so far gone, they died by the thousands each day following liberation. Of 60,000 surviving inmates in mid-April, 28,000 died within a few months. Many perished from eating biscuits and chocolates distributed by well-intentioned soldiers. Fania Fenelon describes her first moments of freedom at Bergen-Belsen in *Playing for Time*. Although Fenelon thought she was drawing her final breaths, she managed to sing — causing the battle-weary soldiers to cry.

Etka Raitapfel Baumstick was there, grateful to be alive. After her Chmielnik friends had marched from Bergen-Belsen, she and a teenager from Warsaw were shoved into a barrack of Hungarian Jewesses. By virtue of being stronger, the two women from Poland were obliged to carry out corpses each morning. Realizing they would die from disease or fatigue, they crept into another barrack full of Polish women who were not Jewish. Etka begged the Kapo to let them sleep on the floor under the beds. "I tried to pretend we were Polish instead of being Jewish," Etka said. "This woman was kind. I think she suspected that we were Jewish. More to the point, I think she was Jewish herself. She was the same person who helped me get my shoes back. I don't know her name. She really saved our lives." The tranquility on the morning of liberation, Etka recalled, sharply contrasted with the explosions of bombs and gunfire the night before. In the eerie calm, Etka and several Polish girls went to the camp kitchen, dragged out a sack of potatoes, built a fire, and cooked. "They gave us bread. They gave us butter. In the beginning, I got sick. Maybe I ate too much."

The Garfinkel sisters' trials and tribulations differed. Of all the places where they were driven, the first stop, Burgau, was the most bearable. "It was heaven compared to Bergen-Belsen," Sonia said of Burgau's Spartan facilities, which, at least, contained primitive latrines. In their new camp, the Garfinkels slept on wooden shelves, or bunks, instead of on the floor. They received rations of soup and bread daily instead of sporadically. They had access to water from a faucet, rather than from contaminated snow. They also toiled from sunrise to sunset.

Each morning, buses transported prisoners into the forest, where they assembled military aircraft called Messerschmitt, named after the manufacturing plant. Zaifman was part of the labor pool, which was divided into small groups assigned to different shifts. "It was dark. I was half-asleep," Sonia said. "Getting ready in the morning was not like it is today," she said with a touch of gallows humor. "I didn't have to wash myself. I didn't have to put on clothes. I wore the clothes I slept in. I jumped from the bunk and got on the bus. It was easy."

Sonia used paint guns to spray the planes in camouflage colors: blue under the wings and green and brown on top. "The Germans told us, 'You have to finish those planes or we'll shoot you.'" Burgau's work force included Jewish electricians, engineers, welders, and other skilled craftsmen from virtually every European country. From them, Helen heard rumors. She feared that, after the planes were finished, the S.S. would kill all of the prisoners to keep the hiding place secret.

On two occasions as she arrived at the planes, Helen discovered small paper bags containing half of a sandwich and an apple. Like Nathan in Skarzysko-Kamienna, she thought there would be reprisals for eating the food. Initially, she thought it was a trick devised to punish the finder for stealing. Helen could not resist, however, and she ate without adverse consequences. She believes a kindly German supervisor left out food to help prisoners.

Bela and Regina do not recall Burgau in detail. The S.S. dispatched them to a nearby munitions factory, according to Sonia. Her three sisters rely heavily on Sonia's memories of their final months in captivity. That is because they were alternately sick, feverish, or falling into semi-consciousness while Sonia was relatively healthy. "I was ambitious in camp. If not for me, I don't think Sonia would survive," Helen asserted. "Sonia was always weak, but here, she was the strongest. In the end, Sonia was strong." Sonia attributes her stamina to her lifelong habit of eating lightly. "At home I wasn't a big eater. My father always told me I eat like a bird. Helen was always hungry. Bela was always hungry. Regina not so. I got food from dreams, really."

After a few weeks, German soldiers expelled the women from Burgau. The next stop, Türkheim, teemed with misery. The prisoners slept in primitive, underground shelters with exposed dirt walls and floors. Sticks, straw, and mounded dirt served as roofs. The weather turned cold at night in late March and early April, but rising temperatures during the day caused lice and insects to crawl from the earth. Warm weather made the bites itch more. "Lice by the millions. It was filthy. It was impossible. The straw was full of lice," Sonia said. Each morning, women disrobed outside, shook their clothes, and picked the flesh-colored pests off their skin. "It was a place to wait and die. You went out, you saw so many women dying all over." The Germans limited food rations because there was little work in Türkheim.

Repulsed by the so-called barracks, the four sisters wandered aimlessly. The outside, just like the inside, resembled a scene from Dante's Inferno. "Everything was bad, but the train and this place, Türkheim," Helen said, unable to finish her sentence as she contemplated the dark and dank cellars. "I don't remember this too much. We weren't there too long. We would have died from cold and disease."

One of Sonia's most piercing images is of Türkheim's Jewish policewoman, a blonde wearing high, black boots, and brandishing a whip. She zealously beat the women, concentrating the blows on Czechoslovakian Jews, Hungarian Jews, Romanian Jews. She spared the Polish Jews, because she was their compatriot. She was the wife of a Jewish authority who had helped save Regina in Kielce's labor camp. Helen remembers, too: "She was a beautiful woman. She was healthy. She had these high boots. I was afraid of her. To be a Kapo, you have to be a certain human being. I don't think I could be a Kapo." Helen shook her head.

The couple well illustrates extremes in camp behavior, particularly among prisoners holding positions of authority. The S.S. laid the groundwork for corruption and injustice within the camps. They forced some of their Jewish victims to become oppressors by designating them to serve as Kapos. "They say if a German looked, they beat us," Sonia said. "Germans ordered them to beat us to get us to work. Some Jewish people do this so the Germans don't beat us as bad." Some appointees responded heroically by taking risks to save lives while others appeared to relish their duties.

Consequently, the Garfinkels are not inclined to generalize about Germans, Nazis, or Jews, particularly against the backdrop of the Shoah, which brought out the worst and best in individuals regardless of ethnic background. Sonia, Nathan, and Helen feel that, if not for the basic decency of Jan Laskowski, a Nazi, they would not be alive today. Laskowski's assistance, which is best defined as a lack of cruelty, must be qualified. "Laskowski helped us there in Skarzysko," Sonia said, "but he couldn't help us in other camps."

Likewise, Sonia still feels animosity toward the Jewish policewoman for beating her fellow Jews. "Those skeletons, those poor souls, she beat them. I saw how she beat them," Sonia said. "I said if I lived through the war, I would kill." Years later, after the couple left Germany, they lived in the country, according to several survivors. "They couldn't live in the city," Sonia said. "If other people (survivors) saw them, they would kill her."

The Garfinkels have heard of a few other survivors who keep to themselves for similar reasons. Jewish policemen and foremen known to have been abusive within the camps became targets of revenge after the war. Some Jews were actually charged with crimes and tried in Israeli courts, according to Simon Wiesenthal's memoirs, *The Murderers Among Us*.

The policewoman's blatant favoritism toward Polish Jews — evident in her floggings of Jews from other nations — highlights discrimination among Jews themselves within Nazi Germany's evil empire. "In Bergen-Belsen, there was a Czechoslovakian Jew who was a foreman," Helen recalled. "She gave less soup to the Polish Jews, and she beat the Polish Jews."

Cesia Zaifman said she did not personally see the floggings in Türkhiem, but she never dared to lift her eyes when a beating was underway. "She was like a Kapo. She was taken to look after us," Zaifman said. "I was like a little mouse. Whatever they told me to do, I do, so I wasn't beaten. Yes, there were beatings. You don't want to see it. You close your eyes. I don't know names."

Evelyn Szczebakowska Cala said she never saw the individual in question strike anyone. "She wasn't a Kapo. She has no position of authority. We asked her to be in charge on the train to Bergen-Belsen. She helped the group to stay together." For that reason, the beautiful, blonde Jewess wearing the high, black boots wasn't popular among all the women, Cala said. She recalls only that the so-called policewoman once berated a prisoner in Bergen-Belsen for emptying a bucket of excrement near the barrack door instead of carrying it to a latrine. "It was very hard to be in charge in that condition where we were. There were always people who would say something bad. Don't listen to them. I would give my life for her. I cannot say nothing. I didn't see."

The days and weeks following Türkheim were traumatic for the Garfinkel sisters, who were evacuated with about 1,000 prisoners. Despite their fatigue and weakness, they were anxious to leave the camp's squalor. The march, supervised by German soldiers, seemed endless. "We walked day and night," Sonia said. "We walked maybe a week, maybe another couple of days. Many girls could not walk further. They fell down. The Germans shot them or left them to die." The ill-fitting, cumbersome, wooden clogs were then an advantage, although Sonia is amazed she and her sisters didn't get frostbite. "Many marched bare-foot. If the trees could talk in the forest," Sonia said of the silent witnesses of suffering and death. "If the ground could say something."

Zaifman also marched from Türkheim. "We were four girls together," she said of the columns of four women abreast. As time passed, she noticed how hundreds of women outnumbered the few German soldiers. As the sun set, Zaifman took her chance. "I said to the other girls, 'Only one soldier is here, and we all go like cattle. Let's go try to run. Let's go and hide. One soldier can't kill all of us.' One girl was very sick. She couldn't even walk. When we run away, we dragged her. She's alive today." Under the cover of fading light, Zaifman and her three companions slipped away, alternately running and walking. They hid in a barn for two days until American troops searched the area. "I looked out and saw a soldier with a different uniform," Zaifman said. "I was talking to him. He didn't understand. It was so funny. He said, 'Slow down.' He made a motion to slow down."

Once again, Cala's long, black hair influenced her destiny and that of her sister, Regina Szczebakowska Zalcman. As wretched as Türkheim and its inmates were, the S.S. came there to recruit a few workers. Impressed by Cala's neat braids and striking face, they chose her to work in a restaurant in the nearby town of Türkheim. Cala and Zalcman, with short blonde hair, reported to the kitchen every morning. They returned every evening with some food — a potato, an onion, anything they could snitch. Two days before the Allies reached Türkheim, a German woman helped the two sisters hide in the restaurant. "Everyone remembers me with very long hair," Cala said. "I was the only one with long hair at liberation."

As Cala, Zalcman, Zaifman, and others met freedom near Türkheim, which was converted to a refugee center, the Garfinkels remained in the pitiful group winding its way through the forest. Helen remembers walking in villages where German women tossed bread, potatoes, even clothes to the prisoners, whose uniforms by then had disintegrated into grimy tatters. Predictably, soldiers beat prisoners to prevent them from eating the food or keeping the clothes. Sonia regards Helen's memory of this as a fever-induced hallucination. "No one threw us food," Sonia said. "I remember seeing a German woman with a baby. When she saw us, she went back inside her house."

Helen also saw a chicken coop in a garden. She crawled into it to search for eggs, which she devoured, shell and all. The soldiers greeted Helen with blows. "Hunger is the worst thing," she said. "If you're hungry, you don't look at the consequences. If you're hungry, you don't wait to eat later. You eat right away." Hunger dominated. Some women ate grass. Hungarian Jewesses combed the grass with their fingers to find insects to eat.

Bela's summary of the deplorable march is brief but to the point: "There's no place where to sleep. There's no place where to wash. You're filthy. You're dirty. You don't have a brush to brush your hair. There's no food. A dog is better treated. In America, you buy cookies for a dog. You take dogs to a veterinarian if they are sick." The Jews were less than dogs in the hate-filled rhetoric of the Germans. They were *Untermenschen* and, as such, did not warrant decent treatment or a quiet death.

As she struggled to march, Sonia recalled what her mother had said in 1940: that of all the Garfinkel children, Sonia would be the one to survive. Sonia thought about how she had nearly given up in Skarzysko-Kamienna and was wishing to die in 1943, but even then she heard her mother's words: "You will survive no matter where they send you." During the death march, those words made Sonia stronger. She gave all her food to her sisters. "It was always in my mind what my mother tell me — even in my darkest hours when I wanted to die. My mother have faith in me," Sonia said. "Something pushed me inside to live. Something inside of me said I have to take care. Like I would be their mother. Not that I had anything to give. I just wanted to carry them. I took over. I was determined."

The march was an excruciating punishment. "We could hardly walk," Sonia said. "Regina was sick. She was burning with fever. Regina could not walk, and we dragged her. She put her head on my shoulder. Her head was burning. We could not leave her there. How could I live with myself if she fell down and she get shot? We promised ourselves we all live together or we all die together." One night, they collapsed in a ditch, expecting either to be shot or to perish from exhaustion. They lay in the comfort of the mud — warmed earlier that day by the April sun. It began to rain again. They tilted their faces to the sky and opened their mouths to catch the drops. Deprived of water by the soldiers, they had been thirsty for days. Sonia said to her sisters, "This is the best way to die."

Chapter Twenty-Eight
STEP BY STEP

While his sisters jumped at the first chance to leave Bergen-Belsen's horrors, Nathan was content staying in the equally abominable Buchenwald. Although he was weak, Nathan did receive occasional rations of what passed for bread and soup, and he could conserve energy by lying in Block Number 65. The drastic reduction in labor assignments there in late 1944 and early 1945 contributed to his survival. Had Nathan been forced to work, his crushed and raw hand would have been noticed, and he surely would have been shot. Clinging to life in Buchenwald with his crippled hand, Nathan awaited the war's end.

Consequently, he felt extreme anxiety the morning the S.S. counted him among 1,600 prisoners sent to the camp's gates. "We were afraid we might be executed. We were afraid we would be shipped to a death camp," Nathan said. "We didn't know what to expect. This was an unknown thing."

What transpired after Nathan's departure from Buchenwald and his sisters' transfer from Türkheim didn't have a name at the time. Historians adopted the term used by survivors: "death march." Nathan's was one of many to snake through Germany, Austria, Poland, and other countries during the war's final weeks. The Germans devised the marches to rid camps of witnesses before the Allies arrived and to kill the remaining Jews. The forced walks, supervised by armed guards, S.S., and soldiers, culminated years of suffering with the worst and final agony. For many, it was fatal. An estimated 250,000 people died or were murdered on the marches, some of which continued after Hitler had committed suicide on April 30, 1945, and after the Soviet Army had seized Berlin on May 2. Germany surrendered to the Allies on May 8.

Nathan walked in one of several groups dispatched from Buchenwald in early April, 1945. As far as he knows, his was one of the few marches from Buchenwald to boast of survivors: 164 from a total of 1,600 prisoners. Reference books state that thousands of Jews traveled hundreds of miles on foot from Buchenwald south toward Flossenburg. An underground network of prisoners working within Buchenwald's administration succeeded in slowing down the evacuations. "The death march affected me most of all. The one month in the death march was worse than all the years in the death camps," Nathan said. "In camp, I always tried to stay away from the perpetrator. In the death march, I was always near my perpetrator. I walked with the criminal together. The day was a year."

Unbeknownst to Nathan, Kuba Zaifman, the young tailor who had been forced to sew in Chmielnik, Kielce, and Czestochowa, had also been expelled from Buchenwald. Zaifman's journey, mostly by train to Flossenburg, Mauthausen, and, eventually, Czechoslovakia, differed from Nathan's, and it occurred earlier in 1945. Zaifman and his fellow prisoners were locked in cattle cars for more than a week at a time. With no food and very little water, the men suffered terribly. One of Zaifman's most distinct memories is pushing his hand through a small hole in the boxcar's side. A peasant thrust a loaf of bread in Zaifman's outstretched hand, but it couldn't fit through the opening. Most of the precious food was lost as Zaifman drew his hand into the boxcar. Prisoners grabbed the bread sticking up between his fingers. All that remained for Zaifman were the few crumbs in his clenched fist. At one point, the Germans released prisoners from the train to dig ditches in Flossenburg. In the middle of the field, Zaifman saw his former boss, General Shlicht. Zaifman brushed the dirt from his striped rags. He held himself erect just as he had done while delivering the gray leather coat and suede gloves to Shlicht in Kielce. "Herr General, is there any tailor work for me?" Shlicht sneered, "What you think this is, Chmielnik? We have nothing here."

Zaifman attributes his survival to the relatively comfortable work he had had as a tailor for several years. In the final months, Zaifman had enough strength to dig ditches and endure starvation.

In *Every Day Remembrance Day*, Simon Wiesenthal posts April 8, 1945, as the date the S.S. began to empty Buchenwald. Nathan departed on April 9. Two days later, on April 11, American soldiers entered the camp and freed an estimated 21,000 prisoners, including Elie Wiesel, a Romanian Jew. Then a teenager, Wiesel later conveyed his experience of the Shoah in eloquent memoirs and novels. He won the Nobel peace prize in 1986 for his life's work, championing the cause of persecuted ethnic groups, such as the Vietnamese boat people.

The day Buchenwald was officially liberated, the killing had begun on Nathan's death march, a journey that defies description, much less comprehension. For every Jew who survived the month-long march, nearly 48 others died each day, on average. "The conventional killing of human beings I can understand," Nathan said. "The Nazis' provocations to justify killing, this bothers me. The Nazi would say to someone coming out of the barn, 'You came out a minute too late,' and he would kill that prisoner... Sometimes they made prisoners run. Then they shot them and said they were trying to escape."

The guards — most of whom were from the Ukraine, Hungary, Romania, Czechoslovakia, the Balkans, the Baltic nations, and other regions east of Germany — murdered daily. They killed with sadistic abandon, but they tried to find reasons to warrant their actions — what Nathan calls "justifiable killing" — as though they had consciences.

Nathan narrowly escaped such death within the first week. As the group waited for a train to pass, prisoners noticed a ditch, the type used by farmers to store vegetables in during the winter. Nathan now believes the guards deliberately stopped there to tempt the prisoners and to create an excuse for killing. Nathan was among the first to jump in. He clawed the dirt frantically and filled his pockets with whatever seemed remotely edible. He bit ravenously into a rotten potato.

Within seconds, 50 or 60 prisoners leapt into the earthen cellar. Then the frightening staccato of machine guns punctured the spring morning. Nathan felt a warm liquid on his neck. He touched it with his hand. There was blood. Startled, he slowly realized he had not been wounded; the blood was from other prisoners behind him who had been shot. The guards began yelling, "*Raus! Raus!*" (German for "Out, out!") Those still alive scrambled from the ravine. The guards mowed down whoever was limping or bleeding, so Nathan hastily wiped his neck to avoid becoming a target.

That atrocity well illustrates the guards' cruelty and the prisoners' desperation.

They had hurled themselves into the vegetable ditch because they were starving. With one disturbing exception that occurred later, the guards did not feed their captives. The prisoners subsisted on the one slice of bread distributed when they exited Buchenwald. They ate grass and other plants along the way. A Hungarian medical student, who also happened to have the last name of Garfinkel, advised Nathan which grasses were safe to eat. Other prisoners, from all over Europe, were not so lucky; they died from illness, diarrhea, and dehydration. They pilfered the livestock troughs at farms where they spent the night. The guards forbade such foraging and shot prisoners for it.

The reaction of German farmers, appalled by the prisoners' filthy and ragged appearance, was mixed. Some complained about stealing. For example, one farmer yelled in protest after seeing a prisoner take bread from an outdoor oven. The guards later forced the so-called thief to dig his own grave. That individual, Chil Kaufman, a neighbor of the Garfinkel family in Chmielnik, dug for a few minutes and then began running, shovel in hand. He was gunned down, meeting the fate of his mother, Getela, who was shot in the Kielce labor camp for being too old. Earlier in the march, Chil Kaufman had torn apart a live chicken with his bare hands — so great was his hunger.

Some sympathetic farmers subtly helped the starving prisoners, Nathan said, by providing water and leaving out extra food for the livestock. "That is why I believe in humanity." Pigs, the best-fed barnyard animals, received a mixture of potatoes cooked with milk and flour. To this day, mashed potatoes remind Nathan of the times he and other prisoners furtively scooped handfuls of food from the outdoor troughs.

One guard, in his own twisted way, helped Nathan and four other prisoners assigned to push the cart carrying his belongings. The cold-hearted Yugoslav prepared a batch of horsemeat soup after the group had come across some dead horses in the forest. The guard cut off a leg, stuck it in a pot of water, placed the brew in a larger pail containing fire, and hung the contraption on the cart. The other prisoners were so hungry, they begged Nathan and his companions for the repulsive broth. "How can you explain this? This Yugoslav, the worst murderer, was trying to feed us," Nathan said. "Why didn't he just give us a piece of bread? Why degrade us with the horsemeat? This is what we call dehumanization."

Yet the horsemeat aided Nathan in his resolve to live. "The struggle for survival on the death march was more than the whole time in the camps. We knew we were close to liberation," Nathan said. "If this were the middle of the war, maybe I would give up. We knew this was the end. I told myself, 'One more day, I am free. One more day, I am free.'" Visualizing his family helped Nathan. "I kept thinking about my sisters. I was wondering where they are. I was wondering whether they are separate or if they are together. I was hoping that they are together. That way one would help the other."

From carrying soup cans in Skarzysko-Kamienna's labor camp, Nathan had learned he could avoid beatings and executions by being inconspicuous. That is why he shunned special tasks even when extra food was offered as an incentive. He made an exception, however, when the guards asked for volunteers to push the carts from Buchenwald. An intense desire to live prompted Nathan to assess each new situation, to calculate his odds for survival, and to adapt accordingly.

Nathan figured that working would give the impression of strength, health, and usefulness. If he worked, the guards would not suspect his injury. Nathan positioned himself at the cart's left side and pushed with his right hand. He hid his crushed left hand in his pocket and draped a blanket over his left shoulder. The cart, carrying the Yugoslav guard's clothes and food, was not heavy. It served as support. Nathan could lean against it as he walked. To be maneuvered, the cart required five prisoners, one at each corner and one to steer from behind in the middle. Fleish Hecker of Lodz, now a rabbi in New York, steered Nathan's cart.

Curiously, another cart remained empty. Its purpose was revealed on April 10, the second day of the march. If prisoners fell from exhaustion near villages and farms, the guards forced them into the empty vehicle. After entering the forest, the lame prisoners were forced to dig their own graves. If they were too weak, other prisoners finished the job. Then guards shot the lame prisoners into the graves. The executions occurred in unpopulated areas devoid of witnesses.

Ten to 20 prisoners collapsed each day. If they weren't shot immediately, they were mowed down later. "There was no fighting, screaming, or pleading for mercy," Nathan said. "They submitted to death. They gave up. Maybe they were relieved to die." As a practical matter, shooting prisoners in small groups each day was easier, Nathan said, than orchestrating the digging of a common grave for the massacre of all 1,600.

One acquaintance from Chmielnik, Lysor Bugeinsky, could no longer walk, so Nathan carried him while pushing the cart. At Nathan's insistence, Lysor stood behind Nathan and put his left arm over Nathan's left shoulder. Lysor's right hand gripped the cart under Nathan's right hand. Nathan bore Lysor on his back, but Lysor's feet dragged. "He said, 'Nate, let me go. I can't walk anymore.'" An irate guard commanded Nathan to drop Lysor and pushed Lysor into the cart of condemned prisoners.

During a visit to Israel in 1980, Nathan informed Lysor's brother, Chaim Bugeinsky, of exactly how Lysor died. Survivors of the Shoah often assume the responsibility of telling each other of the final moments of friends, relatives, and other loved ones. During a 1989 trip to Los Angeles, Nathan told Abraham Kleinhandler that his younger brother, Kalman, died of starvation in Buchenwald.

Recounting his experiences and preserving memories are top priorities for Nathan. "In labor camp, in Skarzysko, we made agreements to talk after the war," Nathan said. "I made about 10 agreements, but none of these people survived. That's why I speak out."

Nathan's death march left a trail of demonic murders. The guards hung one man from a tree by his leg, the same leg he had used to kick a German shepherd that had attacked him. The guards entertained themselves by watching the unfortunate man dangle. The prisoner tried kicking the rope with his free leg to relieve pressure on the leg that was tied. The guards finally shot him. One guard murdered a Jew by stepping on his throat to choke him. Several guards drowned a prisoner by tying a water hose to his mouth.

"Conventional killing I would understand — a bullet to the head. Or beat him to death — I accept this, too. But these bizarre exhibitions? The guards were laughing, and they clapped. Are we human? Sometimes I look at the mirror. I look just like them," Nathan said, referring to his ruthless captors. "I am ashamed of being part of the human race."

The late Primo Levi wrote extensively about shame — felt by himself and other Holocaust survivors — in *The Drowned and the Saved.* Prisoners' brutal treatment of each other and their lack of willingness to help each other in the Auschwitz death camp horrified Levi, an Italian chemist. His conclusion that "man is wolf to man" drove Levi to commit suicide in 1987. For another Shoah victim, writing under the pen name Ka-Tzetnik 135633, shame results from realizing the roles of captor and prisoner could have been reversed. In *Shivitti: A Vision*, Ka-Tzetnik 135633 writes: "The German facing me with the death's skull insignia on his cap, his hands deep in the pockets of his black S.S. coat — could have been in my place... and this is the paralyzing horror — I could have been there in his place!"

No words can express the sheer evil of the Shoah and Nathan's death march. Even Levi's staggering conclusion that "man is wolf to man" falls short, in Nathan's estimation. "It's worse than that. A wolf doesn't kill because he hates me. A wolf kills for food. It's beyond human understanding."

Part of the shame Nathan felt lies in his own desire to retaliate. "Many times I thought about killing a Nazi. Anybody could kill a Nazi. I found out if I commit a crime, if I kill a Nazi, they kill me but they also kill 10 others, 20 others," Nathan said. "Every day, I fought to control myself. I was afraid I can be explosive. On the death march, I was afraid, every day, of losing my sanity. If you see those things, you know you're next."

Nathan knew that living, ultimately, would be the best revenge. Living would give him the last word.

Along the way, Nathan was nearly murdered in a sinister manner reminiscent of Fritz Bartenschläger's favorite execution method in Skarzysko-Kamienna. One of Nathan's few encounters with German civilians led to the close call. A sympathetic utility worker gave Nathan six cigars in apology for not having any food. Employing the other Jew named Garfinkel as translator, Nathan exchanged one cigar for bread from a Hungarian guard fond of smoking. The guard confiscated the other five cigars but said he would give Nathan more bread the next day. After the guard broke his promise, Nathan complained. The guard pulled out his revolver and ordered Nathan to open his mouth.

"I knew he was going to try to execute me the way Bartenschläger had," Nathan said. "I said, 'Give me the bread first, so I can eat it. Then you can shoot me.'" Nathan repeated the final request he had made to Bartenschläger. "I didn't think he would shoot me. I knew he wouldn't do it." The guard kicked Nathan instead. Nathan never got the bread he was owed, but his life was spared.

The guards zealously hunted down escaped prisoners even though the military was retreating. After Appell, they released German shepherds into the barns where the prisoners had slept. The appropriate signal from the dogs prompted the guards to plunge pitchforks into haystacks. Sometimes blood spurted out. Nathan believes that Chil's uncle, Shlome Kaufman, of Chmielnik, died that way.

In a strange turn of events a few weeks into the march, the guards began disappearing. "We felt something is fishy here." Later, it dawned on the captives that their oppressors were afraid of being caught by the Allies. The effort to avoid enemy soldiers and civilians made the march long and winding.

The guards forced the prisoners to walk more than 20 miles a day, Nathan estimates. From Buchenwald, near Weimar, they headed south toward Austria. They passed through the German region of Bavaria near Czechoslovakia. The German towns Nathan remembers include Erfurt, Plauen, and Hof. Plotted on a map, the journey is roughly 300 miles, but Nathan figures the circuitous route probably covered 450 miles.

As his shoes fell apart, he reinforced them with bandages from Jan Laskowski. Nathan had concealed the remaining bandages by carrying them as a belt around his waist. At night, out of the guards' sight, Nathan removed the bandage from his injured hand and used it to strengthen his shoes. Then he wrapped a clean bandage around his hand. He did not wash his hand as he had in Buchenwald, Nathan said, because he was afraid of being seen.

Hiding his injury and keeping his shoes intact were simple tasks that became tantamount to survival. Many death-march victims perished. Some who lived lost their limbs to frostbite and amputation. "Lysor Bugeinsky used strips of blankets to wrap around his feet," Nathan said. "Thanks to the bandages, my shoes lasted."

Toward the end of Nathan's ordeal, he saw Allied planes. "They weren't German planes. They didn't have the German black cross. We were glad. Maybe the planes were going to bomb us. The planes were so close we even saw the goggles of the pilots. One of the guards picked up my blanket to hide under it. This was the most pleasurable thing to see, for me to protect my perpetrator," Nathan said. "Certain things don't go through a human brain. A Nazi hiding under my little blanket? How can you understand those things?"

According to Nathan, the survivors of his death march owe their lives to a coarse German woman, most likely a prostitute. One night, nearly a month after they had left Buchenwald, the prisoners overheard a conversation outside the barn in which they lay resting. The woman, a *Gassenfrau*, argued with a guard. "We heard the S.S. officer say, 'We need to get rid of those Jews. We cannot escape before we get rid of them,'" Nathan remembers. "She said, 'Don't kill the Jews. Leave them alone.'"

Chapter Twenty-Nine
THE LAST CAMPS

On the rainy night they collapsed from exhaustion, the Garfinkel sisters expected the muddy ditch near Allach, Germany, to be their grave. Sonia's reaction upon opening her eyes the next morning was: "Look, we're alive. They didn't shoot us." Sensing a change in the soldiers, she realized the war was ending, if not over. "The Germans behaved different to us already," Sonia said. "They didn't shoot us in the ditch."

The march resumed although the women could barely drag themselves from the sodden trench. Delirious with fever, unable to walk, Regina fell. "If I wouldn't have had my sisters to hold me, I wouldn't be here. I was on their arms," Regina said. At one point, "They actually pulled me. I was on my knees. They were pulling me. I was pleading with them to leave me alone, to let me die."

A day or two earlier, the soldiers would have shot Regina, as they had murdered hundreds of women. Instead, they put her and several others who couldn't walk in a horse-drawn wagon. The group included Gizela Leinkram, Sonia's friend from Krakow. The soldiers, in an abrupt departure from past behavior, gave a potato to each woman in the wagon. Her appetite lost to fever, Regina feebly tossed the potato to her sisters, but other prisoners destroyed the precious ration in their fight for it.

Sonia didn't try to catch the potato because she was so dejected about losing Regina. "I gave Regina up. We saw that they didn't shoot us anymore." Sonia begged the soldiers to tell her the wagon's destination. Dachau. Yet another camp to the Garfinkels, Dachau was Nazi Germany's first detention center, established near Munich in 1933 to hold political prisoners. A sign on the camp's gate reads: "*Arbeit macht frei*," or "labor liberates." The S.S. exploited the inmate population, about one-third Jewish, as a labor force for a network of satellite camps and nearby munitions factories.

The grief of separation surpassed Regina's physical pain. "We were all crying." Regina did not know whether she would see her sisters again. She might not live. Her sisters might be killed. How would she ever find them? Regina had no idea where she was headed, but she remembers seeing warfare. Americans were invading Dachau. As she lay on the rickety wagon, Regina saw bombs and gunfire. "The sky was lit up. There were many lights and commotion."

Sonia, Bela, and Helen also associate their final march with combat. "Dachau is where we saw the guard houses burning. We heard bombs. We saw fire. We knew this was the end of the war, but I didn't know if we would live," Helen said. "A lot of girls start running away. We didn't run away because I was holding my sister's hand. At that time, I didn't think about it. I was weak already. I had sores and open wounds. I was malnourished."

Bela remarked, "I hear so much noise. I see planes. Someone said, 'This is American planes.'" Bela could hardly register being near liberation because she was so close to death.

Although she was absorbed in helping Bela and Helen, Sonia felt the intensity of approaching freedom. "It was a beautiful day. The sun was shining. We saw the English planes. We said, 'Oh God, throw a bomb. Throw a bomb.'" Helen looked up. "We saw the pilots, the planes were so low," Helen said. "The Germans were afraid. They took off their jackets and marched between us."

Yet the soldiers insisted on forcing the women to march until dark. They arrived at a camp called Allach. Bela was taken from Sonia's arms, presumably to a medical clinic. A sea of death overwhelmed Helen. "I saw mountains of dead people. The others were dying of starvation." Helen knew she was next.

Sonia helped Helen walk to a crude building, similar to the

barracks of Bergen-Belsen. There were no bunks or shelves. Hundreds of women lay on the floor, some dead, some alive, and most others hovering between life and death. Lice crawled on all of the bodies. A small table stood amid the filth and misery. "I said to Helen, 'I'm not going to sleep on the floor. Let's sleep on the table,'" Sonia said. "The table was very narrow. I held on to Helen, and Helen held on to me." Helen, too, succumbed to fever. "I was so hot. I was sick. I couldn't move," Helen said. "There was a table. Sonia picked me up and put me on the table. She stayed on the table with me until the next day. She didn't want me to fall down."

The next morning, April 29, 1945, the day of their liberation, Sonia took Helen to the medical clinic where Bela was. Then Sonia was alone, unsure of their condition and Regina's location. She wandered aimlessly about the camp, but bombs jolted her from her dazed state of mind. Terrified, Sonia ran into a building and realized she had stumbled upon the S.S.' living quarters. She couldn't believe the scene before her eyes. "I was in a beautiful barrack. I saw a German woman and man in uniforms. The woman took a picture of Hitler and the swastika off the wall. She tore them up and threw them away." Sonia fled, certain she would be blamed and punished for what the German woman had done: defiling fascist symbols. With the Allies near, the S.S. soon abandoned Allach. "We didn't see the Germans," Sonia said. "That in itself made us so happy, we didn't care that we didn't have anything to eat."

Jewish prisoners who were doctors and nurses began caring for the sick and dying, but they wouldn't allow Sonia to visit Bela and Helen who were nearly dead from typhus. Still thinking of her sisters, Sonia found some potatoes among the limited food supplies. She boiled them in a pot of water and asked the nurses to give the soup to Helen and Bela.

Prisoners hoisted a white flag, and American soldiers entered the Allach camp in late April. Some details are hazy to the Garfinkel sisters, but one image stands out. Whenever they describe liberation, Sonia and even Helen, who was critically ill, say they cannot forget the bright red fingernails and lipstick of the American nurse. "The nurse picked up a prisoner," Sonia said. "The soldiers were crying. I couldn't cry anymore. I couldn't shed any more tears." Sonia was 22 years old.

Dying prisoners did not even realize they were free, much less comprehend it. Helen and Bela were so sick they did not know they lay near each other in Allach's medical clinic. The nurses later told Bela that, at one point, they assumed she was dead and covered her with a sheet. Bela moved. "I remember white sheets. I was completely dead. I couldn't walk, and I couldn't talk," Bela said. "The doctors came, all with masks. A doctor talked to me. Tears were streaming down his face."

Later, "I saw tables with food: white bread, fishes, salami, eggs. People walked, people crawled to the food, and they died." Bela referred to the "canned-goods victims" of whom historian Martin Gilbert writes in *Holocaust*. Food, the obsession of prisoners for years, was so irresistible, many ignored medical precautions. "I didn't care if I die," Bela said. "I wanted so badly this food, but I couldn't walk."

The doctors prescribed intravenous fluids. The nurses explained to Bela that she could die from eating, that her digestive system was too dehydrated to handle food. Eventually, they gave her bits of bread. They tried to soothe Bela, telling her she was free, that the Germans were gone, defeated. They helped Bela sit up and taught her to walk again. She was recovering physically, but her emotions were in atrophy. Bela had just turned 24.

"They told me I would never have children. This I will never forget," Bela stated. "You think I was sad when the doctor said, 'You won't have children'? You think I cared? Who wants children? Who cares? I didn't even care whether I got married. Who was thinking of children? All we cared about was having food."

In Dachau, Regina first found herself on a basement floor with other sick and dying women. "They took us to Dachau to die. They didn't want us to die on the road. They didn't want to leave any traces on the road." Records seized on April 29, 1945, when the U.S. Army captured Dachau, list 67,665 prisoners, including 22,100 Jews. Soldiers who stormed the camp that day, including retired Air Force Colonel Joseph A. Rosalia of Orlando, Florida, recall seeing thousands of cadavers, many of them piled in train cars. Of the estimated 33,000 survivors, fewer than 10 percent, or 2,539, were Jews.

Martin Gilbert wrote in *The Macmillan Atlas of the Holocaust*: "Some of the photographs taken after the liberation of Dachau are so terrible that they have never been reproduced, nor have I felt able to reproduce them here." Rosalia donated his photographs to the Holocaust Memorial Resource and Education Center of Central Florida.

The horror of Dachau made a deep and lasting impression on Helen Rozenek Jurysta although she was nearly dead from typhus at the time. "You saw these piles of dead people. It was unbelievable what you saw there." One night, she crawled from the barrack to use the latrine. It was so dark she lost her sense of direction and couldn't find her way back. To her horror, she realized she was in the wrong place. "I laid down where all the dead people were. I started touching. There was all dead people there."

Although white flags signaled the much-awaited moment of freedom, many prisoners in Dachau remained in a fog and were slow to react, according to Jurysta. "We didn't know what to do with ourselves. We didn't know if we should be happy. We hug each other and start to cry." Some women expressed joy by jumping up and down. Others released their anger by breaking into the German canteen and stabbing portraits of Hitler with knives. Jurysta fainted from weakness and delirium. "I weighed like 70 pounds. Maybe not even that."

The next time Regina regained consciousness, she was lying on a cot in a hospital. American soldiers lifted her arms and legs one by one to take photographs. They also weighed and measured her. She was too ill to speak, to ask questions, or to fathom that they were documenting Germany's inhumane treatment of Jews. After the war, Regina dreaded Holocaust documentaries. "I was afraid if I went to see movies, I thought if they show these pictures, I would recognize myself."

When Regina awakened again, a Catholic priest was giving the last rites to the woman on the next cot, a Jewess from Krakow. The Garfinkel sisters cannot remember her name, but she was a friend of Gizela Leinkram, also of Krakow. She had been baptized a Catholic before the war, but that did not spare her from persecution. Nazi Germany based its genocide on ethnicity, not religion, so Jews who became Christians were also targeted for destruction. Even Jewish families who had converted to Catholicism several generations before World War II were sent to the gas chambers.

Gizela's friend had confided in Sonia that she planned to return to Poland to live as a Catholic after the war, that she didn't want to suffer anymore. As far as the Garfinkels know, the woman did just that after miraculously recovering from typhus. Sonia said she was so angry at the woman's denial of her Jewish heritage that she forgot her name.

The priest, having prayed for Gizela's friend, turned to conduct the last rites for Regina. Realizing what was happening, Regina began screaming, "'I am Jewish. I am Jewish.' I was hysterical. I don't know what I was upset about — because he was a priest or because I was going to die. Maybe I was just simply afraid."

Apologizing for his error, the priest tried to console Regina. He stroked her forehead and murmured, "It's okay. It's okay." The irony of that incident, occurring when Regina was only 15 years old, didn't sink in until later. After years of suffering for being Jewish, Regina wasn't even recognized as a Jew at the war's end. Germany had annihilated nearly all of Europe's Jews, but the stereotypes persisted. "The priest gave me last rites because he thought I wasn't Jewish."

Chaper Thirty
THE FINAL STEPS

The Buchenwald inmates died in greater numbers each day. Remarkably, Nathan survived his injury for many months — from late 1944, when his hand was burned, to early May. The cold weather staved off infection, but sleep deprivation, hunger, and stress finally undermined his resistance. Nathan fell dangerously ill with fever. Being sick, however, may have saved his life; it certainly made the circumstances of his liberation that much more unbelievable.

The prisoners spent their last night of captivity, May 6, 1945, in an empty women's jail in Lebenau, near the Austrian border. The next day, no guards burst in shouting the customary order: "Raus, raus!" Silence filled the jail as time passed from dawn to late morning. The prisoners peered through the window to see empty carts. The guards' belongings were gone.

Finally, the jail warden, an old man in his 70s, entered and said, "I bring you good news. You are free now. The guards are gone. The Americans are three or four kilometers away in Laufen." The prisoners stared. Years of oppression, mistreatment, and psychological manipulation had made them suspicious, distrustful, unresponsive. They were afraid to leave.

The warden returned with some bread. Then three American soldiers entered, one of whom spoke a little Polish. He repeated what the warden had said, but the prisoners did not react. "They told us we were free. We didn't believe them, either," Nathan said. "A uniform is a uniform. Maybe it was a different branch of the

Nazis. To us, a soldier is an enemy. To us, every soldier is a criminal. Every soldier is a murderer. Every soldier is a killer." Emotionally numb and physically weak, the prisoners remained in the jail, some of them unable to walk. "We told them to bring us food. We were waiting for food," Nathan said. "We were afraid of soldiers. We were afraid to go out. We were afraid to live."

Late that night the soldiers arrived with translators: two American Jews, civilians, who had been trapped in Germany during the war and held in a detention camp in Laufen. Their status as prisoners of war supposedly entitled the American Jews to better treatment and to assistance from the International Red Cross.

One of the American Jews, in a bizarre coincidence, was a cousin of one of the prisoners. The two had met in Poland before the war, but the American did not recognize his severely emaciated relative. The chance reunion, causing the cousins to laugh and cry simultaneously, served to convince the prisoners that they were indeed free. "The reaction was like going out from a hot shower and jump in the ice water," Nathan said. The date of his liberation, May 7, 1945, was the day before Germany surrendered to the Allies. "It was a shock. We understood what they were saying, but we still couldn't comprehend. What's going to happen to us?"

The U.S. soldiers brought C.A.R.E. packages of food and toiletries. The prisoners immediately ripped them open. "One man began eating the soap. He knew it was soap, but he ate it because soap has fat in it. Soap is lard." Gripped by fever, Nathan was too sick to eat. He swallowed a few spoonsful of canned, condensed milk and fell asleep. Other prisoners devoured chocolate bars and biscuits that were far too rich for their malnourished condition. Four of the 164 death-march survivors died within hours. They had either overeaten or eaten foods they could not digest. Dr. Pauling, the physician who initially examined Nathan, was surprised only four prisoners died that way.

On the next day, May 8, the soldiers brought Red Cross vehicles to transport the ragged group to Laufen's tiny hospital. Their disheveled and filthy appearance shocked the nuns serving as nurses. The nuns feared approaching the new patients, let alone touching them. Nathan, for example, had not bathed for at least five months; he had taken his last shower in Czestochowa in late 1944. The prisoners resembled skeletons. Nathan weighed 84 pounds, compared with his usual weight of 155.

The doctors lectured the nuns about caring for the prisoners. The women cut off the torn, lice-infested uniforms and burned them. They bathed the men, cut their hair, and helped them to cots. The nuns explained the dangers of eating and gave them a sweet liquid to drink. Eventually, they introduced soup and bread.

An extra stroke of luck contributed to Nathan's survival. A visiting U.S. Army doctor provided penicillin to the hospital and instructed his German colleagues to prescribe it to Nathan. The new "wonder drug," available only through American troops, combatted Nathan's infection. He immediately felt better, but the doctors said they might have to amputate his left hand. "I said, 'If you take my hand, take my head.'"

Chapter Thirty-One
A MIRACULOUS REUNION

The subsiding of Nathan's fever, spurred by penicillin, was a small blessing compared with the news that his sisters were alive. The Red Cross and Allied forces displayed the names of surviving Jews at post offices, train stations, and refugee camps. Former prisoners healthy enough to search for relatives were also a source of information. The nuns at Laufen's tiny hospital wrote down their patients' names, and that list soon circulated.

Within a few weeks, Sonia saw the name, Nathan Garfinkel, on a list at Funk Kaserne, the displaced-persons camp where she was living. "I didn't believe. I thought it was another person named Nathan Garfinkel," Sonia said. The last time she had seen her brother was in Czestochowa in late 1944. Word of his accident convinced her he was doomed. "I was sure Nathan would not survive," Sonia said. "I knew what they did for any little thing. They would shoot him."

A Jew who helped survivors locate relatives, neighbors, and friends asked Sonia for characteristics to identify "Nathan Garfinkel." He would be a handsome man, age 25, blonde hair, blue eyes, from Chmielnik, Poland. He was fond of cycling and philosophical discussions. Most importantly, he would have an injured left hand.

Nathan remembers a Jewish visitor conversing with patients at Laufen's hospital. The man's eyes fixated on Nathan's bandaged hand while he intently asked Nathan for his name, hometown, camp experience, and family. How many sisters? "He told me all my sisters were alive. I started crying when I learned this," Nathan said. "It was hard to believe. I thought everybody's death march was the same as mine."

When the man informed the sisters that the "Nathan Garfinkel" listed was, indeed, their brother, they were overjoyed but incredulous. "When I found out my brother is alive, I could not believe it," Helen said. "I thought for sure he's going to be killed. My brother, Nate: it's only a miracle that he survived."

Though just barely recovered from typhus, Helen and Bela went to Laufen to find Nathan. Sonia and Regina were too weak to travel. At first, the hospital's nuns barred Helen and Bela from seeing Nathan because they believed he had tuberculosis. But the odds of reuniting three death-camp survivors in one family — let alone five — were so unusual, they allowed the visit.

Nathan recognized his sisters immediately. He tried to stand, but he could not walk. He fell to the floor. Helen and Bela fell on top of Nathan to hug him. Nuns unaware of the family reunion thought the two women were attacking Nathan. "We were laughing and crying at the same time," Nathan said. "I expected to see my sisters but not so soon." Bela was shocked to see Nathan bedridden. "I thought he was dead," Bela said. "At the hospital he looked so old. He was very sick for a long time."

Sonia remained unconvinced "Nathan Garfinkel" was her brother until Bela and Helen returned from Laufen. After that first meeting, the Garfinkel sisters took turns visiting Nathan each week at various hospitals. Traveling was not easy. The sisters walked long distances and boarded trains designed for cargo.

"When I found out that Nate was alive, it eased my pain a little bit," Sonia said. "That helped me. We were all raised the same, one for the other. We would go anyplace. I felt somebody should be in command, like a father. I knew Nate could direct us."

Etka Raitapfel Baumstick was surprised to hear about the Garfinkels. "We thought for sure they didn't survive. People were saying that any of these people who left Bergen-Belsen, they didn't survive," Etka said. "I was amazed by that. I don't know of anyone who had so many in one family."

Mandzia Wajchendler Mapa, liberated with her sister and father in Czestochowa, had assumed that all Jews shipped to Germany were dead. That group included her brother, Abraham, as well as the Garfinkels. "We didn't think he was alive. When he came back, it was like he came from the sky," Mandzia said. "Everybody said after the war that my brother went through a lot. He was burned. He was lucky to escape... To have my brother, my father, my sister. We were one of the luckiest."

Chapter Thirty-Two
ANOTHER KIND OF PRISON

Before the miraculous reunion with Nathan, Sonia helped in the Allach camp. This passed the time while her sisters recuperated in clinics. A Jewish doctor from France gave medicine and shots to the sick and dying. Sonia followed him with pails of water, but she closed her eyes. "I couldn't look and see those half-dead people," Sonia said. "Once, I almost fainted there."

Like her sisters, Sonia was bewildered that the Allied soldiers distributed such small portions of bread. "We waited so long for liberation, and they didn't give us anything to eat," Sonia commented. "I was very upset. I asked." Citing Bergen-Belsen as an example, Army doctors explained that starving people easily die from overeating and food poisoning. The amount and variety of rations increased gradually over a period of several months.

First Helen, then Bela, and later, Regina, joined Sonia. The U.S. military assigned them to Funk Kaserne, a displaced persons, or DP, camp near Munich, Germany. The camp consisted of vacant buildings that formerly had housed German officers. The Garfinkel sisters shared a room. For the first time in years, Sonia had a bed to herself, one in which she could pull up the covers. The novelty of such luxuries magnified her feeling of emptiness.

"People think that once we were liberated, that we have food, that they give us a place to sleep, that we would heal. No, it was very, very sad. We were very bad, emotionally, all of us. In a way, we didn't believe it. We couldn't cope with it. Before, in camp," Sonia said, referring to the slave labor and concentration camps, where she and her sisters almost died, "we fought to survive. We fought for a slice of bread. We fought for everything. We were working.

"All of a sudden, we weren't working. We were waiting. We just waited to come down to the kitchen. They gave us soup to eat. We waited. There was no future, nothing. If you think it should be better, it wasn't. It was very hard. If you don't have a future, you don't have nothing. It was very bad. It was the saddest time in my life. I didn't want to upset my sisters. I didn't talk with them about it: no place to go, no one to care for us, what to do. Everything came up.

"You wake up from a bad dream. You feel like an orphan, without parents, without a home, without nobody to care about you. I wasn't a prisoner but, inside of me, I was a prisoner. I wasn't free. Deep down, I couldn't take it. I didn't want my sisters to know. I myself felt if I have somebody to talk about emotional problems, I need this more than food. I was sure I would go out of my mind. I didn't want to burden them. Then if they give us a psychologist, a psychiatrist, we needed it badly. Then was the time."

The Funk Kaserne displaced persons' camp accommodated 7,000 men in soldiers' dormitories and 80 women in officers' quarters. The group of Jews and non-Jews from different nations — all former prisoners — included two Gypsies who were sisters and Mr. Stachurski, a Polish teacher from Chmielnik. Some former prisoners planned a dance, but Sonia didn't have shoes. She was wearing rags on her feet. This reflected the extreme shortages of some goods in the post-war years. Several men, including a Jewish captain in the U.S. Army, offered to find her shoes, but only one fulfilled his promise. A Pole brought Sonia a pair of men's shiny black oxfords that laced.

The Garfinkel sisters visited Nathan often. To be closer, they moved to a private home near Lebenau and Laufen, picturesque towns near the Austrian border. The U.S. Army arranged for the sisters to live in a room of that house. After a few months there, they moved to the nearby Ainring displaced persons' camp, a former German Air Force base near Freilassing. The sisters and other women occupied officers' rooms in a two-story building. Most former prisoners stayed in soldiers' barracks nearby.

While Sonia struggled silently with her emotions, Helen threw herself into the refugee community. She attended vocational classes, where she learned to operate a sewing machine. Confident of her singing talent, she joined the camp's theater troupe. They performed *Tevye the Dairyman,* a musical that later inspired *Fiddler on the Roof.* For her volunteer work, Helen received extra rations of cigarettes and chocolate, which she bartered for items she needed. The camp occasionally showed films, including the first movie Helen saw, *Gaslight,* starring Ingrid Bergman.

"From bad to good was very easy to get used to. From good to bad is hard," Helen said. "Now I look back and say, 'How could I live in that one room in DP camp with my brother and three sisters?' Now I can't live with my children. I like my privacy." Helen kept herself so busy she didn't think about Chmielnik or her missing relatives, much less the murders of 6 million Jews or the magnitude of the genocide she had survived. Helen was 18 years old at liberation. "We had food. We had where to live. We got some clothes. We didn't think about anything," Helen maintained. "I don't remember thinking about my parents, my little brother, my little sister. I think more now about them. We never talked about the concentration camp. We didn't talk about it for a long time. Now we talk about it."

Regina inched toward adjusting. "I remember being given a dress and then another dress. I thought, 'What am I going to do with two dresses? What do I need two dresses for?'" Regina said. "As I got better, it slowly sunk in that we are free." The concept of freedom was difficult to grasp. Regina was only 15 years old — a fact that astonished Ainring's residents. Since age 9, she had been a captive of the Reich, restricted by its invasion of Poland, enslaved by its death camps, persecuted by its racist dogma. "I realized there was a difference between camp and a DP camp. In the

DP camp, nobody told us when to go, how to go, what to do, but I still didn't know what the meaning of being free. I had nothing to compare it to." Freedom was something more than attending the theater in Munich, vacationing in the mountains with her sisters, or choosing among several outfits to wear. Regina could not completely understand freedom until she better understood her wrongful incarceration and the evils of the Shoah. "Slowly I began to realize it, what it was all about, and where I am at. I began to realize that that wasn't right, that wasn't natural, it shouldn't have been," Regina said. "It was a big shock to the mind." The denial in which she had existed during the war continued. "No one talked about my parents. No one spoke of individual incidents." So Regina cried by herself. Before the war, "...what helped me was I didn't realize what was going on," Regina said. "That helped me cope with it. I didn't stop to think, and I didn't ask questions." After the war, Regina began asking herself questions. Composing the answers was a painful process. Like Helen, Regina distracted herself by participating in the refugee center's activities. She took sewing lessons from a German woman, attended English classes, and started enjoying plays, movies, and newspapers. "I wanted to learn in general." Regina was eager to catch up because the war had cut short her education.

Many Jewish survivors were the sole members left of their families. Rachel Wygodna Herszlikowicz lost her widowed mother, six older married sisters, and their husbands and children to Treblinka's gas fumes. She lost her hopes and dreams there, too. Before the Germans razed Poland, Herszlikowicz imagined becoming a teacher of Judaic history and culture, emulating Mr. Laks. "I hoped to continue to go to school and be something because I was very good in school, but the war broke out, and that was the finish of it." Until then, Herszlikowicz had always pictured herself living peacefully in Chmielnik, attending synagogue, taking evening strolls with friends. "It was a very nice life. It's a pity it's not anymore." Instead, Herszlikowicz exiled herself far from Poland.

She moved to Melbourne, Australia.

Some prisoners created their own families. "After they took away my mother, they assigned a girl my age to my perch," Helen Rozenek Jurysta said, referring to her bunk. From the time Lola Hajman became Jurysta's barrack mate in Kielce, the two women never parted. "We got so close, I called her my sister. We were very dedicated to each other. We made a promise to each other that we would go with each other." Consequently, the two women dug ditches side by side in Przedborz, nursed one another through illness, supported each other during Appell, and walked arm in arm on the death march. Lola Hajman trusted the disciplined and frugal Jurysta to save food rations for her. Together they withstood the cruel evacuations to Czestochowa, Bergen-Belsen, Burgau, Türkheim, Allach, and Dachau. After the war, they became sisters-in-law. "We had a double wedding. I married my husband. My brother married Lola."

Jakob Sylman is typical of Jews forced to wait out the war in the Soviet Union. He barely endured banishment to Siberia with his brother, sister, niece, and brother-in-law. None of Jakob's relatives left behind in Chmielnik — including a brother, three sisters, and his parents — lived. Jakob reconstructed their fate by talking to other survivors. The Sylman family remained in Chmielnik even after three large deportations of Jews to Treblinka had occurred. "Father (Leibl Sylman) was in good relations with the Germans because of his beer parlor," Jakob said. "They kept him there until the end. My brother and sisters could have gone to work camp if they wanted to because they had connections, but they wanted to stay home." The Sylmans' tavern was only a temporary reprieve. Jakob heard from some survivors that a German shot his sister, Miriam, for being sick. As far as Jakob knows, the rest of his family was gassed in Treblinka.

The Garfinkels, intensely aware of their good fortune to have each other, remarked among themselves that some people gave them "the evil eye" at the Ainring displaced persons' camp. "I'm sure without my family I would not have survived. I might have survived labor camps but not concentration camps," Regina concluded. "In the beginning there were people who were very helpful to me because I was the youngest there. Although there were nice people and kind people, nobody could take on the responsibility for another person. Everybody had to look out for themselves. In the end, without my family, there would have been nobody to hold me up," she said, recalling that she couldn't even walk.

In the refugee center, Regina talked about going home to Chmielnik, but she elicited only a "maybe" from her siblings. In retrospect, she recognizes they were pacifying her. Slowly, Regina understood what her siblings already knew: Poland represented a large cemetery for Jews. When she attended the funeral of an acquaintance, Regina felt envious. That person had a tombstone with his name on it. She had no idea where her parents and younger siblings were buried or whether they were buried at all. Kalman, Sara, Rachel, and Fishel had no marker. "In DP camp we were told stories. We were told how lucky we were to be alive. Then we began to realize in bits and pieces what had taken place," Regina said. "I think it just came gradually to me. I came to terms with it, that I wouldn't see my parents again. It didn't happen to just one family. There were a lot of people there who were just single people left with nobody."

Some survivors who returned to Chmielnik met hostility. "After '46, I was looking for my brother," said Tosia Fastag Bottner. "All they greeted us with was: 'We thought they killed all the Jews. Now all the Jews are coming back.'" That reaction soured Bottner and many survivors from staying in Poland or even visiting later. "If somebody offered me a fare to go to Poland, I don't think I would have any use to go to visit." Israel "Irving" Buchbinder traveled to Chmielnik via Czechoslovakia. The Polish caretaker of his grandmother's house was incredulous. "Are you still alive?" he asked. "You had better get out of here." After two days, Buchbinder proceeded to Germany. "None of the Jews were secure in Poland, especially in small towns."

Esther Pasternak Tarek and her sister, Bela, went to Lodz, Kielce, and Chmielnik with some trepidation. "In the beginning, you search. You ask," Tarek said. "There was a little hope that they (my parents) were alive." One neighbor greeted the Pasternaks warmly, but he was in the minority, Tarek recalled. The sisters soon became disillusioned. They were especially disappointed to observe some Holocaust survivors trying to profit by selling the property of dead Jews. "We were young. We didn't have any experience," Tarek said. "This was a terrible war." Poles always shortchanged Jews in such property deals, Buchbinder said, but Jews had little bargaining power. They typically accepted what was offered. Returning to Chmielnik from the Soviet Union in 1947, Jakob Lederman noted the unwelcome reception and sensed he was in danger. "The Poles ask me, 'Why you came?' Poles were afraid the Jews wanted their homes back," Lederman said. "I heard stories. A lot of Jews got shot. I got scared." Lederman left.

Mandzia Wajchendler Mapa said fear, violence, and uncertainty dulled the joy of liberation. In her hometown of Skarzysko-Kamienna, Jews and Poles alike looted stores to get food, clothes, and anything else they had been deprived of during the war. "There wasn't a law. If a German was still hidden, they took him out and shot him." Such instances of vigilante justice were few compared with the continued maltreatment of surviving Jews, some of whom were murdered in Skarzysko-Kamienna. Although that city's mayor honored Mandzia's father's claims to buildings and other property he had owned before the war, staying in Skarzysko-Kamienna was not feasible, she said. "My father said, 'Children, we have to go away.' It was more safe to be after the war in Germany than in Poland."

Fay Skrobacka Goldlist, who also found freedom in Czestochowa, heeded the Soviet soldiers' dire warnings. "They said we shouldn't go out because we would get shot. There was fear. Somebody could come in camp and kill us all. We didn't know where to go. Everybody had to find shelter." Goldlist joined a group of Jews who took refuge in a hospital in Czestochowa. The men ventured outdoors to find food, but the women stayed inside, Goldlist said, because they feared being raped by Soviet soldiers. After a few weeks, she reached Chmielnik. "That's when the real tragedy started for me. Somebody told me they saw my sister. I was looking and looking and couldn't find anyone. I couldn't get anything from anybody. The Polacks said they don't have it even though I know my mother gave it to them," Goldlist said, referring to family possessions. She searched eight months for her sister, Cesia, and the rest of her family despite reports that Poles murdered surviving Jews. Goldlist counts her blessings that she wasn't attacked during her post-war travels, but she left Poland feeling cursed with a perpetual sadness. "I'm from a family of eight children. I am alone. My mother then was only 48 years old. My father was 52," Goldlist said. "Thank God I have three children; but, when it comes to family, I am always alone. I still feel alone."

Mania Poper Cherston returned to Lodz, where she met her future husband and found a sister who had survived Auschwitz. "I was afraid to go back to Chmielnik. The Poles hated the Jews," Cherston said. She and her husband stayed in Lodz a few years before persuading a French diplomat to give them visas. "I didn't want to give birth to a baby in Poland," Cherston concluded. "We know that Poland is no place to live."

Morris "Julek" Singer; his wife, Mandzia Garfinkel; and their two daughters returned to Poland from the Soviet Union — an arduous journey requiring them to walk and to catch rides on cargo trains. "Anti-Semitism was worse after the war than before the war," Morris said. "There were organized bands of Poles waiting for the transports of Jews coming back. They were waiting on the border to kill Jews and beat them up." For protection, Jews traveled in groups and slept in shifts. Although Morris and his family reached Lodz without incident, he was too afraid to rent their former apartment and to face their former neighbor. They stayed in Lodz only because they were weary of traveling. They left for Israel as soon as they were rested and, eventually, they settled in Toronto.

Although Henik "Henry" Moszenberg Kaufman narrowly escaped Kielce's shameful post-war pogrom, he spent several years in Lodz, Poland. He and his wife occasionally visited Chmielnik, where he had some powerful ties. Henik and his parents had been born in Chmielnik. While Henik and his mother were trapped in Lodz' ghetto during the war, his father and sister were shot in Chmielnik's square. After the war, Henik's mother, Chana Skoczylas Moszenberg, met her childhood sweetheart, Yosel Kaufman, in Chmielnik. In the town's Jewish cemetery, the two widowers vowed to marry because there were no relatives left alive to oppose their wishes. The need to rebuild families was so strong, Yosel legally adopted Henik as his son, and Henik assumed the Kaufman name. Henik helped Yosel establish claim and title to properties the Kaufman clan had owned in Chmielnik before the war. Yosel demanded that Chmielnik's mayor return missing tombstones to the Jewish cemetery; they had been used to pave streets. Yosel helped to find Jews, children especially, who had been hidden during the war. One of Henik's cousins, Langwald, had converted to Catholicism while in hiding and had married a Pole after the war. She wanted nothing to do with her Jewish relatives or heritage. Good contacts with prominent Poles kept Henik, his wife, mother, and stepfather from harm's way. They stayed with Chmielnik's court judge Bucewicz; otherwise, they would have been harassed.

For Israel Steinfeld, returning to Chmielnik was an eerie experience. "Picture yourself. You close your eyes. You come back. Empty buildings. They're not empty. There are strangers in your home." Familiar with every house and every stone, Steinfeld walked around for several hours. Chmielnik, which had once bustled with thousands of Jews, resembled a ghost town. Poles peeked from behind the curtains of former Jewish homes. Steinfeld felt as though he had landed from the planet Mars. The woman occupying the Steinfeld household was hospitable and allowed Israel to sleep in his own room. Steinfeld accompanied a Jewess by the name of Melman to her home, which had also been seized by Poles. She found a Jewish prayer book hidden in the attic. "She wasn't a religious person," Steinfeld said, "but when she found this siddur, she cried in this attic like this house would sink."

Immune to feelings, Steinfeld wandered in a daze. "It was like blank. Who knows where we are going? What we will be doing? The picture is blurred. I felt that no one would be left." Finding relatives in Germany revived his emotions. His sister, Anna Steinfeld Weinbaum, and, more remarkably, his father, Joshua Steinfeld, were in the Ainring DP camp. Anna worked in an organization called *Bricha* to help smuggle remaining Jews from Poland. Joshua, age 46 at liberation, automatically became the DP camp's elder and rabbi. "The rest was kids, 18, 19, 20. He was like a father to those people. They didn't have the Jewish education. He showed them how to say *Kaddish*," Israel said, referring to the Jewish prayer of mourning. Joshua performed several hundred wedding ceremonies, including those of Bela and Sonia. Many survivors could not face the horrible past they had just lived. Israel and his sister, for example, never discussed her experience in the death camps. Likewise, Israel never asked his sister what happened to their mother. "I made the same assumptions that I'm sure hundreds of people did. It's painful even today. I cannot even now talk."

Survivors typically preoccupied themselves with immediate needs. Israel worked for the United Nations Relief and Rehabilitation Administration, known as UNRRA, to distribute food, clothing, and supplies to refugees. The overriding concern for food, so acute at liberation, slowly dissipated, Bela Garfinkel Soloway Hurtig said. "Later we became more civilized. We were interested in going places. We were interested in people, in books." Each Holocaust survivor, including the Garfinkels' spouses, has a unique account and perspective of what is arguably the cataclysmic event of the 20th century.

Bela met her husband, Saul Soloway, at a train station in Lebenau. Saul, like other Jews from Kobrin, in the Soviet Union, just east of Biala Podlaska, Poland, had been condemned to die in Treblinka's gas chambers. He defied fate by jumping off the train en route. He spent most of the war in the forest with partisan resistance groups. "This hiding, it's even worse," Bela said. "You only know that if they catch you, they kill you. Later they went to camp. They realize it's not life, this hiding." Saul got an exceptional work assignment: driving a supply truck. Although two German soldiers constantly accompanied Saul, he always had access to food. Near the war's end, Saul was swept into a grueling death march, during which he saved his cousin's life. All of Saul's other relatives, including his parents, sister, and baby nephew, were gassed. Sadly, the two cousins did not maintain contact after the war, Bela said, because Saul was angry that his cousin had married a German woman.

Disinterested in Saul initially, Bela was looking for Isaac. "I couldn't find him. I don't think he's alive, Isaac. I have no idea where he is." After meeting Bela, Saul rode his motorcycle to Ainring to visit her. He got inside the camp by telling the officers he was Bela's cousin. She refused to see him, not just once but several times. "I said, 'I'm not going down.' I said, 'I don't know who he is.' I said, 'Tell him I don't live here anymore,' but he kept returning. He came again and again and again." During their lengthy courtship, Saul exchanged four packs of cigarettes for a gold ring engraved with the initials B.S. for Bela Soloway. Later, in the United States, they joked that the initials stood for "bullshit." Bela always wore that ring as a reminder of happiness amid her struggles. "One time he brought me three packages of Jell-O. I don't know what Jell-O is." Many men wanted to date Bela, but she chose Saul because he was good-looking and clever in business. He traded his rations for profits so he could live outside the refugee camp. "Saul wanted to be private. He wouldn't stand in line for soup."

Bela and Saul were married, along with two other couples, by Joshua Steinfeld in Ainring in 1946. Then they lived in the German town of Trostberg near Traunstein. The Burgermeister, or mayor, required a wealthy couple to provide living quarters for the Soloways. The German woman was kind to Bela and brought her flowers and fruit every morning. She provided a maid and served Bela coffee. Saul didn't trust the landlady because she denied knowledge of the death camps, gas chambers, crematoria, and the mass extermination of Jews. "Saul was so angry, if he had a gun, he would shoot everybody," Bela said. "Saul wanted revenge against the German people. He give this woman hell. When Saul came home, he didn't take off his galoshes. Saul had friends come in late. He slammed the door. At night Saul would yell, 'She's going to tell me she doesn't know nothing? She's a big liar.' She couldn't evict, so he took advantage. This woman didn't think I was Jewish. She treat me good. I couldn't say nothing. What can I say? I really didn't care. In a way, Saul was right."

Of the Garfinkels, Bela was the first to marry and the first to have a baby. Bela named her daughter Sandra, which she thought to be a modern, American variation of the name Sara. "We love our mother so much, each of us named our first child after my mother."

Regina married Saul Muskovitz in Graben, Germany, in March, 1949. Saul was from Radomsko, Poland. He also endured the war years with Jewish partisans in the forest, where they scavenged for food, shelter, and ammunition. They expended much of their energy trying to avoid German soldiers, anti-Semitic Polish patriots, and other potential enemies.

In Radomsko, Saul Muskovitz' parents, sister, and four brothers hid in an underground bunker. They depended on household servants to bring them food, to keep their whereabouts secret, and to otherwise help them. After Soviet forces liberated Poland, Saul found the bunker silent and empty. Then he turned to see the following words chiseled on the concrete door: "If anybody is alive, take revenge." Saul recognized his brother's handwriting. Through acquaintances, he learned the employees betrayed his parents and siblings and brutally murdered them a few months before the war's end. Fearing Saul would also be killed, the acquaintances advised him to leave Poland. Saul headed west to Germany, where he lived in various displaced persons' camps. He met Regina while participating in a soccer match in Ainring. After their marriage, they continued to live in the camp.

On learning of Saul's tragedy, Regina lost her desire to return to Chmielnik. "We knew we had to be afraid of the German people. The Polish people, you wanted to trust them, but they betrayed you," Regina said. "I just couldn't separate Polish people from the German people. I wouldn't have gone back to Poland for anything. To go back and see everything intact except the family, I wouldn't want to be reminded." Unlike her brother, Nathan, Regina did not try to befriend Germans. She figured Germans older than she knew about the death camps. Ugly stories circulating in the DP camp convinced her of that. Regina heard that, after Germany's defeat, some residents of Dachau prepared lavish meals laced with poison, set the tables, opened the windows, and unlocked the doors. The mock hospitality killed newly-freed prisoners searching for food. "I believe in collective guilt," Regina said. "I usually went by age. I wondered about Germans older than me. I couldn't trust them." Regina's distrust grew with the passage of time. Many years later, during a trip to Belgium, she awakened in her hotel room to hear people — the customers of a nearby beer garden — singing in German. Regina bit her biceps so she wouldn't scream and wake up her husband. "I thought, 'How can I be there? How can I speak this language?'" In that moment, Regina thought she might lose her mind. It made no sense to be so close to her former oppressors. In contrast, shortly after the war, before she fully realized what the Shoah was, Regina didn't feel such a strong aversion to living in Germany or to speaking the language of Nazis. "Then I accepted it more. I didn't have a choice."

The Garfinkels' maternal aunt, Lonia, sent a Jewish smuggler to guide one of Sara's children to Paris. Lonia attached a small photograph of herself to a note. Her resemblance to the Garfinkels' mother, Sara, was striking. Lonia had written in Polish: "I am glad you are alive. Trust this man. Go with him to Paris." Helen was the logical choice. Nathan still required medical attention. The other sisters were obligated to husbands or fiancés. The smuggler gave Helen a Polish military uniform to wear, but he had no identification papers for her. Together, they boarded a train in Munich. The Allies restricted travel within Europe; not surprisingly, inspectors ordered Helen off the train. Helen and Sonia then considered resettling in Palestine, which later became Israel. "From Ainring, they smuggled many Jews to Israel," Sonia said, explaining they crossed the Austrian border and departed from Linz. Sonia and Helen then decided to follow Bela and Regina to the United States, where their husbands had relatives to sponsor them. Nathan, who originally planned to join his maternal aunts in Paris, also opted for the United States.

Helen befriended her future husband, Joseph Greenspun, in Ainring. During the war, he had served in the Soviet Army, had been wounded in battle, and was hospitalized. On a medical discharge, Greenspun returned to his hometown, Mervice, Lithuania, although Germany occupied it. His family, friends, and neighbors had vanished. Non-Jewish acquaintances urged Greenspun to flee to avoid being killed. Nearly all the Jews were dead, they said, except for a few who stayed in the forest and came to the village at night for food. Greenspun joined those remaining Jews. Together, they formed a band of anti-fascist partisans.

Although Greenspun was spared the death camps, life as a fugitive was not easy. "His experience in the forest was terrible," Helen said. "In the winter, it was cold. They couldn't make a fire.

There was no food. They had to threaten the farmers to get food."
Partisans also pressured farmers to meet their demands for clothing, blankets, guns, and, most of all, the promise not to betray
them. Because the Germans tirelessly pursued Jews in hiding, the
partisans moved from place to place, sleeping in barns, in hay-
lofts, and in trees they had chopped down. During the winter,
they took special care not to leave footprints or other marks in the
snow. The prospect of being hunted down by packs of German
shepherds added more stress to a hand-to-mouth existence of the
worst sort.

Greenspun's parents and five of his siblings were among the 6
million Jews massacred. An older sister and her son saved themselves by living in a cellar. Helen and Joseph did not marry until
1951, after they had both emigrated separately to the United States.
"Hitler was our matchmaker," Helen declared with a touch of irony,
noting that many concentration camp survivors who wouldn't have
otherwise met wed after the war.

The visits of Nathan Nothman at the Ainring displaced persons' camp puzzled Sonia. "When Nathan Nothman asked me to
go out, I felt nothing. I never thought I would marry. I never
thought I would have kids. I thought we would live out our lives,
that we would never have kids or marry. There was no place to go
out. We just walked. I don't know why he talked to me. I don't
know. I lost all my emotions, all my feelings being in camp," Sonia
said, referring to the death camps.

Nothman, a Jew from Krakow, endured a series of ordeals,
including that city's ghetto. In the nearby slave labor camp of
Plaszow, he was compelled to work as a death commando preparing women and children to be shot in an open pit. It was in Plaszow
where Oskar Schindler employed and protected more than 1,200
Jews in a pots and pans factory. Nothman was aware of the famous "Schindler's List" but was not on it. During forced marches
and train rides crisscrossing Poland, Czechoslovakia, and Germany,
Nothman became a prisoner in Flossenburg, Gross-Rosen,

Vistergerstoff, and a number of smaller camps. At the beginning of the Holocaust, Nothman jumped from a train bound for Auschwitz' gas chambers. At the end, he escaped from a death march winding its way between the German towns of Regensburg and Laufen.

Nothman played soccer at the Ainring displaced persons' camp. To visit Sonia, he rode a motorcycle or bicycle. During their courtship, he taught her how to ride a bicycle. Joshua Steinfeld married the couple on January 26, 1947, in Laufen. "Nate always told me, 'You're not going to get married with other people in camp. You're going to get married separate with music.'"

As a soccer player, Nothman got double rations, which he used to finance the marriage ceremony. He paid for live music with cigarettes. He borrowed a wedding gown from a German woman via cigarettes and chocolates. He and Sonia accumulated sugar and flour rations for a baker to make a cake. With other rations they bought the wedding feast provisions in Austria or at the *Tausch-Centrale*, or Central Exchange. "A shoemaker made me a pair of shoes," Sonia said and laughed. "They were so tight — still — I could hardly walk in them." Nothman was extremely popular in Laufen. Because buses did not operate on Sundays, the town's Burgermeister dispatched a bus to Ainring to transport about 100 guests to Laufen's *Altepost*, or dance hall. That was his gift to the couple. Only a handful of Germans attended: the mayor; a city hall clerk called Siegel; Dr. Haberkern; and Ludwig Dietrich, a skilled photographer.

After their marriage, the Nothmans lived in Laufen, in a small apartment sandwiched above Dietrich's studio and below his flat. He was their landlord, neighbor, and friend. Sonia spent many hours talking to Dietrich, a kind man with an aversion to fascism. His brother, Karl Dietrich, who operated a photo studio in the nearby town of Freilassing, had been imprisoned during the war for holding dissident political views. Thanks to Ludwig Dietrich, the Garfinkels own many beautiful, post-war portraits of themselves. They are a small consolation, however, for all the pre-war family pictures, heirlooms, and other sentimental belongings forever lost to the Shoah. A master of still photography, Dietrich captured powerful images with his camera: the burning intensity of Nathan Garfinkel's eyes, the wariness of Bela, the raw determination of Helen, the tender innocence of Regina. The photos of Sonia, with her high cheekbones, also stand out because she has a different look for each pose. Through his art, Dietrich revealed the personalities and emotions of the Garfinkels and their friends. One photo conveys Helen's utter adoration of her brother. Several show that Nathan Garfinkel and his German girlfriend were in love.

Many survivors wanted to start families, Sonia said, but she felt nothing. "People went from camp to camp. Boys look for girls. Girls look for boys," Sonia said. "The guys, they drove us crazy. Everyone wanted to go with us." Once, while Sonia read a German book at a train station, some Jewish men began flirting with her. "These Jewish guys were talking to me. They were very fresh. They were talking to me in German." At that moment, Roman Flaum, a friend, passed by and greeted Sonia in Yiddish. "These guys were ashamed." Had they known she was Jewish, Sonia said, they would have been polite rather than vulgar.

Jewish acquaintances often asked Nathan Nothman why he dated that *sziksa*, or non-Jew. They assumed Sonia was German from her blonde hair, blue eyes, and fair skin. "Prejudice always exists. It was ironic that Jewish people thought I wasn't Jewish, but you have to understand how they felt after the death camps," Sonia explained. Some Germans, including Dietrich, the photographer, begged Sonia and Nathan to stay, but Sonia couldn't bear the thought. "There were a few good ones, but I couldn't live in Germany," Sonia said. "I couldn't wait for the day to going away."

Chapter Thirty-Three
FAMILIAR FACES

Laufen's tiny hospital represented the beginning of a long convalescence for Nathan. Within a few weeks, he was among 35 patients transferred to a sanitorium in Gauting, Germany, near Munich. A spot on Nathan's lungs, which still appears in X-rays, convinced doctors he had the highly-contagious tuberculosis. "Anybody who went to Gauting was very sick," Nathan said. As time passed, he felt better and the doctors concluded he wasn't a high-risk case. Dr. Lehmerer and Mary, a nurse who was the doctor's fiancée, befriended Nathan. Together, the three went to Munich to see operas and plays. The couple invited Nathan to their wedding.

In 1946, Gauting's doctors gave Nathan oxygen therapy for tuberculosis. Then they treated his hand. Soldiers' injuries and frostbite cases during World War II spurred the development of plastic surgery. Doctors learned to graft skin by placing a healthy limb over a wound. In Gauting, Dr. Shedlacsek cut a pouch on Nathan's stomach. The surgeon slid Nathan's hand through the opening so the stomach's skin would attach to the hand. A body cast from neck to hips immobilized Nathan for three months to ensure skin growth. "After every war, medicine is progressing," Nathan said. His hand hurt so badly, Nathan offered Mary his cigarette rations for more painkillers. Knowing the exchange could lead to permanent addiction, Mary handed out placebos.

Gauting's doctors referred Nathan to Professor Lange at Bad Tölz' hospital for physical therapy — basically hand exercises using soap and water. The burned muscle and ligaments of his three middle fingers restricted movement. Nathan's left thumb is permanently crooked because it was bent inside the cast. Professor

Lange, a specialist in plastic surgery, operated twice to enhance agility. He wanted to repeat the skin graft, to improve what the other doctor had done. The back of Nathan's left hand is raised because the flesh contains fatty tissue. Had the fat been scraped from the grafting pocket, the top of Nathan's hand would have been flat, Lange said. Cosmetics didn't interest Nathan. He declined another operation, happy to still have a left hand, satisfied he could stretch his fingers a little more.

After recuperating in Gauting and Bad Tölz, Nathan joined his sisters in Ainring. The United Nations Refugee Association created the camp, and the U.S. military managed it. Intent on living in Paris, Nathan hired a French tutor, but several developments changed his mind. His sisters' decision to relocate to the United States prompted Nathan to study the U.S. Constitution. "I read the American Bill of Rights. I loved it." But something troubled Nathan. During outings to Munich, "I saw segregation in the U.S. military — white soldiers played baseball separately from black soldiers." President Harry S. Truman desegregated the U.S. military via an executive order on July 26, 1948. Integration was not fully achieved, however, until the Korean War. Nathan sought Jewish Congress sponsorship to immigrate to the United States.

While waiting for the paperwork, he explored the land of his former oppressors. "I didn't sit in the displaced persons' camp. I wanted to see the outside. I wanted to see the German people." Enchanted with Berlin, Nathan traveled there a dozen times to attend operas and plays. Berlin also was the home of Gizela Krueger, a German woman Nathan had met in Gauting and Bad Tölz. He stayed in the home of Gizela's parents. "These were the people who took me to see *The Merchant of Venice* and *Oliver Twist*. I wasn't angry that they took me to this play. I wondered why. I asked. I said, 'I am not Shylock, what happened 500 years ago. I am not Faigan, what took place 200 years ago.' They didn't answer. It was silent for two or three minutes." Because Nathan refused to condemn all Germans as killers, he expected the Kruegers

not to associate him with Jewish villains. Nathan's need to de-
molish stereotypes and defy convention motivated him to date
Gizela. Multilingual, she worked as a secretary for the British Army.
She was a single parent, having been widowed when her husband,
a German soldier, was killed during the war. "My sisters didn't
like this, that I have a German girlfriend," Nathan said, "but I
wanted my freedom. I do not believe in collective guilt." Nathan's
high ideals clashed with post-war realities. Their tender expres-
sions in photographs indicate Nathan and Gizela were in love, but
it could not last. Nathan planned to leave Germany, and he did
not want to estrange himself permanently from his sisters. Gizela
had already hurt Sonia's feelings with careless remarks about her
cooking. "Nathan defended Gizela," Sonia said. "He put me down
in front of her." Sonia thought Gizela took advantage of Nathan
to get the money he earned from selling cigarettes, chocolate, and
other rations. "Gizela thought Nathan was rich," Sonia said. "She
was smart. He was like a spare tire to her." The unlikely couple
corresponded after Nathan's departure from Germany, but Gizela's
letters stopped when he got married.

Ugly reminders of the Shoah punctuated the simple pleasure
of being able to come and go as one pleased. Nathan saw a fright-
eningly familiar face once during a visit to Bad Reichenhall, a resort in the German Alps. Nathan happened to be sitting with a
German friend at an outdoor cafe. Nathan's hands shook, clatter-
ing his coffee cup on its saucer. Walking by was the Hungarian
guard who had helped lead the death march. Pulling together his
nerves, Nathan talked to the guard and studied his face to confirm
the man was his would-be executioner. "I knew from his accent."
The guard did not recognize his former victim. Nathan went to a
nearby American Military Police office to report the criminal. The
Army officer in charge said he would investigate, after hearing the
Hungarian's response to Nathan's agitated account of the death
march. Nathan later watched the Hungarian enter and leave the
AMP office. Nathan confronted him, asking, "They let you go

free?" The Hungarian replied, "I am free, but you will be dead." Nathan stormed into the AMP office and demanded, "You let this killer free?" The Army officer said Nathan would be contacted to testify at the trial, but he never heard from the AMP. When he returned to Bad Reichenhall six months later, the office was closed. Nathan's frustration with the apparent lack of justice immediately after the war transformed into disillusionment.

Relatively few S.S. and Nazi officials were punished for their role in the Shoah. The famous trials of Nuremberg, Germany, focused on the Reich's upper echelon. Of 22 individuals prosecuted in the first proceedings, 12 were condemned to death, three were acquitted, and most of the others received long-term or life prison sentences. Subsequent trials in Nuremberg targeted 185 Nazi party leaders, judges, physicians, and business executives. More than half received prison sentences, and several were condemned to death.

The Allies conducted similar, but lesser-known, trials in other German cities. For the most part, however, virtually all middle- and-low ranking Nazi officers and S.S. were at large, resuming comfortable, civilian lives. In his memoirs, *The Murderers Among Us*, Holocaust survivor Simon Wiesenthal estimates that thousands of former S.S. live around the world. Of those, presumably hundreds settled in the United States. The Jewish Documentation Center, founded by Wiesenthal in Vienna, Austria, in 1961, is devoted to identifying and finding Nazi war criminals and to bringing them to justice.

Nathan ended up participating in a war-crimes trial by accident. Once, as he changed trains in Leipzig to reach Berlin, Nathan stopped to read a poster labeled "Wanted: Witnesses to Testify." He froze, stunned. The poster bore the photograph of Hermann Lachmann. Nathan stared at the face of the guard who had nearly bludgeoned him to death, knocking out his teeth in the process, during a work detail at Skarzysko-Kamienna's hospital. "This is my killer," Nathan thought to himself.

It was late 1948. Nathan delayed his journey to Berlin in order to find Leipzig's prosecutors, East Germans using judicial guidelines developed by the Allies. Anxious to catch war criminals, they allowed Nathan to speak with Lachmann in the presence of a stenographer. The court officials insisted that Nathan remain composed because other survivors had attacked suspected war criminals. During the encounter between torturer and victim in the Leipzig jail's visiting room, Lachmann denied being the guard who had nearly murdered Nathan. Lachmann said Nathan had confused him with his brother. Nathan remembered that the guard's brother had been killed on the Eastern front. "I said, 'Mr. Lachmann, if you would be your brother, you would be dead,'" Nathan said. "Then he was quiet."

In May, 1949, Nathan returned to Leipzig in order to be a witness at Lachmann's trial. The proceedings revealed that Lachmann had spent time in Trevienka, Poland, where the S.S. had trained more than 4,000 guards to kill and to torture. Accused of killing at least three helpless prisoners, Lachmann received a prison sentence of only 20 years. His defense — that he was a teenager ignorant of his actions during the war — persuaded the judges to withhold the death sentence. As of 1997, researchers in Berlin believed Lachmann was still alive in Bavaria.

The nascent Cold War between the United States and the Soviet Union thwarted efforts to pursue and to punish Nazis. To stem the so-called red menace, the Allied forces cut deals with fascists, who are the natural enemies of communists. Nathan finds it ironic that the U.S. military in West Germany failed to investigate the Hungarian guard, while the communists in East Germany convicted Lachmann of crimes against humanity. "I assume this Hungarian emigrated to the United States," Nathan said. "This is the difference between east and west politics."

In Leipzig, Nathan bumped into Otto Schnitzler, the German who had secretly left out snacks for the Skarzysko-Kamienna prisoners. "I said, 'Mr. Schnitzler, do you remember me? You gave me a piece of bread in Skarzysko.' He said, 'I gave many people bread. I'm glad to meet one of them. Who are you?'" Nathan then realized Schnitzler could not possibly have recognized him. In Skarzysko-Kamienna, Nathan wore rags and probably weighed only 110 pounds. Now he was robust, healthy, and smartly dressed. Schnitzler, a resident of Leipzig, testified against other Nazis. The two formed a friendship, which would not have been possible during the war. Nathan visited Schnitzler a few times at his home, and they wrote letters to each other after Nathan left Germany.

Unbelievably, Nathan crossed paths with yet another war criminal, whose name he can't remember. Shoah survivors had pointed out the former Ukrainian guard to Nathan in Gauting's hospital. Later, Nathan saw him on the ship to the United States, the General Greely. "I confronted him. I said, 'What are you doing over here?'" Even though Nathan didn't personally know the former guard, the man replied, "If I didn't kill you then, I'll kill you here." Disappointment, rather than fear, gripped Nathan. Many S.S. never atoned for their crimes. "I am willing to forgive, but not to forget," Nathan said. "I don't have to forgive because no one offered an apology."

Chapter Thirty-Four
AFTER THE STORM

The Garfinkels faced many challenges as immigrants in the United States, but any difficulties seemed frivolous compared with the six-year nightmare they had lived. Like other Shoah survivors in North America, they worked diligently to learn English, to find jobs, to raise children, to establish businesses, and to buy homes. While they have enjoyed those hard-won achievements, they are always poignantly aware of their greatest victory — having survived the Holocaust. As much as they might wish to forget the genocide they witnessed, they cannot; in many ways, the nightmare continues. Each of the Garfinkels quite literally suffers from bad dreams and insomnia, not to mention the physical ailments of poor circulation, aching bones, swollen feet, and having lost their teeth as the result of malnutrition. Unlike some survivors, they have not succumbed to mental illness or to despair. Rather, the Garfinkels describe their adversities, large and small, pre-war and post-war, with grace.

Sonia often can't sleep at night, so she thinks of how her life would have unfolded in Poland if fascism and Hitler had never existed. She imagines her parents being elderly and wonders how Fishel and Rachel would have turned out as grown-ups. "This radio, this is my life-saver. I listen to this at three or four o'clock in the morning," Sonia said. "All the time, we always come back to the concentration camp. It lives with us. We can't forget, never." At night, Sonia sees the faces of many Jews from Chmielnik who died in Skarzysko-Kamienna, Czestochowa, and Bergen-Belsen. Her memories include the good things that happened and her own accomplishments of adjusting to a new homeland.

The Garfinkels were eager to experience the freedom and pros-

perity of the United States, but the journey there tested their resolve. No one forewarned them about motion sickness.

"It was not a boat, a ship like you have today," Helen said of
the General W.G. Haas, which was easily buffeted by wind and
waves. As the vessel accelerated on rough waters, hundreds of
refugees began vomiting. "We were all sick the whole time. I even
said to myself, 'I lived through so much, and now I die.' I thought
I would never make it." Ironically, "...they gave us a lot of food and
good food, but we could not eat." Like Bela and Regina, who crossed
the Atlantic in different ships, Helen stayed in the cabin below,
fighting nausea. "Sometimes we dragged each other to the deck. I
went up because they told us to go up."

"I was so sick," Regina recalled of her passage on the Robert
Taylor. "If I were up on the deck, I would probably throw myself
in the water." Her husband, Saul, brought what he thought would
be a refreshing and nourishing supplement to stave off dehydration and nausea: fresh citrus. "For years, I couldn't stand the odor
of an orange. That's how sick I was," Regina said.

After vomiting a few times, Nathan Garfinkel tried to suppress his nausea. He stopped eating, spent much of his time on
deck, and drank lots of water and tea. As he had always done in
the concentration camps, Nathan chose a top bunk so other people
could not throw up on him. "Many people got sick. They told me
I was the strongest person because I control myself." Because the
General Greely was a U.S. Navy ship, it stopped in many ports,
prolonging the journey. As the boat approached New York, some
passengers began crying out, "Here it is! Here it is!" They had
spotted the Statue of Liberty. Nathan recognized the famous land-
mark from films and photographs he had seen. For him, facing
the monument in person was a thrill. The happiness and excitement were contagious. "You couldn't believe the change. Even
the sick people throwing up felt better. They know this was the
end," not only of their nausea but also of years of wrongful imprisonment, suffering, and waiting for permission to enter the

United States. "It meant to me that I'm an American now." In one incident common to new immigrants, Nathan's birthday changed from February 12 to December 2. The month and day were transposed because in Europe it's customary to write the day before the month.

Sonia and Nathan Nothman were among parents with small children and pregnant women who were allowed to fly to the United States. The 24-hour flight was bumpy and uncomfortable, causing many people to vomit, but the real scare occurred following a stop in Iceland. After the plane took off, Sonia saw flames and smoke curling around the wings. "It was an old, beaten-up plane. The engine was on fire. Hitler didn't kill us, but I thought we would go down in the plane. Nate always reassures me," Sonia said, referring to her husband. "He told me a plane have more engines."

Sonia and Nathan Nothman arrived in New York on January 24, 1950. Their daughter, Sandra, was only seven weeks old. The Jewish Social Service, which sponsored the family's immigration, helped them get settled. Initially, they stayed in a hotel on Broadway. The manager there gave Sonia two boxes of baby clothes, and she was overwhelmed with the number of items. "We were not used to those things. We appreciated more." The Nothmans moved to Coney Island, where they occupied two rooms of an apartment they shared with an elderly couple. "There was no furniture. There was a broken table, one broken bed. We had two rooms on one side of the long hall." To Sonia, it was a palace even though they shared the kitchen and bathroom. Accommodating visitors was not a problem because they did not consider sleeping on the floor to be a hardship. Oddly enough, there was little talk of the war and even less about the death camps. Survivors busied themselves with working and starting families. Organization volunteers occasionally inquired about World War II, but Sonia felt at a loss to answer. What she had seen, what she had lived, was too unbelievable.

Refugees sponsored by the Jewish Social Service were eager to succeed because the organization had promised the federal government they would not rely on public assistance. The Garfinkels, like many Shoah survivors, pride themselves on never having applied for welfare, food stamps, or other aid. They do, however, receive restitution from the German government. Monthly payments vary, depending on foreign currency exchanges, German inflation, and the survivors' physical and mental conditions. Some individuals have denounced such reimbursement, but others are more pragmatic. "Saul said, 'This isn't money. This is blood,'" Bela recalled. "I said, 'Take the money.' We take, and we build a life." Applying for benefits required interviews. A psychiatrist asked Bela whether or not she could work, manage a household, and take care of her baby. Later, other survivors told Bela she could have gotten more money by saying she had problems coping with mundane tasks and daily routines. Bela was outraged. "What? I'm going to tell them I can't take care of my baby? I can't do this. My child is my whole life."

The Garfinkel sisters often chide their brother for not demanding bigger payments for his permanently-injured hand. Sonia argued with her husband about restitution until the early 1960s. "Some people say, 'You take money from the Germans, you sell your soul, you sell your parents, how can you?' I understand that point of view," Sonia said. Her husband, Nathan Nothman, finally reasoned that not applying would only benefit the German government and economy. Survivors opposed to "blood money" should accept it, Nothman concluded, and give it to Israel, their synagogue, or their favorite charity.

Nathan Nothman's first U.S. job was screwing lids on pickle jars in a New York factory. "He would come home. His hands were swollen," Sonia said. Nothman, who manages to see humor in every situation, soon quit that particular job, which paid 60 cents an hour. "Four dollars and eighty cents a day," Nothman said. "I say I'll give them $5 so I wouldn't have to work there." The

Nothmans had shipped Rosenthal china trimmed in gold to their new home. Nothman had paid for the dishes — enough to serve several courses to 12 dinner guests — with his double rations of chocolate and cigarettes. The crate was so large it couldn't fit through the doorway of their Coney Island apartment. They sold the German china, worth about $1,500.00, for $300.00.

The Nothmans lived near Bela and Saul Soloway. Saul's aunt and uncle sponsored the Soloways' emigration to the United States in 1947 and shared their tiny, Brooklyn apartment. Bela and Saul slept on a "Murphy bed" that folded into the living room closet. Bela was grateful to Saul's relatives, who helped him get a job in a suitcase manufacturing plant, but she thought she would go out of her mind. "They live so poorly. No washing machine. She went to the market. They have very little food in the refrigerator. She bought three apples and five rolls. Saul could eat five rolls in a minute. I'm losing weight. I couldn't believe they live in America. I said, 'Why did I survive? I come to America for this?'" Bela sought the Jewish Social Service's help to find another place to live, an efficiency apartment on Coney Island. A proud man, Saul did not have the patience to wait for free services offered by Jewish American organizations. "People who came from those laagers, they became so ambitious," Bela said, referring to death camp survivors. "Saul was so ambitious. He wouldn't stand in line. Saul wouldn't go to the medical clinic in America because he have to stand in line. He went to the H.I.S. He said, 'I don't want your $27 a week. Please, give me a job, any job. I am young. I am strong.'"

Many Shoah survivors, like the Garfinkels, persevered after relocating to North America. One of the most touching post-war life stories is that of Joshua Steinfeld, who had served as a surrogate father and rabbi in the Ainring displaced persons' camp. Steinfeld moved to Meriden, Connecticut, where he spent many productive years as a rabbi's second assistant. His children, Israel Steinfeld and Anna Steinfeld Weinbaum, begged Joshua to retire in the late 1970s. By then he was nearly 80 years old. He died in early 1995, at the age of 96. "Somehow, he built a new life," Israel said of his father. More importantly, "the honest Joshua" from Chmielnik found meaning and fulfillment after the Holocaust.

The American Joint Jewish Distribution Committee, known as the Joint, sponsored Helen's emigration to the United States in the summer of 1949. The organization assigned her to attend English classes and to live with a woman in Pittsburgh, Pennsylvania. One of Helen's few encounters with anti-Semitism in the United States occurred at a neighbor's home. The housewife, who had Polish relatives and probably did not realize Helen was Jewish, remarked, "It was a good thing what happened to the Jews in Poland." Helen was speechless. "Many times this comes to my mind. I don't know if they knew I was Jewish or not," Helen said. "I never said anything. I left the house. I never visited that woman or talked with her again. If this happened now, I would not do that. I would confront the situation, but then I was quiet."

An organization volunteer paid special attention to Helen, inviting her to dinner, to synagogue, to the movies, and on other outings. It was Helen's first experience in a Reform synagogue, where men were not required to wear *yarmulkes*, or skullcaps. Helen sometimes babysat the volunteer's two little boys. Spending Rosh Hashanah and Yom Kippur with the volunteer's family made Helen feel like an orphan. Alone in her bedroom, Helen cried. She remembered Icekle, the homeless Jew of Chmielnik. She realized she was to her American host family what Icekle had been to the Garfinkel household. Being someone's charity case bothered Helen. Her visits to New York to see Sonia and Bela made her homesick for them. The Jewish Social Service warned Helen she would lose its financial support and educational benefits if she were to leave Pittsburgh. "At that time, education was not that important to me," Helen said, "but now I wish I had stayed." With the help of Saul Soloway's relatives, Helen got a job sewing brassières, girdles, and corsets for the Question Mark factory in New York. Helen made as much money as her brother-in-law.

Once, during a lunch break, some union representatives explained to Helen the purpose of organized labor — higher wages, paid vacations, job protection, and other benefits. Helen signed a card expressing her intention to join the union, and the factory promptly fired her. The union representatives, of course, did not honor their promises of paying Helen unemployment benefits or of finding her another job.

Regina and Saul Muskovitz stopped briefly in New York before settling in Detroit, where Saul had an aunt who had sponsored their entry to the United States. Regina felt lonely and scared. Being away from her sisters and brother intensified those feelings. She had spent more than half of her life in confinement: starting with her childhood in Chmielnik's ghetto, continuing with enslavement in the labor camps, and ending with her coming of age in Germany's refugee camps. Living in the United States, "the land of plenty," was an experience in sensory overload. "It's coming from one small room into a big mansion and not knowing what to do with it. It was too much to comprehend everything. It was very overwhelming, almost to the point of being frightened," Regina said. "I remember when I longed to go back to Germany to the DP camp. I never talked to anyone about this." In Detroit, Regina worked in a meat processing plant that made salamis and sausages. She attended English classes. She wrote letters urging her sisters and brother to move near her. "Little by little, I think we did talk about this. Then we started going to night school. We met people with the same background. You're not alone anymore."

The first to visit Regina, Sonia took her baby, Sandra, on the train to Detroit. She planned to stay, and Nathan Nothman followed after a few months. The Jewish Social Service in Detroit helped him find a job in a dairy, the McDonald Creamery in Oakland, a Detroit suburb. "The next day, he went to work. He said, 'This is great. We have milk. We have ice cream.'" Sonia was happy to be reunited with Regina, but she missed the big city. New York to Detroit — like Lodz to Chmielnik — offered more excitement.

Sonia also missed New York's larger community of Shoah survivors. The pull to family was stronger, however. The Nothmans lived with the Muskovitzes a few months until they could afford to rent their own apartment, a four-room flat on top of Cunningham's Drug Store. The Nothmans stripped off wallpaper and painted to renovate the flat. "The first thing we bought was a TV with a record player. This is how I learned English," Sonia said. "Little by little, we bought a dinette set, yellow plastic with big red roses. We had an old refrigerator." Sonia's prized possession was a baby buggy her brother had bought in Munich.

Nathan Nothman quit the dairy to become a plumber's apprentice. His decision to enter a more lucrative trade demanded the short-term sacrifice of working for half the pay. In a few years, he formed his own plumbing business. The Nothmans bought a 1949 green Ford, a duplex, and, finally, their own single-family home in Oak Park. Sonia eventually had Bela, Regina, and her brother as neighbors. "This was my happiest time," Sonia said. "We struggled, but it was good times."

Sonia had persuaded Bela and Saul Soloway and her brother, Nathan, to move to Detroit. Saul joined the McDonald Creamery, where he spent his career often working 14 hours a day. Bela got a part-time, minimum-wage job at the bakery across the street from their apartment. "They give me $1.30 an hour. They give me bread and cookies to take home. I'm in seventh heaven." Saul didn't want Bela to work, but she enjoyed it and tried several jobs. She sold Avon cosmetics. She became a seamstress. She also clerked in a chain of women's clothing stores. "I am a modern woman. I like to work. I like to have an extra dollar in my pocket." Bela's encounter with anti-Semitism in the United States has been, for the large part, indirect and impersonal. "I read about discrimination in the newspapers." During the 1950s, she applied for a job at Hudson's department store and later learned the retailer did not hire Jews. She heard the same thing about the Winn-Dixie grocery stores after relocating to Florida in 1978. "When we retired, I wanted to work, but Saul says, 'No.'"

Nathan Garfinkel arrived in New York in 1951 on a boat full of Shoah survivors and other refugees. He lived with Bela and Saul Soloway on Coney Island. A factory hired him to pack clothes in boxes. Nathan's first job in Detroit was pushing automobile bodies at the Hudson Motor Car Company's assembly lines. He then joined his brothers-in-law at McDonald Creamery. As a swingman willing to work any shift, Nathan earned an extra 25 cents an hour. He also enrolled in English classes. "Working long hours didn't bother me because I was working toward the future," Nathan said. "Coming here (to America) I knew my life would be nicer than it was." He alternately lived with the Nothmans and the Muskovitzes. Regina introduced Nathan to his future wife, a neighbor's granddaughter. Nathan and Mildred "Millie" Jacobs married in 1953. They soon bought their own home and had three children.

"It was important to me to have children, to build up a family again," Nathan said. "I am not sure if I know what I know now, whether I would have had children. It is a jungle outside, even here in America." As much as the U.S. Constitution, personal freedom, and economic opportunities favorably impress Nathan, crime and what he considers to be misguided politics disappoint him. He resented the Cold War, for example, not only because fighting communism consumed so much energy, but also because it enabled German war criminals to go free. In *The Murderers Among Us*, Simon Wiesenthal documents how and why the Allies protected fascists after the war. They were gathering intelligence about what they perceived to loom as a bigger threat — communism. Widespread ignorance and discrimination also disillusioned Nathan. A few of his co-workers in the dairy talked about hunting for "coons" in Mississippi. Assuming they referred to raccoons, Nathan was appalled to discover they were joking about black people.

Nathan worked for the McDonald Creamery until 1963, when

Foremost Company bought the dairy and then closed it. He picked up a second vocation by attending Lamar Barber School in Detroit. He supported his family by making ice cream for Good Humor at night. After getting a master barber's license, he opened his own business, Nathan's Barber Shop, in 1965. Nathan also attended adult education classes to get his high school diploma. "Everyone knew America was a rich country. I never could have bought a house in Poland. Here it was possible," Nathan said. "I worked very hard. That didn't bother me. I expected to work very hard, because my hard work was not just labor. I found that America was the land of prosperity."

Joseph Greenspun stayed in touch with the Garfinkels — specifically with Bela and Sonia — so he could court Helen. He visited Helen in New York and in Detroit and invited her to meet his American relatives in Cleveland, Ohio. In 1951, they were married in Detroit. They lived in Cleveland, where Joseph had established his own masonry business. Typical of many newcomers to the United States, Joseph worked like a dog to realize the American dream of providing his family a comfortable standard of living. As many Shoah survivors did, he threw himself into his work in order to block out bad memories. After laying bricks 12 to 15 hours each day, Joseph was too exhausted to bathe, to eat, or to even speak, Helen said. Many nights, on arriving home and taking off his shoes, he simply lay down on the living room floor. "My daughter, Rita, said she never remembered her father when she was young. He left at six o'clock in the morning, and he didn't come home until it was dark," Helen remembered. "When he was asleep on the floor, I couldn't wake him up. Once, when he was taking a bath, I called him for dinner, and he was asleep in the bath tub."

True to her independent and inquisitive nature, Helen made many friends in Cleveland, but she felt she had to see Bela, Sonia, Regina, and Nathan at least once a month. She taught herself to drive while she was pregnant with her first child, Pauline. Even though she could barely speak English, Helen drove alone to Detroit. Helen and Joseph stayed in Cleveland until their two daughters graduated from high school. Joseph wanted to relocate to a warm climate — specifically Australia. Helen refused, knowing such a move would severely restrict visits with her sisters and brother. In 1973, the Greenspuns moved to Orlando, Florida, where Joseph invested in real estate. "It was warm. I liked Florida," Helen said. "I thought here is vacation year-round."

Shortly after World War II, the Garfinkels did not think much about their parents, younger siblings, or Chmielnik. It was too painful. The distance of time has brought them closer to those bittersweet memories of being with their family in their hometown. "I keep telling myself my parents would have been such-and-such age now," Regina said. Only now, more than 50 years after liberation, can Regina bring herself to acknowledge fully the loss of her parents. "I was afraid I would forget what they looked like. That picture of my mother: it was a copy of a copy," Regina said. "I don't even have a photograph of my father. Once, years ago, I saw a movie on TV. The man had a little beard. I thought, 'That's what my father would look like.'" Regina often pushed away the past to concentrate on the immediate needs of caring for her three children and on adapting to life in the United States. Reminders sometimes punctured her superficial amnesia. "I used to live across the street from Bela. Once I looked out the window, and I saw her walking across the street, and she looked just like my mother. It was a flashback."

Regina has silently lived a tragedy greater than grief for her parents and more searing than any physical scar. It was a burden she couldn't shake, and she bore it since the Germans seized Chmielnik. In 1939, "I remember thinking there was something wrong with me or with us," Regina said. "That haunted me until way after the war, even when I came here. I remember thinking for so long that there was something wrong with me or with the Jewish people. Why would somebody pick on the Jewish people?

I wanted an explanation. I searched for it." The lack of explanations and outrage during the German occupation, within the slave labor camps, and in the war's aftermath, caused such questions to linger for decades. Her parents and older siblings had tried to shelter Regina from their worries by saying the situation was only temporary, but she emerged from the war with a skewed sense of what was normal and what was right. Starvation in Chmielnik's ghetto, executions in Kielce's work camp, and torture on the death march were so routine in Regina's childhood, that it took her many years to realize how profoundly wrong and criminal the Shoah was.

"My husband was a very angry man after the war. He won't even talk Polish," Regina said, referring to Saul Muskovitz. "My husband asked the rabbi, 'Why am I alive, and my parents died? They were such religious people and righteous people.' That rabbi had a prudent answer for something that had no answer. He was a survivor. The rabbi said, 'That's what your parents wanted. They wanted you to live. When you're a parent, you'll see. You'll view your child's life as more important.' I found comfort in that answer. My husband didn't buy it, but it helped me. I felt some comfort in that."

Chapter Thirty-Five
FACING THE FLAMES

Each Shoah survivor is a precious eyewitness to a modern-day, man-made catastrophe. The Holocaust is so horrifying many people choose not to read about it, to discuss it, or to watch films depicting it. Those who do, can't comprehend it. The crimes are too many: 6 million murdered. The crimes are too evil: dehumanizing and torturing Jews before killing them. Survivors themselves can barely believe they endured such suffering and beheld such cruelty. What they lived through was so overpowering, some survivors cannot speak of it. Those who do, like the Garfinkels, struggle to communicate what happened. Relating to such an apocalyptic event may be impossible, but approaching it through individual accounts is a start. The Garfinkels enrich history by sharing their experiences. That act requires courage to face the past and intelligence to recognize its importance as a lesson for future generations.

Like other Shoah survivors, the Garfinkels hope to mitigate, if not prevent, racism, hatred, and genocide. They realize that children and high school students learn more about history by listening to the participants than by reading texts. Just as each survivor's story is unique, each survivor's expression of his or her own story is unique. The ability and willingness to recall and to relate memories vary. For example, it is easier for Israel "Ira" Kaminsky to publish *Hed Hairgun*, an annual magazine about Chmielnik and its former Jewish residents, than it is for him to describe personal incidents related to the Shoah. Each year, Fay Skrobacka Goldlist, Sarah Frydman Goldlist, Abraham Goldlist, and Mania Poper Cherston help Kaminsky organize annual reunions for Chmielnik's Holocaust survivors and their families. At those gatherings, Nathan refrained from broaching such a weighty topic although he had always wanted to discuss the Holocaust. "I never told anyone about my tragic background," Nathan said. "A few people would ask me about my war experience. I started talking about it, but they would cut off the conversation. Even Jewish people weren't interested. It was too traumatic for them to listen." Nathan's nervous energy today reflects his long-suppressed desire to bear witness. Exchanging stories with his sisters and other survivors wasn't sufficient.

The 1984 opening of the Holocaust Memorial Center in West Bloomfield, Michigan, provided the outlet Nathan needed. He is among survivors who lecture at the museum, in schools, churches, and other community forums. "I volunteered. No one asked me to volunteer," Nathan said. "I had a compelling need to talk about this. It's still not fulfilled." In his presentations Nathan focuses on World War II history and politics, while disregarding his personal account. He is more interested in consciousness-raising than in attracting attention to himself. "For myself, I have no sadness. To be aware that this can be repeated tomorrow creates sadness," Nathan contended. "I speak for those who cannot see. I speak for those who cannot hear. I speak for those who cannot touch. They have no cemetery. They have no monuments. If I wouldn't be here, other survivors would talk for me."

The proliferating number of pseudo-historians claiming the Holocaust is an exaggeration or a hoax drives Nathan to accept as many guest-speaker invitations as possible. "History is strange because it can be distorted," Nathan said. "More people are coming up and denying it. I am concerned for my children and my grandchildren. Even Germans could be the victim tomorrow. This could happen to anybody, any time." Like his sisters and late mother, Sara, Nathan has a very giving nature and shows his generosity in numerous ways. He introduces himself to classrooms of students by saying, "I don't like captive audiences. Let me be captive to you."

Nathan encouraged Sonia to lecture for the museum, and she began in 1985. "I came. It was very hard in the beginning. I would speak. I had so much to tell, my tears are choking me. I hold back my tears. I try to control my tears. I would cry on the way home," Sonia said. "It got easier. I went to universities and temples. I go twice a week. Sometimes if a survivor doesn't show, they call me... Since I am getting old, I am getting stronger."

Helen first spoke publicly in 1981, during an educational conference about the Holocaust at Valencia Community College in Orlando. "Six years from my past I can't say in 10 minutes. It was painful for me to talk," Helen said. "That's the first time I spoke about my father." As she described to that first audience the Germans cutting her father's beard, Helen broke down in tears. "I never talked to my children about my father, but I talked to them about the Holocaust." Like many survivors, Helen found her past creeping in when her children didn't finish their meals or when they asked why they didn't have grandparents. Helen kept her answers neutral, saying she was once hungry and that Hitler tried to kill all the Jews. She did not delve into the intricate details of her personal tragedy.

That first Holocaust conference in Orlando not only helped Helen recognize her special place in history and use her memories to enlighten others, but it also formed the genesis of the Holocaust Memorial Resource and Education Center of Central Florida. Since the Center opened in 1986, Helen has been a faithful volunteer, speaking at schools, in churches, and for other organizations. "It's like going to a psychiatrist and talking. It's painful, but after you talk, you feel a lot better," Helen said. "What made me want to do that: I thought this would help to educate the people, that I would talk about my past, that it shouldn't happen again." During her presentations, Helen speaks about her family, their simple lifestyle in Chmielnik, how she was forcibly taken to Skarzysko-Kamienna. She describes the grim and Spartan labor camps, the inhumane conditions of the train ride and Bergen-Belsen, the death march and liberation. "I don't talk about religion. I don't talk about politics. I talk only about my experience," Helen said. "I speak for the people who did not survive." Helen also speaks for other survivors. "I have friends who, until this day, can never talk. They can't talk. I think they want to black out the memory, and they can't talk about it." Letters from children inspire Helen to keep lecturing. "If I can reach one child after one day, after one hour, a child can change, if I give my story, I am pleased. I have so many beautiful notes from the children and teachers. I don't care if you're white or you're black. I say no other human being should hurt another human being for no reason. When I saw *Roots* on television," Helen continued, referring to Alex Haley's epic about black slaves in the United States, "and they chopped off his foot, I looked away, but I said, 'You know, that's true.'"

In contrast to Helen, Sonia, and Nathan, Bela did not lecture nor did she tape an oral history. "I want to do different things," Bela said, noting that volunteer work and travel interested her more. "Not everybody can have the same thing." When she played canasta, mahjong, and other games with friends, they sometimes asked about the Shoah. "I don't want to talk about the past. I want to talk about the future. I say it's behind me," Bela said. "I'll never, never explain to them. They are American girls. They were born here. How can you explain people something they're not involved in? I never discuss with nobody. Nobody can understand. I can't understand what I've been through." Much of Bela's reaction is reminiscent of Simon Wiesenthal's closing anecdote in *The Murderers Among Us*: disbelief. Bela couldn't believe there was a time in her life that she wrested bread from the hands of a corpse, that she kicked cadavers in her path, or that she asked God to strike her dead. "If I didn't live this, and you tell me this, I would say you're a big liar. I couldn't believe that human beings do this to each other. You can't even call that barbarism."

Despite her reluctance to speak of the laagers, they were always in the back of Bela's mind. She was reminded when she saw her children and grandchildren discarding leftover food or pouring unfinished beverages down the kitchen sink. "I told them, 'Don't throw away food. Put the sandwich back in the refrigerator. I wish in my lifetime I had a glass of juice.'" Bela did not avoid answering her children and grandchildren's questions about the Shoah. By the same token, she didn't go out of her way to speak of it; for many years, she couldn't. "I listen to my sisters and brother. I have enough. I am very sensitive. To sleep, I have to take a pill."

After imigrating to the United States, Bela threw herself into daily routines. She never thought about the death camps during the day in Brooklyn or Coney Island, but, like a tidal wave, they emerged larger than life every night. She woke up screaming and crying — convinced the S.S. had taken her baby daughter, Sandra. "It was very bad in the beginning. We slept separate for a while. Saul slept on the couch because I scream," Bela said. Saul had bad dreams, too, but not as often, and he tried to reorient Bela to the present. "He showed me the baby. He said, 'The baby is here, Bela. What is wrong with you? Why do you have these dreams?' I said, 'I don't know why.'" Over the years, the frequency of Bela's nightmares diminished. During the 1990s, every few weeks she would wake up in the wee hours of the morning. She was soaked in sweat, and her heart was racing. She dreamt the S.S. were battering the door to drag her to camp. She dreamt the guards of Bergen-Belsen were ordering her to report to roll call. She dreamt she was lying immobile in the deep, muddy ditches of Przedborz. Claustrophobia and panic were about to drown her. "I stay in a deep hole. I want to go out. I want to hold on and go out. There's nothing to hold on to. I say, 'If I don't get out of here, they'll come and kill me.' I wake up and thank God it's not true."

Casual observers who considered Bela to be intelligent, fun loving, and well-adjusted would have been surprised to hear Bela describe herself as a nervous wreck whose moods swung from despondency to optimism. "I cry by myself," she said. "I won't cry in front of other people." In the moments Bela felt she had nothing to live for, she told herself she had everything to live for — her children, grandchildren, siblings, and two happy marriages. Widowed twice, Bela found herself as popular among men in the 1990s as she was as a teenager. They were attracted by her elegance and sophistication. Bela was grateful her brother and sisters lecture about the Shoah and that her two daughters combat discrimination through the second-generation organizations of Holocaust survivors. "This should never happen again," Bela remarked. "If this were to happen again — God forbid — I wouldn't go so easy. I wouldn't do what they tell me. I kill them before they kill me. I would say, 'You want to kill me, kill me now.'"

Regina, who is a private person by nature, says she could not speak publicly the way Nathan, Sonia, and Helen do. Yet once, while Sonia addressed some children at the Holocaust Memorial Center in West Bloomfield, Michigan, Regina found herself joining the commentary as Sonia trailed off. She even interrupted her sister. "I don't actively try to remember it; I might not remember things in detail, but I'll never forget," Regina said. "It's not something you can forget. Nobody has to remind you of it. It's just within you. It's always below the surface."

The museum is a comfort to Regina even though she cannot fully participate. She is especially proud that her daughter, Deborah, an architect, helped design the center and its educational displays. During the opening ceremonies, officials dedicated an eternal flame to the 6 million Jews killed. "I had silent screams," Regina recalled. "I was screaming to my parents. I was saying, 'See, you're not forgotten. See what your granddaughter did.' All day long, those screams went on in my mind. 'See, we have not forgotten. Look what your granddaughter did for all of us.'" Regina values the establishment of Holocaust study centers throughout the United States because they are meaningful to all victims, dead and alive. Such museums not only educate the public but they also provide a legacy to the children and grandchildren of survivors. "I think it helped Nate. He was very frustrated. I'm very happy for my sisters and brother. They can talk so openly about it. I couldn't talk about it. I was closed off. My children pieced the story together." Regina said she is indebted to Deborah, who also worked as a consultant to the Holocaust Memorial Resource and Education Center of Central Florida. "I feel that Deby did something for me. Since Deby helped build that center, it's easier to talk about it. The story shouldn't just die with us."

Of all the Garfinkels, Sonia has been the most steadfast in observing Shabbat. She rarely goes out on a Friday evening. Instead, she stays home to light the candles at sunset, to say the blessing, and to let the flames burn to the wicks' ends. "I would not miss Friday. There's something in me I cannot change. It's part of my life growing up. This way I remember my parents." Preparing the candles provides Sonia a few moments of solitude before her children and grandchildren arrive for dinner and conversation. "In Europe, everyone was religious, but now people go away from this. I don't criticize. I don't tell anybody. I'm doing what's good for me. My husband, Nate, doesn't care much, but he respects my wishes." As she strikes the match, Sonia is reminded of her mother, Sara, performing the same ritual more than 50 years ago in Chmielnik. "Whenever I pray over the candles, I see the picture: my mother walking into Treblinka with Fishel on one side and Rachel on the other side. I always see this without fail." Each Friday, as Sonia faces the candle flames alone, she brushes away her tears.

Chapter Thirty-Six
AFTERWORD

As a journalist obsessed with written records and independent verification, I went to Germany to see what traces of the Holocaust remained. Would I find evidence of the Garfinkels' imprisonment in the concentration camps of Dachau, Buchenwald, and Bergen-Belsen? Could I locate the court documents of the war-crimes trial in which Nathan Garfinkel testified? What would the Nazi death camps look like more than 50 years after World War II? Figuring that Ludwig Dietrich had died, I wondered whether any of his children or grandchildren had followed his footsteps in photography.

The quest for more information was rewarded within an hour of my arrival in Munich, near where the Garfinkel sisters were liberated. At the train station, a map of the city's subway system showed Allach as a metro stop about half-way between Munich and Dachau. I froze. During my library research in the United States, I could never find any references to Allach, not even a spot in the Atlas. Allach was the final destination camp of Sonia, Helen, and Bela after their cruel death march. I knew I would go there.

First, I went to the Dachau memorial, which is much smaller than the original gulag. It was there Regina Garfinkel Muskovitz was taken as a dying prisoner in a rickety wagon. It was there Regina was liberated, but she was too sick to realize that the terror had ended. A few old buildings remain, along with a reconstructed barrack, the foundations of dozens of barracks, and a museum. The wrought iron gate reading *Arbeit macht frei* is surprisingly small. Beate Michl, a staff historian at the memorial's archives, found the names of the Garfinkel sisters in the prisoner card catalogue. Helen and Regina are listed under their Jewish names,

Hanka and Ryweia. The prisoner card catalogue also provides birth dates and places, liberation dates and places, and home addresses before deportation. The last addresses cited for Bela and Sonia are in Lodz. Each of the sisters is labeled, "Jewess, Pole, in protective custody."

Most remarkably, the prisoner card catalogue contains identification numbers for the Garfinkel sisters: 143 449 for Bela, 143 453 for Sonia, 143 461 for Helen, and 143 508 for Regina. The Garfinkel sisters do not remember being assigned numbers, so they are baffled by the contents of Dachau's prisoner card catalogue. They were under the impression their oppressors didn't know their names — the sisters certainly were never called by name — so, they ask, how could they have been assigned numbers? Apparently, unbeknownst to them, the Nazis maintained meticulous records.

I asked Michl, the historian, about Allach, which appears on the Dachau memorial's map of satellite camps. She said the factories and barracks of the Allach slave labor camp no longer stand, but there is a small sculpture commemorating the numerous death marches that wound their way through Bavaria. Besides a book by former French prisoner Henri Laffitte, little is written about Allach. Michl suggested I contact the archivist at the BMW Corporation headquarters in Munich.

The BMW Story — A Company in Its Time acknowledges the automaker's production of arms, aircraft engines, and rockets for the Third Reich. Allach is mentioned in the book as one of the contributing factories. What isn't mentioned is BMW's use of political prisoners as slave laborers during the war. BMW's archivist, who was on the brink of retirement in 1996, gave me proof of Allach's existence: photographs of the camp's barracks and prisoners working on the assembly line. The same archivist, Rita Strothjohann, of Munich, also had produced a documentary film about one of the death marches.

From Munich, I traveled to Laufen, the picturesque town

where Sonia had lived as a newlywed. The name of the street that had been Sonia's address was changed from Hindenburgstrasse to Rottmayrstrabe. The Altepost where she married Nathan Nothman still operates a few doors away from their former apartment. The photography studio is gone — closed by Ludwig Dietrich in the early 1950s, when he moved to Oberndorf, Austria, near Salzburg. Ludwig died in 1981, and his negatives, mostly glass plates, were discarded. His son, Udo Dietrich, owns a camera shop in Freilassing. After my visit, Udo Dietrich did some sleuthing and learned that the barracks of the Ainring displaced persons' camp no longer exist. However, he reports that the women's jail in Lebenau, where Nathan Garfinkel was liberated, was converted into a juvenile detention center; the hospital in Laufen, where Nathan recovered, is now a retirement complex. Oddly enough, Dietrich spends his winters in Florida, so he has renewed his acquaintance with the Nothmans and Garfinkels after more than 50 years. Helen remembers him as a "skinny, little teenager." When he first met the Garfinkels and other Jewish Holocaust survivors his father had befriended, Udo Dietrich was a photographer-apprentice in Salzburg and he visited Laufen on weekends.

Because of its location outside Weimar and its decades-long isolation behind the Iron Curtain, the Buchenwald camp memorial is more raw, less sanitized than its counterpart in Dachau. Many of the S.S. buildings are preserved, functioning as administrative offices for the memorial and its archives. The grounds are huge in comparison to Dachau's memorial but not big enough to hold all the suffering that occurred there. Visitors who wander can find the railroad tracks and platform where Nathan Garfinkel and thousands of prisoners had arrived. Contemplating the freedom we so often take for granted, visitors can walk the same path prisoners took to the barbed wire enclosure. The barracks are gone, but their foundations are visible on the rocky hill sloping down toward the museum. For many years the Communists showcased Buchenwald as a monument to Soviet martyrdom with no hint of the genocide of Jews, the atrocities suffered by anti-fascists, and the post-war revenge against German soldiers. German reunification, along with increased tourism, has resulted in more complete information in the displays.

Buchenwald's archivist, Sabine Stein, found Nathan's name in the camp records. The large identification number, 115117, dwarfs the name, "Garfinkiel, Natan." The prisoner card shows Nathan is a "Pole, Jude," born in Chmielnik on February 12, 1918. His occupation — given as Bäcker or baker — perhaps reflects Nathan's wish for a work assignment near food, although his paternal grandparents owned a bakery in Chmielnik. The card is stamped January 18, 1945, the day he arrived at Buchenwald. Other documents provided by Stein show Nathan's assignment to barrack No. 63 and his transport to Buchenwald. The handwritten lists reveal he arrived among a group of 2,740 Polish Jews from Czestochowa.

Finding the court records of Nathan's testimony against Hermann Lachmann was tricky because the trial occurred in East Germany, under Soviet control in the late 1940s. The court file could be anywhere — in the former East Germany, in the former West Germany, in Poland, or even in Russia. I went to Berlin because Nathan Garfinkel, during his visit to Germany in 1992, had been told the records were there. After a lot of running around within Berlin, I found a historian who was confident of locating the records. That individual, Johann Legner, is the communications liaison for Der Bundesbeauftragte für die Unterlagen des Staatssicherheitsdienstes der ehemaligen Deutschen Demokratischen Republik. That particular archive, specializing in East German secret records, houses materials related to World War II. Legner's confidence contrasted with the pessimism I encountered at the Bundesarchiv in Berlin. Some of the archives operated by the German government are in transition, with records being moved from one place to another.

Nonetheless, the Bundesarchiv and Legner's archive both

mailed me photocopies of documents linked to Lachmann's trial. The records show he was among 23 guards who were prosecuted for war crimes they had committed in Hasag's slave labor camps in Kielce, Skarzysko-Kamienna, and Czestochowa. Lachmann was accused of killing at least three people, including Feingold. Although Lachmann confessed to killing Feingold during the trial, he was sentenced to only 20 years in prison. The records indicate that, if Lachmann had not been so young (a teenager during the war), he might have been condemned to death. Nathan's name appears on a list of 87 witnesses who participated in the Leipzig trials, which took place from May 24, 1949, through June 17, 1949. Transcripts of Nathan's testimony and Lachmann's response are also available. Lachmann served little of his sentence and is probably living in Bavaria.

Of the three concentration camps I visited, Bergen-Belsen is the most remote and least yielding in terms of written evidence. Near the war's end, the Germans destroyed files before turning over the camp to British forces. However, the hellish misery of Bergen-Belsen — piles of corpses, emaciated prisoners barely breathing, and excrement — were recorded on film by Mike Lewis, an army photographer now living in Australia. In a documentary shown at the museum, Lewis says he never viewed his own film nor does he care to; seeing the camp with his own eyes in 1945 forever altered his perception of the world. The British soldiers were so horrified by the ghastly conditions, they burned down the barracks. They later regretted that hasty attempt to reduce epidemics of typhus and other diseases — realizing they had destroyed tangible signs of Bergen-Belsen's existence. Since 1993, school children in the region have worked on an excavation project to expose the barracks' foundations. The vast memorial site contains a dozen burial mounds for thousands of prisoners and several monuments honoring the victims of different nations. Sounds of gunfire — target practice at a nearby military installation — disrupt today's stillness, as if to jolt visitors into an awareness of Bergen-Belsen's terrible past. As I stepped on the uneven, spongy soil, wet from a light rainfall, I wondered how many tears and how much blood the ground had absorbed. I thought about Helen digging in the snow to find leaves. I tried to visualize Sonia and Regina dragging the iron headboard across the camp. I remembered Bela's description of the stench-filled barracks. A cement reservoir sits at the excavation site, outside the landscaped terrain; it had contained the water the prisoners so desperately needed but to which they were denied access.

Despite the impossibility of imagining what the prisoners lived, historians continue to study Bergen-Belsen and the camp officials' strategy of killing Jews through systematic neglect and starvation. Thomas Rahe, the memorial's scholar, and Arnold Jürgens, a researcher in Hannover, have reconstructed a list of prisoners by circulating questionnaires to Holocaust survivors and by relying on a few, original documents they obtained from sources outside Bergen-Belsen.

Jürgens has a photocopy of a transport list identifying 500 women who were shipped from Czestochowa to Bergen-Belsen in February, 1945. Most of those women, all Polish Jewesses, were taken from Bergen-Belsen on March 5, 1945, to Burgau and to Dachau. Jürgens' list contains the names of the Garfinkel sisters, their birth dates, hometowns, and identification numbers — which happen to correspond with the numbers in Dachau's prisoner card catalogue. Jürgens' list includes the names of other eyewitnesses mentioned in previous chapters: Bela Jakubowicz, Fasia or Tosia Fastag, Hanka or Helen Rozenek, Ewa or Evelyn Szczebakowska, Regina Szczebakowska, and Cesia Zajfman or Zaifman. Reading the names is disturbing. The Garfinkels know many of the women, some of whom died on the death march. Jürgens received a typed copy of the transport list from a Polish citizen who had been a former inmate of Bergen-Belsen. Jürgens believed the original list was most likely in an archive in Warsaw. Following that tip, I wrote about a half dozen archives there. Within eight months, I received a photocopy of the handwritten original list from the Instytut Pamieci Narodowej.

That I found written records surprises some Holocaust survivors. Even though they are familiar with the German stereotypes of neatness and orderliness, they cannot believe the Germans would provide proof of the Garfinkels' Holocaust experience. Nearly all of the people who helped me were born after the war. I would like to think the task of historians and journalists transcends nationality. We're all after the same thing: documentation, which leads to the truth. What surprised me was how easily and quickly I got the documents. I arrived in Germany with no forewarning, no appointments, no credentials. I don't even speak German, so I was deeply concerned that no one would take me seriously. Thankfully, many of the historians speak English, and they kindly referred me to colleagues who could enhance my research. Within two weeks, I found nearly all the pertinent paperwork.

The research trip to Germany exemplifies the trail followed by many journalists: one thing leads to another, which leads to another, and yet another. When I first arranged to interview Helen for a magazine article about the Holocaust museum in Orlando, I didn't anticipate writing a book about her family. Much later, when I began asking Helen and her siblings about their epic past, I figured I would verify their story through library research; I hadn't planned to contact other survivors from the camps. However, the annual reunion of former Chmielnik residents made that possible. Despite the frustration I felt over not being able to work full-time on *Sara's Children*, I continued plodding along, trying to make the best possible use of my spare time. After mailing what I thought was a presentable version to dozens of potential publishers, I went to Germany to look for documents. Improving the manuscript, adding yet more voices and vignettes remain a priority. During a recent vacation in Australia, I sought out yet another survivor from Chmielnik: Rachel Wygodna Herszlikowicz.

The Holocaust never ends. For each tale of survival, there are at least one hundred, perhaps one thousand, stories of lives cut short. Each is a shameful indictment of mankind's capacity for evil and a searing reminder of how much we take for granted. The Garfinkels' bold and brave testimony serves as inspiration while educating readers about the Holocaust's widespread horrors. They, along with other survivors, are evidence of goodness and the irrepressible power of life.

Images
of the
Tarkeltaubs
and the
Garfinkels

A pre-war photograph of Mr. & Mrs. Tarkeltaub.

Golda Tarkeltaub

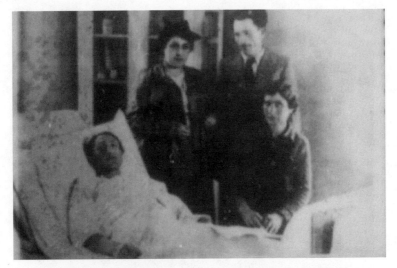

A photograph of Nathan Garfinkel in the hospital with his mother, Sara, sitting at his bedside. From this photograph the only remaining image of Sara was taken.

Sara's Children's Post-War Images

Nathan Garfinkel

Helen Garfinkel

Bela Garfinkel

Regina Garfinkel

Sonia Garfinkel

*No known
photographs of
Sara's children
Rachel & Fishel
exist.*

Sara's Children's 20th Century Images

Nathan Garfinkel

Helen Garfinkel
Greenspun

Bela Garfinkel Soloway
Hurtig

Regina Garfinkel
Muskovitz

Sonia Garfinkel
Nothman

Photos by Judy Watson Tracy

No 143.442   743.469

Zug Tag	Nr.	Name	Vorname	geboren	Veränderungen
5.3.45	143 442	Reich	Fela	5. 12. 09.	
	443	Goldberzt	Rysia	10. 12. 24.	
	444	Melcer	Bronia	15. 12. 95.	
	445	Radzynska	Rozia	25. 12. 22	
	446	Fuks	Lola	1. 1. 23.	
	447	Miodek	Anna	6. 6. 20	
	448	Miodek	Dora	16. 3. 22	
	449	Garfinkiel	Bela	15. 5. 20.	
	450	Herszkowicz	Eva	11. 11. 11.	
	451	Furberg	Hena	2. 2. 11.	
	452	Moszenberg	Anna	10. 6. 22.	
	453	Garfinkiel	Sonia	29. 3. 22.	
	454	Szafir	Sara	19. 4. 22.	
	455	Goldber	Henryka	2. 6. 16	
	456	Goldber	Iza	5. 5. 17.	
	457	Zajdman	Hela	12. 6. 19.	
	458	Zajdman	Roza	12. 2. 24.	
	459	Milewicz	Rachela	5. 4. 23.	
	460	Sztrowajs	Rut	3. 2. 13.	
	461	Garfinkiel	Hela	9. 7. 25.	
	462	Gruszka	Eva	21. 1. 11.	
	463	Krause	Gita	13. 7. 20.	
	464	Rozlich	Mizia	25. 7. 22.	
	465	Prejs	Cesia	7. 10. 07.	
	466	Salomkiewicz	Fania	6. 2. 20.	
	467	Gorncaritz	Rywka	29. 3. 27.	
	468	Orbach	Leosia	22. 6. 18.	
	469	Maszkowicz	Mania	24. 12. 20.	

A handwritten Nazi transport list, found by the Author in the Polish Archives lists #449 as Bela Garkinkel, #453 as Sonia Garfinkel; and #461 as Helen Garfinkel, Regina Garfinkel is listed a few pages later, on page 743.498, as # 501.

Photo By: Judy Watson Tracy

Suzan E. Hagstrom, a native of Salina, Kansas, is a Phi Beta Kappa gradu-
ate of the University of California at Berkeley. She completed her junior
year abroad at the Universida de Madrid, Espana, and then received her
Bachelor's degrees in Spanish and Journalism. Suzan researched and
wrote *Sara's Children* in her spare time while working as a financial
news reporter for *The Orlando Sentinel* in Florida. In her early journalistic career, she was a reporter for the former *Richmond News Leader*, an
afternoon daily in Virginia. She is now a free-lance writer for several
California newspapers and a resident of San Diego. Suzan has won several awards, including the Knight-Ridder Specialty Fellowship, and has
authored many nationally-published articles and book reviews. She is a
member of the United States Holocaust Museum, Washington, DC, and
a strong supporter of the Holocaust Memorial Resource & Education
Center of Central Florida.